Self-Determination Theory in Practice:

How to Create an Optimally Supportive Health Care Environment

by

Jennifer G. La Guardia, Ph.D.

FORWARD

Health behavior change can be incredibly challenging. Clients are better able to navigate these challenges when they experience their healthcare providers as true partners in their care. This manual describes how our teams work collaboratively with clients to make health behavior changes (e.g., improve diet, increase physical activity, lose weight, reduce and/or stop smoking) in a manner that respects clients and honors their personal goals.

Our treatment approach is guided by Self-determination Theory (Deci & Ryan, 1985, 2000; Ryan & Deci, 2000a, b; 2017), a humanistic, person-centered approach to motivation. The underlying premise of SDT is that motivation is elicited from within a person (not imposed on or given to them) and that supporting clients' basic needs for autonomy, competence, and relatedness will best promote the initiation and maintenance of behavior change.

Perhaps unlike other treatment manuals you may have read, the SDT approach is a philosophy and "way of being" with clients that does not easily fit into a step-by-step, "how to" manual. Why? Well, simply put, people are complex and the behaviors that they are trying to change are complex. So, it is impossible to distill this complexity into a key set of phrases to say or set of linear steps to follow. That being said, this manual will help you to understand basic principles and techniques that embody the SDT approach and it will provide examples of how it is put into practice so that you can use these tools flexibly to address the varied and interesting challenges that clients bring your way. Some of these techniques will be familiar to you, as good interviewing and client-care skills cut across many different theories and approaches. But, the philosophy and framework will help you to structure (or restructure) your interventions to bring this approach to life. We provide guidelines for how to translate this approach into various treatment modalities—individual, group, and mobile health. Finally, we provide information on potential ways to develop your organizational culture to support this approach. So without further ado, let's get started!

TABLE OF CONTENTS

SECTION I

Motivation and Health Behavior Change

CHAPTER 1.

Health behavior change and maintenance:
Challenges and opportunities

Over the past 50 years, the developed world has seen a major shift in the leading causes of illness and death. Illnesses including cardiovascular disease, diabetes, hypertension (high blood pressure), dyslipidemia (high cholesterol) and several cancers now represent the primary risks to people's health (WHO Global Status Report on Noncommunicable Diseases, 2010). Luckily, these diseases can be both prevented and managed in part by lifestyle behaviors such as engaging in regular physical activity, maintaining a healthy diet, and abstaining from tobacco use. However, initiating and maintaining healthy lifestyle behaviors is challenging – both for the individuals who are attempting to engage in them and for practitioners who are supporting clients in making these changes. Why is this so?

Health behaviors are complex. Making changes to diet, physical activity and tobacco use behaviors requires juggling multiple – and at times competing – motives. It requires developing self-regulatory skills and making fundamental shifts in how individuals orient to the world around them. For example, nearly every smoker is aware of the health risks of smoking cigarettes and using other tobacco products. In any given year, 70% of current smokers attempt to quit smoking, yet very few succeed (CDC, 2011; U.S. Department of Health and Human Services, 2014). Similarly, many people set goals – including New Year's resolutions – to make other health changes such as losing weight, eating healthier, and being more physically active. However, most people fail to achieve their new year's resolutions, despite being confident in their ability to do so. The fact that so many people attempt to make changes to their behaviors suggests that they are motivated to change. That fact that they often fail to achieve the changes that they seek reflects the complexity of the behaviors involved and the challenges that exist in initiating and maintaining change.

Why might this gap exist? Traditionally, health behavior interventions have focused on the nuts and bolts of the behavior change itself. Trying to quit smoking? Clear your personal space of all smoking-related paraphernalia (e.g., ashtrays, lighters, secret stashes of cigarettes), declare your home to be smoke free (e.g., no smoking indoors), and set a quit date. Trying to be more physically active? Develop a physical activity plan, join a gym, or go for a walk during your lunch break. Trying to make healthier choices around eating? Buy more fruits and vegetables, and buy less junk food. Although all of these strategies can help to get people moving in the direction of the changes they seek, they fail to consider the broader context in which these changes occur.

What do we mean by this? Health behaviors are complex not only because the behaviors themselves are complicated, but because changing health behavior is almost never just about the health behavior. For example, people often smoke to help them cope with negative emotions or relax in stressful social situations. Being more physically active involves experiencing unpleasant physiological sensations – like sweating and muscle discomfort – and spending less time doing other things like unwinding from a busy day with some couch time in front of the TV. Eating healthier may mean developing a taste for new foods as well as eating less high fat, high calorie foods that have been used as a tool to soothe negative feelings during stressful times or as part of celebrations or cultural traditions. Thus, changing health behaviors involves developing new ways of coping, developing new tools in the tool belt.

Changing health behaviors also involves shifting relational dynamics (e.g., making physical activity a part of social events; changing up an after-dinner routine of having a smoke with one's spouse to catch up on the day's events; having regular sit-down family meals during the weekdays) as well as changing potentially longstanding norms and traditions (e.g., adjusting favorite family recipes to accommodate new health goals). The challenge of shifting these relational dynamics is both social and personal. That is, people often experience pushback from their social environment when they try to change their behavior, and they also experience a sense of significant personal loss as they make behavior changes, as if an important part of their history and tradition is gone forever. Thus, both intrapersonal and interpersonal dynamics are deeply impacted by behavioral changes.

To further complicate matters, problematic health behaviors tend to co-occur. For example, people who smoke are more likely to have a poor diet and tend to be less physically active. Even for those who don't smoke, having a poorer diet tends to also be associated with being less physically active. Clients often attempt to change multiple behaviors simultaneously. For example, weight loss efforts often focus on making changes to dietary intake (both the amount and kinds of foods eaten) as well as level of physical activity. Further, changes to one health behavior often require attention to its interplay with other health behaviors. For example, quitting smoking can sometimes result in weight gain. For some, the negative consequence of weight gain can itself derail efforts to curb smoking habits. So, efforts to quit smoking might also need to catalyze behavioral changes to diet and physical activity to address potential weight gain. Thus, effectively managing multifaceted behavioral changes can be challenging for both clients and practitioners.

Finally, most interventions focus solely on jump-starting health behavior change, without considering the fact that how you initiate behavior change may have important downstream consequences for how behaviors are maintained over time. Indeed, in much of the research literature, behavior change initiation and maintenance are treated as entirely separate processes. There are, of course, some key differences between initiation and maintenance of behavior changes. For example, when clients are first initiating a health behavior change they may need assistance from practitioners to create a plan of action, articulate goals, and develop the requisite skills necessary to enact change, whereas in maintenance, tasks may shift to refining skills, developing new skills and interests, and taking on greater challenges. The ways in which practitioners engage with clients in the earlier stages of initiation can influence how clients navigate maintenance of their behaviors over time. Many of the intuitive approaches to jump-starting behavior change – incentivizing health behaviors (e.g., paying people for completing a program or reaching a particular goal) and providing clients with ready-made goals and action plans – may not serve clients well when it comes to maintenance. For example, making behavior change contingent on getting a reward sets up a person to expect and "need" the reward to engage in a behavior. So, when the reward isn't there, the likelihood of engaging in the behavior is reduced. Clearly, once seduced by a reward, it's hard to go back from that expectation. Another example is when practitioners drive the initiation process by giving clients ready made plans or goals. These packaged programs don't readily allow clients to connect the behaviors they are trying to change to what is meaningful or important to them (e.g., living longer to be with family), what is manageable in their lives, and what *they* ultimately want. Successful behavior maintenance requires clients to internalize and own their behaviors such that the behaviors they are adopting are self-endorsed and consistent with their broader goals and values.

5

Thus, from the start, it is important for practitioners to engage with clients in ways that elicit clients' own goals, interests, and plans.

The SDT approach recognizes and addresses the complexities of human behavior. It is focused on helping clients develop their own value for and interest in health behaviors and make plans that support changing goals from initiation through maintenance. Essentially, the foundation of this approach is about understanding what motivates people's behavior and how can we create the circumstances that optimize motivation and support well-being. So, let's talk about what it means to us to take a motivational approach to health behavior change.

CHAPTER 2.

Why motivation matters

People who design interventions to address health behavior change have continuously grappled with two key questions--"What gets people to initiate behavior change?" and "What keeps people maintaining those changes over the long term?". These are essentially questions of motivation.

Interestingly, theorists have differed quite a bit in their conceptualizations of human motivation, and these different conceptualizations have had important implications for how treatments are constructed. Below we discuss some of these basic differences and outline the main assumptions of the SDT perspective on motivation.

View of human nature

Simply put, there are basically two schools of thought about the nature of motivation. The first, which follows from the behaviorist tradition, suggests that people are moved to behave in response to contingencies from the environment. People are not thought to be agentic and initiate behavior, but rather behavior is produced when the environment sparks it. According to this philosophy, the key to intervention is to determine the "right" reinforcements (rewards) that will result in an increase in the desired behaviors and the "right" punishments that will extinguish undesired behaviors. Thus, behavior is best understood as a function of learning these contingencies and continuing to employ these contingencies in the environment to maintain the behavior.

The second school of thought is that humans are naturally oriented toward growth and well-being, and they actively engage their environment to achieve these ends. Thus, motivation is something that comes from within the person and can be either fostered or thwarted by the environment. From this perspective the key to intervention is to help clients draw on their own motivation and work to facilitate the kinds of motivation that are likely to result in long-term maintenance of behavior. Different theoretical approaches under this broad umbrella certainly emphasize different ways to achieve this, but nonetheless, these approaches broadly see the client as a partner in the behavior change process. The SDT approach clearly falls in this second camp.

Quality of motivation is important

Motivation is often defined as "psychological energy that is directed toward a goal". Early distinctions of motivation reflected the idea that either you "have it" or you "don't". So, people were considered to be motivated if they were engaging in some behavior (e.g., exercising) whereas they were characterized as unmotivated if they weren't doing the behavior. This way of thinking about motivation suggests that *quantity* of motivation is what matters most. From this perspective, the main target of intervention is to find ways to get people to be *more* motivated, with the intervention judged to be successful if people simply do the targeted behavior more frequently.

However, many decades of research have shown that motivation is much more complex than you "have it" or you "don't". Rather, motivational *quality* -- or in other words, the different reasons that fuel people's behavior -- is important. In fact, these reasons are critical to whether people will even try to engage in a health behavior and whether they will maintain it over the long term. Having a more differentiated view of motivational quality also has implications for how health care providers intervene, such that the target of intervention is not simply to get people to do more of a given behavior but it is to help them to do the behavior for personally meaningful reasons. This takes a bit more explaining, so in the next chapter we dive into these issues more deeply. But for now, the main thing to remember is that the SDT approach pays attention to *why* people are engaging in a behavior, not just that they are engaging in a behavior.

Motivation is dynamic

Behavioral change is a dynamic process. That is, people's reasons for engaging in a behavior may shift within and across days. Why is this so? People will have multiple choices about how they engage behaviors (eating, physical activity, smoking) throughout the day, every day. At any given time, multiple motives for the same behavior may be operating simultaneously. Moreover, because people have many different behaviors that they engage in each day, the energy that people have for any given behavior can naturally fluctuate as a result of other competing demands. Thus, successfully navigating behavioral change requires getting clarity in this "motivational soup"[1].

The SDT approach helps clients to articulate the many reasons for engaging in health behavior changes and helps them to make sense of these many motivations. Further, the SDT approach helps clients harness other "big picture" reasons for engaging in health behaviors (e.g., being a good role model for my kids; being able to be active with my spouse) which in turn helps them to orient everyday behavioral choices toward these big picture goals. Again, there is much more to be said about this, and we will elaborate on this in later sections.

Goals provide direction for motivation

A core part of the behavior change process is the formation and revision of goals. People have overarching goals (e.g., I want to lose 30 pounds) as well as more proximal goals (e.g., I

9

will eat a healthier lunch) that guide their everyday behaviors in the service of their overarching goals. Thus, goals help to provide direction for clients' motivational energies in the behavior change process.

Most interventions focus simply on formulating a target goal without considering the reasons motivating the aims. So, for example, a client might want to lose 30 pounds because she wants to be more attractive and have people regard her more highly whereas another client might want to lose 30 pounds because it will allow her to be more active with her kids. As mentioned just a moment ago, the reasons that fuel behavior matter to persistence. So, in SDT terms, not all goals are created equal, and thereby would be expected to yield different outcomes.

Another important issue pertains to the dynamic nature of goals. Most goal theories suggest that goal setting is an iterative process, with constant feedback loops and revision of both overarching and proximal goals. However, in practice, goal setting is often treated as a one-time event that happens at the beginning of treatment. Goals, in fact, need to be transformed to optimally challenge clients' skills and abilities. As skills develop, what was challenging initially may no longer keep one's interest and energy. Thus, goals must evolve to create new and interesting challenges to tackle. Further, goals often shift naturally over time, such that the reasons why people start to engage in a behavior and why they maintain it can be quite different. The SDT approach attends to helping clients develop and evolve goals both in response to their changing skills and abilities but also their changing interests and values. Again, the focus is on setting meaningful, self-endorsed personal goals, a focus not always found in other approaches to treatment. We elaborate on how to do these things in upcoming chapters.

Motivation and emotion go hand in hand

Lifestyle behaviors inherently have an emotional experience tied to them. Many people get pleasure from sweet treats but also feel regret after the sugar rush is gone. Many people feel energized after a good workout but also dislike feeling sweaty and sticky. Many smokers feel more relaxed after a cigarette but feel self-conscious about taking a smoke break. Thus, lifestyle behaviors can have a mix of emotions tied to the experience itself.

Behavior change also often generates negative feelings for clients before it makes them feel good. For example, clients often feel uncomfortable when they change a behavior—anxious when they cut back on cigarettes, craving foods that they are trying to cut out of their diet, and fatigued and sore from moving muscles that they haven't been moving. They also experience disappointment and feelings of failure when there are bumps in the road to change. Thus, the process of change brings with it a potentially new set of emotional challenges which can make it more difficult to persist.

Finally, stress from other life circumstances can have a significant impact on how well clients navigate health behavior changes as well. Clients often use food, drink, tobacco, or inactivity to soothe their negative feelings---for many it's a primary coping mechanism in their tool belt. As such, changing health behaviors requires clients to develop new tools for coping amidst learning other new skills as well as incorporate new knowledge that is fundamental to the behavior change, which for some clients is an overwhelming task.

It should now be abundantly clear that the emotional landscape of behavior change is intimately tied to motivation for health behaviors. Thus, the SDT approach focuses significant energy on illuminating and addressing this interplay. Again, we expand our discussion of this in upcoming chapters, but for now remember that this becomes a central point of attention in our intervention, one that is not characteristic of most health behavior change interventions.

Behavior change is a journey

Behavior change is an ongoing *process,* with new and evolving challenges. On such a journey, one expects bumps in the road, times when the pace needs to be slowed, and other times when it feels like smooth sailing. Thus, drawing on one's motivation to persist through the natural ebbs and flows of this journey becomes an important skill for both initiating and maintaining behavioral changes.

The SDT approach helps clients to view behavior change as a process, thereby focusing clients on the "long game". We also are choiceful about the behavior change strategies that we do and do not employ through treatment, as we know that although some seem to spark initiation of behavior change (e.g., incentives), they have a detrimental effect on long term maintenance. Thus, the design of our intervention tries to keep in mind the totality of the behavior change process and aligns momentary interventions and practices with this overarching aim.

Summary: Why motivation matters

In summary, motivation is the fuel that energizes the initiation and maintenance of behavior. It is dynamic and is intimately tied to emotional experience. Thus, adopting a motivational lens to intervene can help us to account for the complex and varied challenges that are a part of health behavior change. The SDT approach provides the theoretical framework to understand health behavior change and the practical tools for translating theory into practice. We now turn to illuminating these features.

SECTION II

Understanding Motivation:

The Self-Determination Theory Perspective

CHAPTER 3.

The many types of motivation

In the previous chapter we talked about the idea that there can be many different reasons why people may engage or disengage from a particular behavior. Now, let's dive into these issues more deeply.

When people are not engaged in the behavior

When people show relatively little or no action or intention to behave we call this *amotivation*. So, why might people be amotivated to engage in a particular behavior? It turns out there are three main reasons why. Let's use the example of trying to lose weight to illustrate these three reasons. People might not be motivated to try to lose weight because losing weight is *not viewed as personally important or other behaviors are a higher priority.* People also might not be motivated to try to lose weight because they *don't believe they have the ability* to carry out behaviors that will help them to achieve weight loss. Or, people might not be motivated to try to lose weight because they believe that *even if they try they won't actually be successful* at losing weight. So, although on the surface it might look like everyone who is disengaged may be similar, there is often more going on behind the scenes.

So how might these different reasons for not engaging in a behavior have implications for how health care providers intervene? If we were just concerned with <u>quantity</u> of motivation we would treat all of these people the same. That is, we would simply give them instructions on how to increase a particular health behavior and we might also set up some rewards or consequences to ensure that they keep up with what is prescribed. However, knowing *why* someone is amotivated will steer the intervention in a different direction.

When clients say that they <u>don't view change as important</u>, the core task for health care providers is to take genuine interest in and understand why this is. For some clients, this is genuinely their viewpoint---they are freely choosing to not engage in the health behavior. For these clients, no manner of coaxing or convincing (no matter how compelling you think your pitch for change is) will move them to behave differently.

However, for other clients, saying that they don't view change as important is a way to dismiss a behavior or set of behaviors that they don't feel very capable or confident about engaging in. If a practitioner takes genuine interest in and is curious about clients' reasons for not finding the behavior to be important (and does not have a hidden or not so hidden agenda to change clients' behavior), clients can better clarify whether they are freely choosing to not engage in the behavior or whether they have disengaged because of perceived inability or lack of confidence to achieve their outcomes. For those clients for whom the latter is true, as well for those who are explicit about the fact that they find it difficult to carry out the behaviors or don't have faith that they will get their desired outcome, the intervention is focused on how to meet them at their knowledge and skill level to develop a manageable path for change. For some people this might mean beginning with very basic knowledge and concrete skill building exercises. For others it may mean exploring ways to increase interest or challenge in what they are already doing.

For those who appear amotivated, taking time to do a motivational assessment is an important process in itself, as it helps clients to give voice to their perspective and begin to own it. Sometimes this exploration grows value for the behavior and interest in trying to change it, while at other times it confirms their reasons for not engaging in the behavior. Later in the chapter on working with ambivalence, we will talk about specific ways to shape this assessment (e.g., how to ask questions with curiosity and not an agenda to push them to change). But, for now let's talk a bit about when motivation (in some form) is already present for clients.

When people are already motivated for behavior

Many of the people that health care providers see already have some motivation for health behavior change—they have shown up to the office or clinic for some services and they already have a problem they want to solve, a goal that they want to achieve, or a new goal is identified during the course of routine care (e.g., check-up reveals that blood pressure is high). Even though they are already motivated for changing a behavior on some level, differentiating the *quality* of their motivation is important.

SDT outlines several different types of motivation -- the different reasons that fuel behavior (Appendix A). Let's explore these different motives more deeply, using the example of why people might engage in physical activity to lose weight to illustrate these different motives.

People might engage in a behavior because they <u>feel direct external pressures to achieve a reward or to avoid punishment</u>. So, people might get rewards if they exercise and lose weight (e.g., reduced premiums for health insurance) or they might get punished if they don't (e.g., pay extra doctor bills and expenses because they are overweight). People might also <u>feel internal pressures</u> (e.g., "I should" or "I have to") <u>in order maintain their self-worth or to avoid feeling guilty</u>. So, people might work out to lose weight so that others (e.g., doctors, family, friends) won't be disappointed with them[2] (to avoid feeling guilty) or because they believe that working out will help them look better so others will be more attracted to them[3] (to maintain their self-worth). People might also <u>value the behavior and how it serves other important personal goals</u>. For example, people might work out because working out is a means to losing weight and improving their health, which is something that is important to them. They might also value playing with their kids and doing more activities with friends, and losing weight makes it physically easier to do both. Finally, people might just do the behavior because they <u>really enjoy</u> being physically active and find it <u>fun and challenging</u>, and because feeling physically good makes them also feel more psychologically alive and vital.

Each of these reasons might fuel a person's behavior, and in fact, at any given moment some or all of these motives may be vying for attention. For example, consider a client who is thinking about going out for a walk that she had scheduled with a friend. She has had a long day and has a bunch of other pressing tasks to do before she goes to bed that night. She might feel rather pressured to abandon her plans and turn attention to the other tasks she has to finish. Yet she might also feel pressured to go on the walk because she knows that she "should" do it to better her health and she would feel guilty for cancelling on her friend. She also knows that she really enjoys the time she has with her friend and knows that getting out of the house and getting her heart pumping usually feels really good and gives her a new sense of energy. Clearly she has several different motives that are operating simultaneously.

On the whole, the balance of these different reasons is what is most important. Are people driven more so by internal and external pressures (or what we call controlled reasons) or are they driven more so by value, interest, and enjoyment (which we refer to as more autonomous reasons)?

Research has shown that balance matters to persistence in the behavior as well as the person's overall well-being. The more that people are driven overall by value, interest, and enjoyment, the more they take ownership over their behaviors, and as a result, the more likely they are to initiate and maintain their behaviors over the long term. In contrast when people feel more controlled and pressured to engage in behaviors (e.g., they are doing things because others tell them to, so that others will like them, or so they can get rewards or avoid punishments), it is harder to get started and harder to maintain behaviors (e.g., exercising, eating healthier) over the long term (See Ng et al., 2012 for review).

Let's explain this in a different way. When people are pressured to behave, it doesn't feel good. In fact, pressure typically results in feelings of resentment, anger, annoyance, guilt, and defeat. People don't want to feel this way, so naturally they will tend to avoid behaviors that kick up these feelings. Or if they do engage in the behaviors they will be miserable doing them and will likely be more reluctant to continue engaging in the behaviors (and feeling bad!) over the long term. By contrast, when people deeply value the behaviors they are engaging in, they feel interested and energized and are more likely to actively engage in those behaviors without even being prompted. And, when there are obstacles in the way or negative feelings creep up, they will be more likely to try to push through those obstacles and negative feelings and engage in the behavior because they know that the behavior can afford a return on their investment, such as revitalized energy, a more centered self, and/or getting them closer to a personally important goal.

Remember our client who was deciding about whether or not to go out for a walk? What gets her out the door to actually go on the walk versus deciding not to? It is true that on any given day one set of motives might outweigh the others and drive behavior in a particular direction. That is, even if she highly values a particular behavior (e.g., walking) and is interested in engaging in it, there are some days that she won't engage in the behavior. Even when she decides that she doesn't want to go for that walk that decision will likely feel okay because she listened to what her body and mind really needs, and having weighed the pros and cons, she has freely chosen to not engage in the behavior—and thus is autonomous in that choice. On average though, if she is motivated more so by autonomous reasons of interest, enjoyment, and value, she will be more likely to get out the door (even when she doesn't really feel like it) and will feel better about engaging in the behavior afterwards (e.g., feeling good or at the very least feeling less stressed).

By contrast, if our client is motivated to go out for a walk mainly for controlled reasons, such as avoiding the financial consequences of being overweight, avoiding feeling guilty, or trying to make herself more attractive and desirable for others, she will likely have more trouble engaging in the behavior. Why? Typically in response to external or internal pressures, she will either disengage from the behaviors altogether (and maybe even sabotage her own efforts by overeating or being sedentary) or if she does go for a walk she will likely feel miserable, making the experience even more unpleasant. And, when other stressors have dominated the day, taking care of herself will typically be the first thing that goes by the wayside. Thus, when a person behaves mainly in response to feeling pressured or controlled, the chances of continuing the behavior will be less likely.

So how do people become more autonomously motivated? SDT outlines three basic psychological needs that when fulfilled not only produce greater autonomous motivation but also promote greater overall psychological well-being. SDT also defines the ways that the social environment can provide support for these three basic needs, thereby providing the roadmap for how others can facilitate motivation and well-being. We now explore these features in detail.

CHAPTER 4.

Basic psychological needs

SDT argues that every human has basic psychological needs for <u>autonomy</u>, <u>competence</u>, and <u>relatedness</u>. Let's take a moment to briefly describe each of these three needs (Appendix B).

First, *relatedness* refers to the need to feel close, connected to, and valued by important others and it is the foundation of self-worth--the sense that one is significant, lovable, and worthy of care. Experiencing relatedness is perhaps best captured by the sense that one can be authentic, or in other words one's "true self", and have that appreciated by others.

Autonomy refers to the idea that people need to feel willingly engaged in their behaviors and feel a sense of ownership over their actions. In essence, people need to feel like they have a say in what they do and that their perspective and their feelings actually matter to others. The opposite of feeling autonomous is feeling controlled or pressured to behave in a particular way.

Finally, *competence* refers to the need to feel effective and capable and develop a sense of mastery over one's behaviors. People most often experience competence when they have the opportunity to be actively immersed and engaged in their behavior and feel optimally challenged to stretch, extend, and grow their skills and abilities.

Over 40 years of research has shown that when people feel their basic psychological needs are being satisfied by their healthcare environment their behavior is more likely to be autonomously motivated (driven by value, interest, and enjoyment), and as a result they are more likely to persist at their behavior and experience greater well-being (See Ng et al, 2012 for review; see <u>www.selfdterminationtheory.org</u> for the most up to date references providing empirical support). It should be intuitive that feeling connected to others, having a sense of authorship over one's behaviors, and feeling capable to engage in the world effectively would be associated with the markers of well-being—greater vitality and energy, more positive mood, and life satisfaction. But why would having each of these needs fulfilled lead to greater autonomous motivation and sustained behavior change?

First, let's explore how support for autonomy translates into greater autonomous motivation. Health behaviors, on the whole, are not intrinsically motivated. That is, they are not done just for their inherent interest or enjoyment but rather are performed in the service of another purpose or goal (e.g., to improve insurance premiums; reduce personal health risk; be more active with one's kids; be more attractive to others). The social environment clearly has an impact on the content and direction of these goals. When health behaviors are mainly driven by directives, guilt, or pressures to maintain one's self-worth, the social environment is often actively contributing to creating such pressures. Under these conditions, health behaviors are sustained to the extent that these continued pressures are present. However, if these pressures cease and the person has not developed their own value for the health behaviors, the health behaviors will cease as well. In contrast, when the social environment affords opportunities for people to direct the course of their behaviors by doing what is most personally interesting or meaningful to them, people are able to internalize the health behaviors and integrate them with other core life goals, values, and pursuits. Thus, a more autonomous form of *self*-regulation is created. This form of self-regulation can be sustained without the presence of external prompts, pressures, or contingencies--a point critical to maintenance of behaviors over the long term.

How autonomy support facilitates autonomous motivation may seem rather straightforward, but what about competence and relatedness needs? This may be less clear initially, so let's explore this briefly.

21

When people feel competent, the behaviors they are engaged in are doable and reliably yield expected outcomes. Remember the concept of amotivation? One of the main reasons why people do not engage in health behaviors is because they don't feel they have the requisite skills or abilities to make the things they want happen. So, at a very basic level, people need to have a sense that they are capable of carrying out a behavior, and this sense helps people to engage in that behavior. But, simply being able to successful at a behavior or accomplish a particular goal is not enough to sustain behavior. There are many behaviors that people *can* do, but if these behaviors don't matter to them then they won't continue doing them. So, to sustain behavior, capabilities need to be aligned with personally important goals---or in other words, competence (feeling capable of doing the behavior) and autonomy (doing things that they value) must go hand in hand.

There is one other important point about how autonomy and competence are synergistic in behavior change. As we mentioned a moment ago health behaviors tend to not be intrinsically motivated, at least at first. However, over the course of engaging in health behaviors some people find that as they are exposed to new experiences and acquire new skills they develop interest in and actually enjoy health behaviors for their inherent reward--because they are fun, challenging, and stretch their experience (e.g., cooking a good meal; walking). Thus, together autonomy and competence fuel intrinsic motivation, the most autonomous form of self-regulated behavior.

Finally, what about relatedness? Relatedness support is important in several spheres and is often the gateway for both initial and sustained engagement in health behaviors. What do we mean by this? First, when providers show genuine care for their clients, clients are more likely to trust them and invest in treatment. Also, when clients engage in treatment with others who share their common experiences and struggles (e.g., treatment group members), they often develop deep and abiding connections that further contribute to their commitment to treatment. Continued engagement in treatment in itself provides the opportunity to grow clients' skills, develop their interests, and help them deeply integrate health behaviors into their lifestyle. That is, in essence, remaining connected to treatment providers or others in treatment provides the opportunity for clients to transform motivation so that they can be more autonomously self-regulated. Beyond initial engagement, connectedness becomes especially important when challenges arise. So, even when clients have self-endorsed (autonomous) goals, providers and other group members offer needed encouragement and shore up clients' self-confidence to help them stay engaged and persist through challenges. In this way, relatedness becomes the necessary backdrop---the pillows to fall back on---to persist at personally meaningful goals during times when other factors may make engaging in health behaviors more difficult.

Beyond the immediate treatment environment, clients need to have good supports in their social world, or at the very least not have people that are thwarting their every attempt to change. At minimum, when clients experience relatedness, others do not punish, reward, guilt, or praise them in an attempt to move them to behave. Or, when pressures or reinforcements are coming from other sources, good supportive partners will help clients to quiet those pressuring voices so that clients' own interests and values can be listened to and followed---or in other words, so clients can be more autonomously motivated. When clients truly experience relatedness it is a result of others showing non-contingent regard for them. In the case of health behaviors this means that no matter if the person loses weight, changes their diet or level of physical activity, or quits smoking they are still cared for--regard is not contingent on their behavioral outcomes.

Thus, support for relatedness promotes greater autonomous motivation by allowing clients to be authentically engaged and free themselves of the pressures to behave otherwise.

Summary: Basic Psychological Needs

For behavior to persist, it needs to be aligned with personally important goals and a person must feel capable of carrying out the behaviors. Important others shape the circumstances in which clients are attempting to initiate and maintain health behaviors. To the extent that others provide opportunities for clients to explore and develop personally meaningful goals and provide the guidance and resources to help clients grow skills to carry out behaviors, then behaviors will be more likely to persist. But, autonomy and competence support is not enough. Clients can be volitional about wanting to change and have some skills to do it but if they don't have a supportive others who value them and what they are trying to do, it will be an uphill battle, and for many, one that they just give up trying to engage in. Thus, fulfillment of each of the three needs is important for internalizing health behaviors so that they are more autonomously self-regulated. This in turn can have a profound impact on long term persistence.

It is clear that support from the social environment--- friends, family, children, co-workers (and healthcare providers too!)--plays an important part in whether clients experience need satisfaction, develop more autonomous motivation for their health behaviors, and persist in their health behaviors over the long term. Let's take a deeper look at the specific ways that these relationships exert an influence when it comes to health behaviors.

CHAPTER 5.

How does the social environment affect health behaviors?

Every person is embedded in several social groups (e.g., family, peer groups, workplace) that may impact their health behaviors. Further, each group can be thought of as its own ecosystem with its own unique balance. For example, each environment has their own norms about health behaviors ---what, when, and how people eat, the extent to which people are physically active versus sedentary, and whether smoking is accepted or even encouraged. Workplace norms can be further driven by the organizational structure (e.g., management, regulations) and the type of work being done (e.g., rhythm of a nurse's day can be dictated by the medical urgency of patients' needs). Beyond the group level, each person within a group has their own motives that drive their behavior and each person has a stake in how the system runs. Thus, there is the potential for both cooperative and competing motives between people within a system.

So what happens when one or more members of a group want to change their behavior? When a member or members of the system try to change (e.g., trying to eat healthier), the shift in the balance creates ripples that are responded to with support or are met with pushback. Systems differ in the extent to which they are flexible and the extent to which players within the system are willing to adapt to the changes of a particular member or members of that system. In other words, systems differ in the extent to which they are supportive overall as well as the extent to which the key members of the system in particular (e.g., spouse, boss, best friend) are supportive.

Let's give an example. Say a married mom with two kids wants to lose some weight. She has determined that the best way to do this is to eat healthier. So, she starts to stock up the fridge with more fruits and veggies, gets rid of the "junk food" in the pantry, she stops ordering pizza and picking up take-out meals that the family has grown accustomed to, and she starts experimenting with homemade, healthier recipes. Although the family says they are in support of her efforts, they regularly complain about the changes in the household because it's her (not them!) that is on a "diet". They further protest by starting to hijack her efforts (e.g., bringing home junk food or take out). So despite her value for health behavior change, the obstacles that get in the way of change are not just within her but are being actively created by key members of her social system.

Clients don't just need their relational supports to be cheerleaders that offer encouragement. Rather, they often need the social system to shift its practices. For example, some workplaces have a practice in which they celebrate each employee's birthday (or any good news for that matter) with a cake or some other treat. This amounts to a constant barrage of high-calorie sweets that employees are expected to partake in (otherwise it would be rude!). Further, at home, couples often have an implicit contract--a structure by which basic functions of the relationship (e.g., who pays the bills) as well as more elaborate functions are organized (e.g., the roles and responsibilities of each partner; how much time they spend together and what they do). So, for a husband to carve out some time for physical activity he might get less time with his spouse and might need his spouse to take up some new responsibilities or shift some other regular responsibilities within the family.

In both the workplace and marital examples the social system has to renegotiate its contract about the expectations and responsibilities of the different players in the system.

Whether the social system is willing to renegotiate the terms of the contract of the workplace or relationship is a core factor in whether clients can reach and maintain health behavior goals.

Interestingly, despite knowing that the social system is so important to health behavior change, most interventions are still largely focused on clients only, with little consideration for clients' complex relationships. In fact, we would suggest that many individually-based interventions have failed to achieve long-term maintenance in part because interventions fail to address the fact that individuals live their lives in dynamic social contexts that can both support and impede their basic psychological needs and thereby directly impact behavior change efforts.

The SDT intervention approach incorporates conversations between healthcare providers and clients about how clients' relationships support or undermine their basic psychological needs and thereby play a role in their health behaviors and treatment decisions (La Guardia & Patrick, 2014). Specifically, providers help clients to identify who can be important sources of support or who will otherwise create real and substantial challenges to them initiating and maintaining behavior change. Clearly, it is not enough to simply be aware of these social dynamics. Another core function of the SDT approach is to help clients solidify and grow their existing relationship supports outside of the healthcare office in order to better maintain behaviors long after formal treatment ceases.

Practitioners help clients shore up as well as grow opportunities to connect with supportive others. Practitioners also help clients develop communication skills to ask for the support they need from relational partners who present obstacles as well as learn when to disengage their energies from those who continue to be unsupportive. Thus, an SDT intervention helps clients to understand how their important relationships influence their own motivations, it gives them the opportunity to become more choiceful about their own value for health behaviors rather than simply being pushed by external or internal pressures and controls, and it helps clients to become more effective at garnering support from others.

Finally, in addition to the need support that important others provide clients in their everyday lives, SDT is concerned with how practitioners support clients' basic psychological needs in the context of treatment. Indeed, treatment provides a critical model for need support. To understand the quality of providers' support, we first need to consider the underlying motivations of providers. Why? Just like clients, healthcare providers can be motivated by their values and interests as well as by pressures (external and from within themselves). These motivations will influence how they engage with clients, and in turn how clients' engage in the behavior change process

Motivations of the healthcare professional

Most health care providers (e.g., doctor, nurse, mental health professional, dietitian, exercise physiologist, tobacco counselor) and health-focused mentors (e.g., trainer or coach) choose their profession because they value health, they are interested in and passionate about their area of specialty, and they want to play a role in helping others achieve better physical and/or emotional health. These motives fuel the enthusiasm and energy that healthcare professionals bring each day to help their clients navigate the often challenging road of health behavior change. In turn, providers' interest, value, and passion can generate a sense of hope and confidence in clients to carry out behavior changes and successfully sustain them. These motives are what make providers true advocates and collaborative partners in the journey of managing clients' health.

Health care providers also have other motives that might drive how they interact with their clients. Let's face it---most professionals work within a system that requires them to produce objective outcomes of client engagement (e.g., clocking enough billable hours to meet a quota, getting clients to attend greater numbers of sessions, getting a greater number of clients to complete programs) and client performance (e.g., lose weight, reduce their cholesterol, quit smoking, etc.). These are real pressures from above that drive salary, membership on insurance panels, program funding, and sometimes even whether professionals keep their jobs. So, of course healthcare professionals will be pulled by these demands and in turn push their clients to perform.

A subtler, but no less potent pull, is the want to be seen favorably in the eyes of others. At some level, everyone wants to be seen as the "good" child, student, employee…fill in the blank. Healthcare professionals are not immune to this. They want their clients to show up and perform well so that they look competent and are well-regarded by their colleagues and others. And, on the flip side, when clients don't meet their goals or don't show up, healthcare professionals' egos can get bruised. No one likes a bruised ego. So, healthcare professionals often try to prevent their egos from getting bruised by subtly (or not so subtly) pressuring clients to meet their expectations, make them feel like a "good" professional, and look good in the eyes of their colleagues and others. Unfortunately, when professionals are focused on their own goals and get wrapped up in making sure they are seen as competent, they can make tasks over-challenging for their clients, resulting in exactly the outcomes that they were trying to prevent (e.g., clients not meeting their goals or dropping out).

Finally, the ugly truth is that some (although luckily not many) healthcare practitioners get into and stay in the business not because they primarily want to help others, but rather, because they desire the power and authority afforded by a position of status. Oftentimes, professionals who are strongly driven by these motives believe that they "know what's best" for their clients and "encourage" their clients (read: prod, guilt, or shame) to meet their expectations. This form of feeding the ego has more to do with the providers need to promote and protect their own self-worth, with clients becoming casualties of the process.

In summary, professionals have a variety of motivations that can influence their interactions with clients. Without an understanding of their own motives it is harder for health professionals to keep both the noble helper motives as well as the more pressured motives in check, and as such, health care professionals may respond more to their own values (rather than to those of clients) and subtly (or not so subtly) amplify pressures on clients to change. When this occurs, treatment is no longer client-centered and clients' voices are no longer the loudest in the room. And, as a result, healthcare providers run the risk of missing opportunities to connect with clients, better understand their goals and how they want to go about achieving those goals, and keep clients engaged in the treatment process. The SDT approach pays attention to providers' motivations and creates time within the organizational structure to check in with providers, help them become more aware of their varied motives, and be optimally client-centered. The last chapter of this book focuses squarely on how to pay attention to one's own motivations as a provider and how to change the culture of one's workplace to foster provider practices to specifically to meet the goal of being more client-centered.

So what happens when providers' motivations are aligned with providing client-centered, optimally need supportive treatment? That is, what does it functionally mean to support clients' basic psychological needs? Let's explore what providers do in treatment to build a foundation of need support.

CHAPTER 6.

Principles for creating a need supportive treatment environment

In this section we provide a primer as to how each need is functionally supported (summary in Appendix B). What you will notice is that although each psychological need has its own unique or signature features, at times the functional ways that providers offer support may serve one or more of the needs. Another important feature to note is that although we talk about each need separately, the needs dynamically interact, such that supporting (or undermining) one will also likely impact the others. Thus, creating an optimally supportive environment means that providers will need to keep in mind supporting all three needs simultaneously. At first this might seem like a daunting task (I have to attend to 3 things at once!) but in reality once you adopt the client-centered, humanistic way of being with your clients, support for all three needs emerges more naturally. Let's begin with describing the fundamentals of supporting each need and then we will explore some of the ways that needs dynamically interact.

Facilitating Support for Relatedness

Clients need to know that they can trust you to care for them and that you will be their advocate. This foundation is developed first and foremost by creating an atmosphere of warmth, genuineness, and empathy, or what Carl Rogers called <u>unconditional positive regard</u> (Rogers, 1961).

Warm regard starts from the moment clients walk through the door and is conveyed not only by basic kindness and compassion but also by the respect that providers show for clients' time and efforts. This regard must be genuine, such that providers are sincere, candid, and transparent in their interactions with clients (no hidden agendas or judgments). Moreover, the tone of anything a provider says or does must be attuned to the clients' thoughts, feelings, and perspectives and convey empathy—understanding, validation, and acceptance. Thus, true unconditional positive regard is achieved by making time for and truly listening to clients and caring for their absolute worth, regardless of their behavioral outcomes.

It is oftentimes mistakenly suggested that unconditional positive regard means that providers simply need to accept all behavior. However, there is an important distinction between *endorsing a behavior* and *accepting the person*. Specifically, a practitioner can genuinely accept and empathize with the feelings and motives that might underlie a person's behavior without liking and endorsing the actual behavior itself. Here's an example of what we mean. Let's say that your client is trying to lose weight. She has a big event coming up and was hoping to have lost more weight by now. At your next meeting she tells you that for the past two weeks she has been trying a fad diet that has her fasting on most days so that she can drop some extra pounds more quickly. Practitioners can support relatedness by conveying to the client that they appreciate that she is upset about wanting to have lost more weight and that she is anxious about her appearance for the upcoming event. But, relatedness is also conveyed by expressing care and genuine concern about how her fasting behaviors might negatively impact her health. Further, practitioners can set clear limits on what they will and will not help clients do, such that they do not have to support behaviors that violate their own professional ethics. When these conflicts around endorsing or supporting a particular behavior occur, it is important for practitioners to have an open dialogue with clients and appreciate clients' reactions to these limits. Thus, supporting relatedness does not mean "anything goes" but rather is focused on showing care for the client and being genuine with them while still respecting a providers own professional ethics.

One other thing to note---this isn't a carte blanche pass to fire a client because he or she is not following what you want them to do or how you want them to do it. We've noticed a recent trend in training and in practice is to coerce clients to "be good patients" or else give them the boot. Clients are already struggling with changing their behaviors and are often feeling pretty bad about themselves for needing assistance. Firing clients abandons them precisely when they are in need and serves to confirm those beliefs that their challenges are unmanageable and they are not worthy of care. So, to be clear, setting limits in practice is about setting reasonable limits (e.g., when the client's behavior may cause significant harm and I cannot in good conscience help with that). It should be an extremely rare event in a practitioner's practice (if ever) that clients are shown the door because they violate the practitioner's ethical principles or practice rules. Frankly, if a practitioner is at this point, the more likely route is to orchestrate a referral and transition the client to another provider to manage other more pressing psychological or physical health issues.

Beyond the relationship to the practitioner, another key factor in providing support for relatedness is working with clients to understand how their basic needs are getting met or undermined in their important relationships outside of treatment. Providers do this by helping clients recognize the direct pressures they are experiencing (rewards, punishments) as well as quiet the introjects (e.g. the internal directive voices such as "I should", "I have to", "I must") that are the loud and often dominating forces undermining clients' behavior change. They also provide opportunities for the clients' personal values and interests to take center stage and model acceptance of clients' own needs as important and valuable. Finally, they help clients develop the communication skills to convey to important others both their need for unconditional regard and the concrete ways that others can functionally provide this for them.

33

Facilitating Support for Autonomy

The crux of supporting autonomy is to be client-centered. This is accomplished in several ways. First, providers need to <u>know about the client's perspective</u>. Naturally the first step is to ask about clients' experience of their health behaviors in the past and present and be curious about how their experiences have impacted them. Learning about clients' perspectives also extends to learning about their personal values and goals as well as their interest in putting energy toward these goals. In essence, the provider attempts to understand all that is important to the client and how different areas of their life influence their behavior. This seems simple enough. However, there are lots of ways of asking questions--some lines of inquiry look more like a detective on a fact-finding mission with a specific agenda while other lines of inquiry are unclear or seem to have no purpose at all. Providing a framework for what will be asked, a rationale for questions (e.g., how it will help to craft treatment), asking open-ended questions, and offering an opportunity for clients to shape the scope of the conversation (e.g., adding what they think is important or pertinent to them) helps clients to participate in the process. Further, reflecting back your understanding of what you have heard, acknowledging their point of view, and recognizing the motives behind their behaviors will help clients recognize that you have "got it". In essence this is a process of discovery, marked by a curious and interested provider who conveys to clients that their experience and perspectives have been heard.

Second, autonomy is supported by collaboratively <u>devising a menu of possible options</u> for behavior change with clients. To devise a menu of options, clients contribute their own ideas about potential ways they might want to address behavior change and providers offer options that they can effectively deliver. Devising a menu of options is not an unlimited set of all possibilities. The menu is constrained by what you can effectively offer, and if other treatments are desired that are not within the scope of what you can offer, you can direct clients where to pursue desired alternatives and facilitate these referrals. Clients are not expecting that you are a one-stop shop. Or in the words of a colleague, clients aren't going into an Italian restaurant expecting that the menu will have all other possible cuisines (e.g., Chinese, Mexican, etc.) to choose from[4]. The idea is to create true possibilities for choice, *including the possibility that clients will choose to not change some or all of their behaviors.*

Third, if clients desire information and further guidance, providers offer a meaningful rationale for each option, including the potential benefits and drawbacks as well as the likely consequences of each course of action. Fourth, to create true opportunities for choice, providers actively explore clients' thoughts and feelings about the options generated, eliciting and acknowledging clients' feelings and perspectives without judgment. Further, providers offer opportunities for clients to ask questions and time to ponder the possible choices, including choosing not to make any changes at that time. Only with this consideration can asking clients what they would like to do be truly autonomy supportive.

Finally, if clients do decide to change their behaviors, part of autonomy support is to help clients develop personally relevant and meaningful health behavior goals. As we have talked about in depth earlier, people will have the most energy for and are more likely to persist at the activities that they like to do and the activities that they personally value. Thus, providers specifically help clients to articulate macro-level and proximal health goals that serve to support their core values and, if possible, also spark their interest and enjoyment.

Facilitating Support for Competence

The foundation of building competence is to provide structure and foster a mastery approach to learning, including devising optimal challenges, experimenting with and honing the tools to navigate these challenges, and developing skills to provide self-directed feedback.

First, let's talk about structure. Clients often come with a fair bit of anxiety and uncertainty about how treatment will unfold. Developing structure is about providing both a basic organizational framework for treatment (e.g., how often you meet with clients, the general format of sessions, the resources you can provide) as well as articulating the process of treatment. The *process* of treatment is not simply handed down to clients as a set of rules or expectations, but rather is developed through a collaborative dialogue with clients to determine shared expectations about the scope of your work together but also how you will interact (e.g., providing opportunities to maximize client input and participation in the process). When clients know what is coming and what to expect, some of their anxiety and uncertainly can be reduced and their ability to integrate new information will be also enhanced. Further, by shaping the structure of treatment with you they are more effective in being their own advocate to shape the pace and direction of their behavior change.

Second, an intervention cannot be a one-size-fits-all approach because people start with very different knowledge sets and tools to carry out behaviors, they have different strengths to capitalize on, and they have different challenges to overcome. To support competence, providers have to meet clients where they are in terms of their skills and abilities. To understand where clients are first requires an understanding of their basic knowledge about a given behavior, the tools that they have to manage the behavior, and their own assessment of their strengths as well as challenges. It further extends to asking clients about what they think are the needed inputs to guide their behavior.

Competence building also involves formulating a plan of action. Formulating a plan of action is a collaborative process that involves making proximal goals optimally challenging --- *specific, reasonable, and challenging enough* so that clients are stretching their skills but do not feel completely overwhelmed. Thus, creating optimal challenges is about outlining manageable steps toward change. Because there are many ways that clients can approach any given health behavior change, providers can create structure and guidance in this planning process by offering clients tools to support self-management (e.g., exercises on goal setting, building contingency plans, time management) that might help them to more effectively tackle a behavior change. Planning also involves identifying barriers to behavior change, including practical constraints as well as challenges that might come from family, peers, or other relationships. These barriers inform the development of optimal challenges and help to identify what other supports are needed in order to be most successful at behavior change pursuits. Ultimately providers are offering the scaffolding to guide clients' progress and are relying on clients' judgment to gauge what seems reasonable and manageable to them.

Competence is then grown by translating planning into practice. That is, clients practice skills that are instrumental to making healthier choices and experiment with what is most effective for them. Your work with other clients can help generate ideas about solutions, but it is important to first have clients generate strategies. Clients are quite resourceful and creative if given the chance.

Providers work with clients to evaluate progress on self-relevant goals by helping them to learn how to self-administer <u>informational feedback</u>--developing creative solutions to challenges that come their way as well as capitalizing on their strengths and what is working well in their efforts. Notably, informational feedback is not about providers simply delivering their opinion as to what clients should do or how they should resolve a challenge. Actually, if the provider too quickly sees the solution and rushes in to provide it, the client is robbed of the opportunity for self-discovery and mastery. Rather, informational feedback is about talking with clients about what they think about the situation, how they understand the problem, what they might imagine would be some options for a solution, and helping them to consider all the possible sides so that they can choose the next steps. It can, if the client is interested, mean that providers share an opinion and validation *vis-à-vis* patients' goals. But, it is not a given, as unsolicited feedback can actually backfire and end up feeling shaming, demeaning, or patronizing to clients.

Finally, part of competence support is also about helping clients <u>develop realistic expectations</u>--assessing the challenges in behavior change and acknowledging the need to revise plans--and helping clients <u>cope with disappointments</u> when plans don't work as intended. Clients often have pretty high expectations for themselves, they expect change to be easier than it actually is, and they end up flogging themselves when things don't go how they imagined it would. So, when clients don't have realistic expectations of themselves, providers can help to reframe challenges to support initiation, build confidence, and appreciate efforts and successes (even small ways). The goal is that clients will learn to reframe plans that don't work as challenges rather than failures, and begin to do this for themselves moving forward.

When the needs and need support interact

It likely has become clear as you read through the sections above that oftentimes offering support for one need will have an impact on another. There are several common ways in which this occurs. First, attempting to learn about a client's perspective (autonomy support) is not simply about gathering facts. It goes a step further. The reflections that providers offer their clients convey understanding and validate clients' perspectives. In this way providers are supporting relatedness by promoting acceptance of clients without judgment. Thus, autonomy and relatedness go hand in hand.

Second, developing a menu of options and choosing a set of personal goals (autonomy support) also fundamentally involves building competence. That is, goal structures create the scaffolding on which to develop a plan of behavior change. In turn, the various processes which unfold throughout treatment that help to build competence (e.g., determining optimal challenges, designing experiments to test out behavioral strategies, etc.) are guided by clients' personal choices. Thereby, these activities also essentially foster autonomy.

Finally, developing the skills to provide self-relevant feedback and realistic expectations for oneself are also about developing greater acceptance and kindness for oneself. Thus, good supports for competence will also evoke support for relatedness.

Although there many other subtle ways that the needs and need support interacts, these examples illustrate that understanding the interplay of the needs allows providers to be much more mindful and integrative in their approach to treatment. The downside is that because needs must be supported simultaneously to create an optimal treatment environment, failing to support one of the needs will often have consequences for satisfaction of the others. We offer some examples of how this occurs in the next chapter.

Summary: Creating a need supportive environment

Ultimately, need support is about meeting the client where they are and joining them on their journey, providing them guidance and encouragement along the way, and valuing them for who they are, not simply what they do or don't do. Thus, in the spirit of Carl Rogers, the approach is client-centered and is at its core about genuinely caring for the client with whom you are interacting. Although each psychological need has its own unique or signature features, at times the functional ways that providers offer support impacts one or more of the needs. Thus, the needs dynamically interact, such that support (or undermining) of one will also impact others. When practitioners are *need supportive*, clients are more likely to trust and *feel connected to* the practitioner and be invested in treatment. In turn, the more likely they are to become *autonomously motivated for behavior change* and feel *competent* to engage in behavior change, and persist in those behaviors over the long term.

SECTION III

The Anatomy of an SDT Intervention:

Putting SDT into Practice

To understand how to put SDT into practice it is necessary to think at two levels: 1) what is the <u>structure and content</u> of the intervention, and 2) what are the <u>processes that guide interactions</u> within the intervention. Thus, in the upcoming chapters, we provide a roadmap of the basic tasks and structure of the intervention and we also comment on the processes that make the intervention client-centered and optimally flexible, open, and responsive to clients' needs.

Because people are designing interventions using different delivery methods, we have created guidelines to address how to engage in three different methods of delivery—individual face-to-face interventions, group-based interventions, and mobile health interventions. Each of these modes of delivery shares common threads, yet they also have unique components and challenges to consider. In our practices, we often use a combination of these delivery modes in order to best reach our clients and meet the demand of managing costs. We suggest that you read each chapter to decide what delivery mode or combination might best work for your population. Appendix C provides references for applications of SDT interventions in various health domains and these reviews provide important synopses of these literatures (Fortier, Duda, Guerin, & Teixeira, 2012; Fortier, Williams, Sweet, & Patrick, 2009; Ryan, Patrick, Deci, & Williams, 2008; Teixeira, Carraça, Markland, Silva, & Ryan, 2012; Van de Berghe, Vansteenkiste, Cardon, Kirk, & Haerens, 2014).

CHAPTER 7.

Individual face-to-face interventions

The Initial Interview

Clients often feel overwhelmed about behavioral change and are not sure how to proceed. Many have had a long history of failed attempts to change and/or sustain behavior change. Thus, the initial meeting is designed to gather information, build rapport so that clients feel comfortable and trust that you are their advocate, discuss possible pathways toward their desired changes, and build confidence that change is manageable. In this chapter we outline the basic content that we typically cover in this initial phase and the process that guides this session (summary in Appendix D). To demonstrate this approach herein we will use the example of a client who is interested in weight loss, but in Appendix E we also include an example of how this dialogue might unfold if a practitioner is working with a client who is interested in quitting tobacco.

Provide a framework or general outline for the session. Usually we begin each session by describing what to expect out of today's session. We let clients know how much time we have and what kinds of information we might try to learn in this session. But, we also check in with them about what they think about the framework of the session and whether there are other things to add to the agenda. Importantly upfront we set the tone of our collaboration by encouraging clients to ask questions and have open dialogue about how things are going throughout the session.

Ideally (if possible), allow 60 minutes to conduct this initial interview. If this amount of time is not reasonable given your workplace constraints, you can use the client experience questionnaires (Appendices F, G, H, I) to gather some initial data (but make sure you read what they wrote if you do this!) and/or break up the activities of this session into multiple sessions. Taking the time to do this initial assessment right is essential to understanding clients' perspectives and goals and ultimately to retaining their participation in the process. Below we provide a sample of how we might introduce the session. In Appendix J we provide the dialogue throughout this chapter again with sidebar notes to explain how each part of the dialogue provides need support.

Thanks so much for coming in today. Today we have about 50 minutes to talk. In this first session I typically like to use this time to learn a little more about you— your background, your health, and your experiences around [insert health behavior, e.g., trying to lose weight]. I am interested in both the challenges you have encountered and what has worked well for you. I would also like to spend some time learning about your goals and what you hope to get out of our work together. All of this information will help us to understand a bit more about how to create a plan that best addresses your needs and make any changes you want to make more manageable. Near the end of the session we can discuss some potential ways to address some of your goals and determine what we want to do in terms of next steps. What do you think of that plan for today? Anything else you think I missed that we should add to our agenda?

Because our work together is about managing your health it is helpful to have your inputs throughout our work together. So I'll do my best to check in with you about your thoughts and feelings throughout the session but please also feel free to stop me at any time while we are talking to ask questions or to let me know other thoughts you might have.

Introduce your background and role. People often like to know who they are talking to. Many clients will not have seen you before. Some will be anxious about disclosing information and they need to feel like they are working with a person they can trust. By briefly explaining your training background and your experience helping people make health behavior changes you will help clients to develop a sense of who you are and how you might be helpful to them. If you have other team members that will work with you in their care it is also useful to talk about their functions. So, for example, in one of the weight loss programs we designed our team was made up of registered dietitians, exercise physiologists, nurses, and psychological health professionals (psychologist, social worker). Although clients mainly saw one of these professionals for their main point of contact, we let clients know that the team works together to formulate plans and that the other professionals on the team are available for consultation about particular challenges. Thus, clients have the ability to draw on the expertise of many different disciplines in our practice. If you do not have this kind of team readily available, you may want to consider letting clients know about how you utilize other professional and community resources to support your practice and their care. For example, it may be useful to talk about how you can work with their primary care physician to help manage their care. Below we provide a sample of how we might introduce this information.

> *So before I ask you more about yourself, I wanted to let you know a little about my background and the team we have here to assist you in your care. I am a registered dietitian by training, which means that I regularly work with people to help them learn about how good nutrition, incorporating new foods into their diets, and planning meals can help them to lose weight and improve their health. We don't need to just explore changes to your diet. We can talk about incorporating physical activity, managing stress, or other behaviors, such as smoking, that might also be impacting your health. It's up to you how much or little we might work on these different aspects of your health. I have training to address these other issues, but we also have other team members—an exercise physiologist, nurse, and psychologist—who can consult on any specific area of concern so that we can ensure we are doing the best in terms of your care. [Alternative if you do not have a team that you work with: I regularly consult with colleagues—an exercise physiologist, nurse, and psychologist—who can, with your permission, work with us on any specific area of concern you have so that we can ensure that we do the best in terms of your care.]. With your permission, we can also work closely with your primary care physician to coordinate your care. Do you have any questions?*

Getting to know the client. Clients are more likely to stay engaged with providers who show interest and care for them personally. Plus, because each client is unique in terms of their personal circumstances, their strengths, and their challenges, and these factors will influence their treatment, spending time to get to know them personally, learn about their health history, and learn about their health behaviors currently will help to better formulate the "big picture" and tailor treatment to clients' unique profile.

Below are some examples of questions used to gather information in an open, non-judgmental way. Remember, to be open and non-judgmental requires being genuinely curious about clients and working to understand how they have come to be where they are today. Not all questions are used at once. Be flexible with the flow of conversation--questions are best used, as the practitioner feels appropriate, within the context of a conversation.

Personal history. *Tell me a little about yourself. What do you do for a living? What's your workplace like? Family? Any pets?* This brief introduction just gives the practitioner a sense of the basic landscape of the client's world. It is important to listen not only for key pieces of information about their work life (What does their job entail? What are the demands of the workplace?) and home life (Do they live alone? Do they have a gaggle of young kids?) but also *how* they talk about these pieces of information. That is, clients often leak feelings (positive or negative) about their home life and work life. File away this information in your brain, as it will become useful when you learn more about clients' stressors and social supports later in the session.

Understanding the health behavior in context. If we know that clients are interested in changing a particular health behavior and we have the opportunity to contact them before they come in for a scheduled appointment we often use a brief questionnaire ahead of time to get them thinking more deeply about their health behaviors and their motivations for changing them.

A copy of this questionnaire for each health behavior discussed in this manual is found in Appendices G and H. You will notice that we ask not only about the relevant health behaviors but we also ask about current stressors as well as current social supports. Stressors can derail even best laid plans, and as we discussed earlier in this manual, social supports are key to whether behavior change is sustained. Thus, learning about these factors upfront can help the practitioner to better see the complex dynamics that may be impacting behavior change. Below we illustrate how we use these questions to guide the conversation for the initial session.

History of identified health behavior. To lead in to taking a history of the health behavior clients want to change, begin by reflecting on their reason for coming (Transition question: *What brings you here today?*). Here we use the example of losing weight to illustrate a potential follow up conversation.

> *You are here to get some assistance in losing weight. I wonder if you could tell me a little about your experience with trying to lose weight in the past.*
>
> *What did you do to try to lose weight in the past?*
>
> *When was 1ˢᵗ time you tried to lose weight?*
>
> *How often have you tried to lose weight?*
>
> *What has been challenging? What didn't work well?*
>
> *Has anything worked well for you?*
>
> *Any new or additional challenges for you currently that are making it difficult to lose weight?*

There are important processes that dictate this line of questions. First, it is important to periodically (e.g., every few minutes) reflect back to clients what they have said to ensure you have a true understanding of what they said and what they are feeling. Obviously, we cannot anticipate all that clients will say and thus cannot script these responses for you. Good reflections require good listening. However, below we provide some examples of reflective statements that are non-judgmental in tone. Note that reflecting is not simply parroting back the words to clients. Instead, reflections contain brief summaries of core themes, a check-in to clarify information, and/or echo the meaning or emotional experience of events for clients.

> *I heard you say that having kids has really made it challenging to have time for yourself. It sounds like this stress has contributed to not always eating very well or getting time to exercise.* (***brief summary***)

> *It sounds like you felt like you had a better handle on your weight in your 20s because it was easier to exercise and lose the weight. But that doesn't seem to be working well now. Is that right?* (***check information***)

> *My understanding is you have been struggling with your weight since childhood and that it made you feel not so good about yourself, especially when you were a teenager. And from what you said, it sounds like some of those feelings continue even today.* (***reflecting meaning for client***)

It is important to clarify and deepen an understanding of their experience, not only to get more details but also to get a better sense of their feelings about their experience than they might initially offer. For example, clients often have a lot of information to convey and inadvertently leave out important details. They might omit feelings that accompany their experience. So, querying about these features becomes an important part of the conversation. Remember, ask for more information in a way that does not impose a judgment (e.g., *Can you tell me more about that?; I'm wondering what that's been like for you?*)

For some clients, these queries may still not yield more information. You may need to be more specific about what information you are looking for. So, for example, "*Can you tell me more about that?*" might need to be refined to query more specifically about details (e.g., "*So you said that being overweight kept you from doing things that you wanted to. What sort of things did it keep you from doing?*). Querying thoughts and feelings about their experience, as is the case in asking "*I'm wondering what that's been like for you?*" might not yield more information because clients are having difficulty clarifying their thoughts or labeling their emotional experience. In this case it might be useful to consider what they might have felt and wonder with them about those feelings. For example:

> *It sounds like that might have been pretty hard for you* (Alternative: *It seems that you might have been pretty disappointed by that experience.*)

> *Often people feel pretty frustrated and defeated when they try a bunch of ways to lose weight and run into a lot of obstacles. I'm wondering if you might have had this experience as well.*

To figure out what thoughts and feelings might be occurring clients, listen to what they are saying. They are often giving you clues as to their likely experience. You can also draw from common experiences that other clients have had. Remember that when you offer up a reflection it should be in the spirit of allowing clients to "try on" what you are saying and let you know whether you have "got it". So statements are not pronouncements about your observations of the truth but rather are offered in the service of checking in and making sure you are seeing clients' experience accurately through their eyes.

Before transitioning to the next part of the intake session, it is important to check in about any details you may have missed or other important information that clients might want to share. This invites clients to help you to better understand them.

> *So I think I have a pretty good understanding about your experience around trying to lose weight. Is there anything that you think I have missed? Anything else important that you think I should know before we talk about your goals?*

49

Learning about motivations for behavior change and their goals. Understanding

clients' history provides the backdrop to their experience. If this was a movie or a book, you just

gathered the backstory of the character in order to give context to present day behaviors. So, the

next step is to understand what is prompting an attempt at behavior change now and what they

hope to accomplish.

> *So I'm curious about what is making you want to [lose weight] now?*
> *[Alternative: What are your reasons for wanting to lose weight now?]*

This question is fairly open-ended. Remember that just like other questions you ask, the follow

up is important. So, for example, if they say that they want to lose weight to be healthier, a

potential follow up might be "*Is there anything that has happened lately that has made you focus*

more on your health?". The reasons that people give often have a story behind them--they just

don't emerge out of nowhere. So by querying further you might learn more about what is

prompting their focus--was it an aunt who died recently of heart disease, a diagnosis of diabetes,

or the recognition that they just want to be more physically able to participate in activities with

their spouse and kids? The answer helps you to understand the *quality* of their motivation.

Another important point to remember is that behavior change is often not just prompted

by one reason. So, it is important to query about whether there are other reasons that are

influencing clients' interest to change their behaviors. Appendix F can be used to help discuss

the various motivations with your clients.

> *So I'm wondering if there are other things influencing your want to lose weight*
> *now? People often have a number of things influencing their decision to lose*
> *weight---they want to get better health benefits or spend less money on health*
> *care, they are getting pressured from others to lose weight, they want to feel*
> *better physically, or they want to do other things that are important to them (like*
> *travel, play with their kids, or do fun activities with their friends) and losing some*

weight will help them to do that more easily. I'm wondering if any of these kinds of reasons or any others might be influencing your decision as well?

Equally important to understanding clients' reasons for change is to also understand what motivates them to *not* change their behavior. Let's face it--people get some pleasure out of the behaviors that they are engaging in, whether it is direct (e.g., eating sweet treats and high fat foods or smoking to get a physical rush; being sedentary to relax) or indirect (e.g., eating and smoking are often a part of social interactions). Helping clients to recognize what they get out of their behaviors also helps them to begin to understand some of the pulls that keep them from changing and helps them to make a more informed decision about whether or not they will try to change. Here are some potential ways to ask about the benefits of not changing their behaviors.

Any reasons for not wanting to change your current behaviors?

Anything you think you'll miss, or miss out on, if you change your behaviors?

Are there any benefits you get from not changing any of your behaviors?

It is important to reflect back to clients what they have said in order to summarize the different pulls to maintain versus change their behavior. Moreover, it is important to then ensure you have a true understanding of the balance of these pulls.

On one hand you have some reasons to change your behavior such as (insert what they said) and on the other hand there are some pulls such as (insert what they said) that might make you not want to change. I'm wondering what you think about the balance of these different motivations? How strong is each side pulling right now?

For clients who have a strong sense of ambivalence about changing their behavior--that is, the pulls are strong both to maintain their current behaviors and to change their behaviors--it will be important to spend more time sorting through their motivations. We focus the next chapter on doing an in-depth exploration of ambivalence.

For those who have a relatively stronger pull toward making a behavioral change, it is then important to understand the balance of their different motives for change.

> *So it sounds like you are strongly leaning toward changing your behavior. I also heard that there are a lot of different reasons that you have for changing, including* [insert the different reasons for change that they stated earlier]. *Out of those reasons, what do you think is the strongest reason fueling your want to change your behaviors?*

Although you likely have some clue as to whether clients want to change their behaviors for more autonomous versus controlled reasons simply by the sheer number of autonomous versus controlled motivations that they cited already, the frequency or count on each side of the autonomy continuum doesn't tell the whole story. That is, one very strong controlling reason or one very strong autonomous reason might drown out all of the others. Thus, intensity or significance of the reason for wanting to change *will matter*. So, the rationale behind asking the above question is to understand clients' perception of the state of their motivational balance.

Where clients are motivationally will help to tailor responses to them. In all cases, practitioners will want to acknowledge and validate how clients' reason fuels their behavior. For those who are operating out of more controlled reasons, providers will additionally want to address how we might try to develop more autonomous reasons for behavior change and work to lessen controlled motives throughout the course of treatment. For those who are operating out of more autonomous reasons, providers will also want to have clients attend to when controlled motives become louder so that together they can work to realign balance toward greater autonomy. Below we offer some general ways to address the issue of motivational balance, although we encourage practitioners to have deeper discussions with clients about their balance when clients are amenable to such dialogue.

> ***If controlling pressures are strongest:*** *Sounds like you feel pretty pressured to change your behaviors right now. One of the things that we know is that pressure can kick us into gear to get started with behavior change but we also need other reasons to keep doing the behavior over the long term. So, as we work together I am wondering if we can try to see if there are some ways to help you feel less pressured and find your own personal value for these behaviors (and maybe even find ways to help you like it too). How does that sound to you?*

> ***If autonomous reasons are strongest:*** *Sounds like changing your behaviors right now is really important to you personally. The personal value and interest in changing your behavior that you have right now will be important to sticking with these behaviors over the long term. Sometimes over the course of treatment clients find that they start to feel more pressure to change their behaviors. As we work together if you start to feel more pressure to engage in these health behaviors let's talk about how that is affecting you. That way we can try to see if there are some ways to help you feel less pressured and rediscover your own personal value, interest, and enjoyment. How does that sound to you?*

There are two critical points to pay attention to in the dialogue above. First, we do not want to convey that there are "good" motivations and "bad" motivations. Remember, people have many different motivations for engaging in health behaviors, even the most autonomously motivated people. So, people will have a mix of motivations that influence their behavior at any given time. However, it is important to understand that to sustain behaviors over the long term and feel good about maintaining their health behaviors, clients will need to cultivate autonomous motivations for their behaviors. Thus, we want to talk about the process of internalization as an inherent aim of treatment.

Second, it is imperative to check in with clients about what they think about this notion of working toward greater internalization. Some clients might think it is nonsense while for others the idea resonates with them. Learning about how clients think about the process of behavior change will help you to better take their frame of reference and be more understanding of how they orient toward treatment. Thus, the goal is to remain client-centered.

Depending on how much time you have with clients each session and how much time the previous discussion took, this may be a natural point to begin to wrap up the session and set the frame for your work together in upcoming sessions. Here's an example of how to convey this.

> *We have talked about a lot today—I learned about your experience of trying to lose weight in the past and I learned about your motivations for changing your behaviors. The next step is to learn a little more about your current health behaviors, develop some potential options for changing these behaviors, and see what goals, if any, you would like to work towards. I'm wondering if that is something you are interested in doing?*
>
> **If yes:** *Because doing all of this will take more time than we have left today, we can make another appointment so that we can talk more about these things.* [Set up an appointment to follow up within a week]
>
> **If no:** *I am wondering if you can help me better understand what led you to that decision?* [Allow the client to respond, then reflect back what you heard].
>
> *I am wondering whether it would be helpful to you if we make some time down the road to check back in? What's important to know is that the option of whether we follow-up is up to you and I will do my best to offer support around whatever you choose.* [If yes, then schedule an appointment in a month or two from now. This can be a simple phone check in or a formal face to face appointment.]

Learning about current health behaviors. Part of helping clients make behavior changes is to learn a bit more about their starting point. Each person is going to have their own unique habits so taking this history will provide a snapshot as to their daily living and allow you to better personalize and tailor treatment. In Appendix H we provide a detailed set of questions to guide this section of the session. It's worth noting that for some clients it is useful to write down what they are saying so that you can look at the visual together. Make sure to do this only if the client will find it helpful.

In the next bit of time I would like to learn more about you're current health behaviors. If you can help me get the most accurate picture of your current [eating, physical activity, smoking] patterns, this will help us to identify some potential opportunities for change.

Current Diet. *So to start I would like to learn a little more about your current eating habits. Tell me what a typical day looks like for you when you feel you are on target with your goals, when you feel that you are eating in a way that feels good to you.*

Now tell me what a day looks like for you when you are having a bad day, when you feel like you are eating in a way that doesn't feel good to you.

How many days of the week would you say you are having a "good" day? How many "off" days typically?

Current Physical Activity. *Now I am wondering about your current level of physical activity. Outside of exercise, what is your usual level of physical activity each day? So for example, some people sit all day at work while others move around a lot during the day.*

How do you feel about exercising? Do you like it? (If yes: why do you like it?; If no: why don't you like it?)

What kinds of activities did you do?

How often do you exercise each week (e.g., walk, ride bike, elliptical, etc.)? How long did you typically exercise on those days?

Do you exercise with anyone? If yes: How does that go for you? Is it helpful/not helpful to have others around?

What things keep you from being active?

Are there any kinds of exercise that might you be interesting in trying out? Anything you used to like to do? Anything new that sounds intriguing?

Current stressors. *Oftentimes stressors can impact your attempts to change health behaviors. On a scale from 1 to 10 (with 1 being little or no stress and 10 being the most stressed you have ever felt in your life) what would you say is your current level of stress?*

I'm wondering what kinds of things create stress in your life right now?

What is it about those life events are causing you the most stress?

This is also an important point in your conversation to talk with your clients about the timing of making behavioral changes. When clients are overly stressed, it is often difficult to make changes because they just don't have the energy, mental capacity, and flexibility to make even small changes and manage the seemingly inevitable disappointments that will likely come their way. If they are super stressed, sometimes it is useful to help them work on reducing some of this stress before they tackle other health behavior changes. Again, this is not for you the practitioner to decide but it is an opportunity to have a dialogue with your clients about their stress and the potential impact on behavioral change. If their level of stress is quite high, here are some potential ways to query about whether they would like to address these stressors.

> *You said that your current level of stress is pretty high. How do you think that might impact the changes you are hoping to make?*

> *Are there any stressors that you think you would need to tackle to make this behavior change a little easier?*

Social Support. It is important in the first session to query about the kinds of supports clients have as well as who might also impede their attempts to make changes.

> *We know that the important people in your life can influence how easy or difficult it will be to make behavior changes.*

> *I'm wondering...in general, who are the important people in your life that provide you support? Who do you think you can count on for support around changing your behaviors so you can lose some weight?*

> *Are there any people in your life that are making it difficult for you to change your behaviors to lose weight?*

We are listening here not just for who they say are important supports but also who is absent from the list. If clients mentioned earlier that they are married but then do not cite their spouse as a key support, you can ask about that. Also, you can query about how other important people in their lives might react to them when they try to change their behaviors.

I noticed that when I asked you about who are your best supports you mentioned two of your close friends, but your spouse was not someone you listed. I'm wondering how your spouse fits in the picture?

So how do you think your kids/extended family/co-workers will react to you trying to eat healthier?

Any worries about how changing your diet will be received by others?

Health issues. While clients are waiting to begin their appointment we ask them to complete a brief checklist to alert us to important medical history (e.g., example for clients coming in for weight loss can be found in Appendix I). The checklist covers medical, surgical, psychiatric history as well as current medications. We review this checklist for any significant issues or medications that may impact efforts to make health behavior changes (e.g., some medications make weight loss more difficult). We then always check in with clients to obtain more information about how these health factors are impacting them.

While you were waiting for today's appointment to start you completed a checklist about your current medical conditions. I noticed that you indicated a few things on this list. I would like to just go through these briefly so that I can better understand how these conditions are affecting you right now. Does that sound okay?

You indicated here that you have [insert healthy condition]. I wonder if you could tell me more about that? How is this impacting your functioning? Does this create any limitations for you?

Proceed through the checklist. It is always good at the end to ask clients if you have missed anything or if they think there is any other relevant health information you should know about.

Formulation of preliminary macro-level goals. Clients often have a set of goals in mind when they enter treatment. Some will have several specific goals while others might just express more general aims. So, it is helpful to learn a bit more about what they hope to achieve. At this point you do not need to develop specific goals. Rather, just get the broad strokes of what they hope for. Later on, we will dig deeper into the details and clarify the picture.

> *People often have a goal in mind that they would like to achieve (e.g., regain energy and mobility, reduce pain in everyday life activities, be able to be more active to play with their kids or join in activities with their partner or friends). What goal or goals do you hope to achieve through our work together?*

If you did not end the session at the previous break point and you are running out of time in this session, this is another potential place to end the session. Next session you will continue exploring goals, devising a menu of options, and choosing the next steps. If ending here, wrap up the session using the same dialogue as outlined in the previous break point, adding the reflections about what you learned about their health behaviors, social supports, current health conditions, and preliminary goals. If you are continuing the session, it is still good to check in with your client to summarize the information you have heard up to this point and see how the client is doing. The process of disclosing information can be both relieving to clients but also hard. So, it is good to take a moment to slow down the pace, understand how they feel, and offer support if needed.

> *We have covered a lot of territory today. I want to take a moment to check back in with you to summarize what I've heard and see if I have a good sense of important information.*

Convey a formulation of what you heard to be a summary of their history around the health behavior, their current challenges, and their current goals. This formulation should be relatively brief, but thorough. Check back in to see if you are right. (*Anything important that you feel I have missed? Any other goals you want to add to the list now that we have talked more?*) Sometimes the conversation can prompt clients to add new information or new goals to the formulation. So, giving them the opportunity to reflect on whether we have the whole picture gives them a chance to do this.

Some clients may be overwhelmed at this point, while others will be energized by the discussion. Taking a moment to take the temperature (*How are you feeling?)* about where they are is particularly important because the next sections introduce more information about treatment options and initiate an important decision making process about how they want to proceed next, which are two critical pieces to the initial process. If they are overwhelmed you can bet that making a decision about how to proceed will be more difficult. So, if this is the case it might be best to see if they want to continue the conversation again next session, with the explicit agenda for next time to go over treatment options and make decisions about they might want to proceed. Here's how you might consider offering them time to revisit the conversation with them at another date. Use your clinical judgment and listen to what the client wants to do.

> *Because we have talked about a lot today I am wondering whether it would be a good point to take a break and make another appointment to talk again? We can either continue on today to talk about different treatment options and making a plan for how you want to proceed or we can set up another time so that we can spend some more time exploring those issues? It's up to you…what feels doable?*

Discussing options for treatment. By now you likely have a pretty good understanding of the behavioral change landscape for your clients. The next step is to begin to explore treatment options, providing a meaningful rationale for why these strategies have been determined to be the options you have offered.

> *There are different options we can explore to help you to lose weight. Are you interested in hearing information about some potential options?*[If yes, then describe what each involves and provide a rationale for some of the health benefits of each]

59

Eat healthier. *One way to go about losing weight is to focus on eating healthier. There are many ways to eat healthier. Some of things we might focus on are learning about nutrition, portion control, meal planning, cooking strategies and new recipes, and introducing new foods, among other things.*

Get regular physical activity. *Another way to go about losing weight is to focus on getting more physically active. When we focus on physical activity we typically look for ways to increase your daily activity overall (such as standing and getting moving more often during the day than sitting) and begin to incorporate exercise routine into your week. Often we start with walking to get people started but we really would be looking to develop a routine that involves activities that are most interesting and enjoyable to you. We can also add stretching and strength training (e.g. such as resistance bands or weights) to further build your physical fitness.*

Combination of eating healthier and getting regular physical activity. *We also can tackle weight loss by doing a combination of healthy eating and physical activity strategies.*

The potential benefit of changing up your diet and level of physical activity is that it can lower your cholesterol, improve your blood pressure, and improve your sugars, which are all important in lowering your risk for developing heart disease, diabetes, and some cancers. People often also report that changing diet and physical activity also helps to improve their energy levels, improve their mood, and make it easier to do everyday activities, such as climbing the stairs, taking a walk, or keeping up with friends, family, and co-workers.

This is a lot of information for clients to absorb. So it is always important to stop and ask for their feedback, thoughts, and questions they might have about the options presented.

I've given you a lot of information. I'm wondering if you have any thoughts or questions about what I have said so far?

Although you may have a typical menu of options that are dictated by your practice, it is useful to ask about whether there are other treatment options that clients are interested in. For example, in the case of weight loss, clients might be interested in also learning about bariatric surgery, medications, specific diets, and herbal supplements.

These are the typical ways that we address weight loss. Are there other ideas or strategies that you are interested in talking about?

It is important to not go beyond the scope of your expertise here. You don't have to know everything! In fact, feigning knowledge just serves to undermine clients' confidence in you. If you know that there are other typical treatments that they might want more information on, it would be good to have resources for clients (e.g., pamphlets describing bariatric surgery; reputable informational websites) as well as contact information for professionals they might consult with to explore these alternative options.

Develop a collaborative plan for next steps, as appropriate. To develop a motivationally tailored plan, the next step is to understand clients' interest in the intervention options. If they are interested in a particular option, offer them some materials to read before the next session and set the frame for your next session.

> *So we've discussed a number of options, do any of these approaches sound appealing? Any sound more manageable for you right now?*

> *Because our session is almost over for today and because I want to make sure we have enough time for our next steps, next time we can plan on working on setting some preliminary goals and choosing some strategies to tackle changes. In the meantime, I have some materials that can provide more details about how we might tackle [changing your diet, increasing physical activity, both changing your diet and increasing your physical activity]. I am wondering if you would be interested in looking over some of these before our next session?*

It is important here that the materials you give to clients are not overwhelming. So, don't just inundate them with handouts, but rather be choiceful about having prepared some summaries of each approach to behavior change and also provide them web links to other readings that they can follow up on if they so choose. We have also created a print library of materials in our waiting areas and our own websites to choose from. This gives clients choices about selecting those avenues that seem most interesting to them but it also allows them to ease into the informational abyss at a pace that feels manageable.

If clients seem unsure about what is most appealing to them in the menu of options or are feeling overwhelmed by the decision to make a behavior change, you might consider offering them time to think about the options and revisit the conversation at another date.

> *Because we have talked about a lot today I am wondering whether it would be helpful to give you some information about each of these options and then we can make an appointment to talk again about what seems most appealing and doable for you. Some people consider all of their options but decide that making a change isn't something that they want to do right now. So, we can always leave that option open too and make some time down the road to check back in and see if anything has changed. What's important to know is that how we proceed is up to you and I will do my best to offer support around whatever you choose. Do you have a sense of whether you would like more information and set up a time to talk again in a week or two or would you rather hold off on considering making changes right now and maybe schedule some time in a month or two just to check in?*

At this point you cannot be sure whether clients are just simply worn out by the initial session and don't feel capable of making a decision, whether they genuinely want some time to ponder different options and perhaps talk with close others before making a decision, or whether they genuinely do not want to change their behaviors at this time. If clients clearly want to delay the decision process, then follow through with information and resources to help them make a decision and schedule a time to talk again within the next week (or as close to that as possible).

If clients are *not ready to change at all*, it is imperative that practitioners do not challenge that decision but rather attempt to understand their decision. It is then important to reflect what clients have said and express understanding for why their decision makes sense for them at this time. This helps clients know that they have been heard and that you truly are an advocate for their autonomous decision.

> *I respect your decision to not make changes right now. I am wondering if you can help me better understand what led you to that decision?*

Let clients know that they are welcome at any time to discuss their health behaviors. You may also offer a follow-up date to check in (in a month or a few months). This simple invitation can be effective even when clients do not initially wish to change their behavior—because it offers an opportunity to re-open the dialogue later if they so choose. The greatest chance you as a practitioner have to aid clients at some point in the future is to *not* pressure them in the present and let them know you are always willing to help if they ever decide differently.

Summary: The Initial Session

This initial session sets the tone for treatment and provides clients with their first glimpse of how you will support their psychological needs. Although the steps may seem like a long list of procedural details, Appendix J helps to illustrate the purpose and function of each of these steps in the support of clients' autonomy, competence, and relatedness needs.

CHAPTER 8.

Working through ambivalence

Most clients feel some measure of ambivalence about changing their behaviors. That is, there is often a conflict between their motives for change and their motives for not changing. Although the first place where this conflict between motivational pulls may come up is within the intake session(s), ambivalence emerges at different times throughout treatment. That is, ambivalence does not stop when one decides to dive into a behavior change. It continues to rear its head. Thus, the process of working through ambivalence that we will discuss in this chapter is one that we may revisit over and over again throughout treatment. Our goal is to foster an open dialogue with clients to help them identify their various motives, move out of a place of being "stuck" between their various motivational pulls, and develop their autonomous goals, even if these goals consist of not wanting to change their behaviors. What may differ is the form and function of the ambivalence at different points in time.

Ambivalence to initiate change

At the beginning of treatment ambivalence centers around two key themes. The first is a question of whether clients want to engage in behavior change or do not want to at all. The second pertains to clients who do want to make a change but are struggling with *how* they want to change their behaviors.

The first question--whether clients want to change at all--harkens back to our earlier discussion about amotivation. Remember, when clients are amotivated, they are not currently engaged in the target behaviors and their disengagement may be fueled by several reasons. First, amotivation can indicate that behavior change may not actually be important to clients or may not be in line with what they actually want to do. The intervention in this case focuses on illuminating the various reasons to change or to not change behavior, and assesses the relative strength of each side of the balance with clients so that they can begin to move in the most autonomous direction.

Second, clients may not feel equipped to make changes. Even considering a change feels like a high-stakes risk (e.g., personal success or failure is on the line) and attempting to change feels like an insurmountable task. For most clients this is not their first rodeo--most have tried to change their lifestyle behaviors in the past and have experienced disappointment with initial outcomes or have been unable to maintain desired outcomes over the long term. When clients lack confidence in their efficacy and/or are disappointed by prior outcomes, the focus of the intervention is on helping them voice their feelings about these experiences and their current fears about attempting behavior change, and it is also about explaining how the resources you will provide can help them to build knowledge, develop tools, and guide them on their journey. Thus, this approach tries to quiet the fears that clients have and make the challenges feel manageable so that they can envision change as a real possibility. Then, they can more freely explore the pros and cons of behavior change and assess whether they are indeed personally interested in making such changes.

Many intervention approaches use Janis and Mann's (1977) decisional balance exercise to help clients clarify the benefits and drawbacks of changing versus maintaining their behaviors. This exercise includes facilitating a dialogue about clients' perceptions of the pros and cons of engaging in the behavior (e.g., being more physically active) and the pros and cons of maintaining the status quo (e.g., maintaining a sedentary lifestyle or the same level of physical activity that they currently have). We also employ this decisional balance exercise in our practices. This tool can be implemented in a visual format--written out by clients and simply facilitated by practitioners--or it can simply be facilitated in conversation. For example, here is how we might initiate each part of the decisional balance:

Pros of being sedentary/maintaining current PA: *What do you like about your current level of physical activity? What's appealing about keeping everything the same as it is now?*

Cons of being sedentary/maintaining current PA: *What are the drawbacks of keeping your physical activity level the same as it is now?*

Cons of being more physically active: *What kinds of things would you consider to be negative, or not so good, about trying to be more physically active?*

Pros of being more physically active: *What do think are the positives that would come from being more physically active?*

This exercise helps practitioners initially understand clients' perspectives. It also helps clients see more clearly their motivations for maintaining their current behaviors or changing them, as well as acknowledge their own internal conflicts. It is important to note that what makes our approach different than other uses of this decisional balance exercise is that we are also actively listening for and querying about the different reasons that fuel amotivation (importance, competence, outcome expectations) as well as the different motivations that fuel making a behavioral change (autonomous vs. controlled). Thus, we use the queries that we have introduced in prior sections of this book to help clients fill out the motivational picture so that they are poised to make an autonomous decision about change.

If clients are not clear on whether they want to make changes to their current behaviors, providers can ask whether they want to do some experimentation to test the waters of change.

Would you be willing to try to incorporate just a bit of physical activity into your days this week (perhaps walking for a few minutes in the morning, lunchtime, or the evening) and make some notes about what that was like for you?

*Would you be willing to try out cutting back on a particular food or beverage
(e.g., soda) that seems doable for this week and make some notes about what that
was like for you?*

*Would you be willing to do an experiment and quit for half of the day to see what
it feels like? You can use intermittent Nicotine Replacement Therapy (NRT), like
gum, lozenge, inhaler, or nasal spray, if you would like. NRTs are especially
helpful if you have never made a quit attempt, as they can provide significant
relief from withdrawal symptoms.*

If clients are not interested in experimenting with change, negotiate a plan to connect again in the next month or two to reassess interest in behavioral change. This intervention is best done with considerable patience, tolerance, and respect for clients' choice. Remember, this approach keeps the door open for contact and serves as an important invitation for future desired change.

*So it's my understanding that you might want to change up some of aspects of
your diet or physical activity but you want to take some time to think about this
before you start on making some changes?*

*Some people consider all of their options but decide that making a change isn't
something that they want to do right now. I respect your decision to not make
changes right now. We can always leave the option open to make some time down
the road to check back in and see if anything has changed. What's important to
know is that the option of how we proceed is up to you and I will do my best to
offer support around whatever you choose. Do you have a sense of whether you
would like me to check back in with you in month or two?*

Ambivalence that emerges later in behavior change

Later in treatment, even when people have committed to engaging in health behavior change, new challenges come up that make it difficult to still engage in further health behavior changes. For example, as clients' priorities shift so might their intention to make further changes to their behaviors. Sometimes those are choiceful decisions while at other times they are thrust upon the person (e.g., parent, spouse, or child becomes ill, the client becomes the caregiver, and no longer has the resources to engage in further changes). So resolving ambivalence may be

67

about timing--helping clients give themselves permission to take that break and find an entry

way back into treatment at a later time point.

Ambivalence later in treatment may also take the form of grappling with whether to

pursue one behavioral path versus another. For example, clients often struggle with whether to

push the changes they have made to the next level or whether they want to work simply on

mastering and maintaining their current behaviors. In essence they are grappling with whether

the changes they have made are "good enough" for now or whether they want to make more. To

help clients make decisions at this juncture it is important to help them pay attention to their

energy and interest in the next steps. Do they want to push to next level of changes because they

feel pressured to or are they interested in new challenges? Notice again we return to assessing

motivations for behavioral change and help clients pay attention to acting from an autonomous

place. We will say much more about this process in the upcoming chapter.

Summary: Working through ambivalence

Ambivalence is a characteristic feature of most behavioral change. Clients often first

grapple with ambivalence--simultaneously wanting to and not wanting to change their behaviors-

-in the decision to seek and begin treatment. But, even once they have committed to a treatment

path, ambivalence will again likely emerge. Thus, helping clients recognize that they will have

many motivations and hone skills to effectively assess their motivational landscape provides

them the power to make more autonomous, informed choices about their behavioral path.

CHAPTER 9.

The work after the initial session

If clients are ready to begin to make some behavioral changes the first step is to understand the scope of the work you will tackle together and what level of guidance and scaffolding they need to proceed. In essence, you are defining the structure needed to help them build competence. Some clients will need very little education and they will be self-directed with a program, whereas others will need more basic education, collaborative planning on practical details, and guidance to tackle challenges that emerge along the way. Starting from this basic foundational information, a tailored intervention can then be built. In the following chapters we outline the key steps that we have found to be most helpful in the path toward behavior change. What you will notice is that clients are introduced to a variety of behavioral strategies that have been shown in prior research and interventional work to help them succeed in making health behavior changes. These include strategies such as goal setting (develop specific, realistic goals), action planning (help participants create concrete, tailored plans for reaching goals), action implementation (how to follow a concrete plan for behavior change--determining how/what/when/where and the associated behaviors needed, e.g., packing gym bag, schedule exercise in planner), self-monitoring (assessing daily behaviors and adherence to goals by completing daily dietary and exercise log that records time of day and quantity of foods consumed and type, intensity, duration of activity), learning how to give oneself self-referenced evaluative feedback on goal progress (how did I do relative to my plan?), identify and manage cues for eating and inactivity (e.g., home, work, grocery store, restaurants), and identify challenges or barriers and engage in problem solving (e.g., how to change the plan, garner the scaffolding or social supports needed). So, we do not re-invent the wheel--we briefly describe the strategies used, provide examples of worksheets (when applicable), and refer you to other writings to explore other tools to support these techniques. What you will notice however that is that what makes our approach unique is *how* we structure treatment overall and employ these techniques within treatment. In other words, the *process* by which we approach using these behavioral strategies is often different than how they are typically employed in other interventions.

What do we mean by this? First, change is not a linear process. That is, most clients move in and out of the various treatment activities, revisiting different steps along the way as they learn more about themselves and more about what they need to do to succeed in behavioral change. Different clients also move through tasks at a different pace and with different levels of ease. So, some clients may struggle with a particular task while others may find the same task a breeze. Thus, the activities of treatment do not follow a set number of sessions (problem solving could take 1 session or 6 to master, depending on clients' needs) and treatment does not have to adhere to a rigid sequence (e.g., you don't have to wait to talk about the emotional impact of behavior change until session 10 if it is a prominent challenge for clients right now).

Second, in most health interventions, techniques or tasks are prescribed to clients. That is, the program has a philosophy about what is the "right" way to go about behavior change and what you do in treatment follows this prescription (e.g., clients are assigned homework, that homework is reviewed, and then the next assignment in the sequence is made). Although such structure might be useful to some clients, for others it actually turns them off and leads them to quit treatment. In our approach, providers plan treatment *with* the client and continually provide options for how to go about making behavior changes so that the approach fits with clients' wishes, at a pace that fits best with their overall lifestyle. The key for providers is to be flexible and match clients where they are. This gives clients the best chance of remaining engaged in behavioral change.

Third, there are some techniques used in other behavior change treatments that we simply do not endorse or employ within our approach (e.g. setting up reward contingencies, thought stopping). The main reason is that research has shown that these techniques will undermine clients' autonomous motivation, undermine their competence, and/or create conditions in which they feel conditionally regarded. We will note these techniques and provide a rationale for why we do not employ them.

Fourth, we have a more explicit focus on two areas that receive relatively little attention in health behavior change interventions--engaging the support of close relationships and managing stress. These arenas have a significant impact on treatment effectiveness yet typically only comprise a very limited portion of time in lifestyle interventions relative to other skills. Moreover, they are thought of as secondary or later targets of treatment when in reality these are often the issues that sink clients' efforts early on.

Finally, we spend concerted time with clients helping them to plan for maintenance. In fact, from the beginning of treatment we are thinking about maintenance, as we try to foster autonomous motivation for the health behaviors they are engaging in. More than that though we recognize that developing skills and sustaining them can pose different challenges. Thus, concerted time and energy is spent planning for maintenance.

So, what are the core tasks that we typically address during the course of treatment? In this chapter we elaborate on the activities described above as well as the processes that dictate their delivery (see Appendix K for summary).

71

Identifying the scope of treatment

Clients will have left the first session either identifying an initial course of action or wanting to ponder that initial course of action. The first task is to try to get a sense of the initial scope of work that you will be doing together and how to creatively tackle that scope of work.

Some clients will be limited in terms of the amount of insurance coverage that they will have for their care, the time that they are able to commit, or various other factors that might shape the course of your care. Although these issues may just seem to be part of doing the normal business of contracting treatment, it poses an interesting challenge for structuring treatment autonomously and at a pace that is doable for clients. As we know, insurance coverage and other constraints don't often match clients' needs. So, understanding if there are any limits upfront can help to better define a reasonable course of action for treatment as well as any external resources that you might want to begin to harness in order to supplement your work together and/or enable clients to continue their work once your course of treatment is done. Some of this conversation may be borne out more so once you and your clients have talked a bit more about their goals, but here is how we might ask about understanding any limiting factors

> As we start to plan out our work together it is helpful for us to know how much time we will have together and if there are any limits on how we develop our plan of action. So things like the number of sessions we have together and how often we see each other will shape how we proceed.

> I understand that your insurance will cover 12 sessions with me and beyond that any expenses would be out of pocket. I'm wondering what you are thinking about the feasibility of extending treatment beyond 12 sessions or whether you think we should be thinking about how to build up some resources outside of our work together.

Another part of creating the structure of treatment is to establish clear and consistent expectations upfront. In the SDT approach this is a collaborative process so that it is not simply practitioners doling out rules but rather is a contract between clients and providers about the scope of their work together and the mutual expectations of how their interactions will be conducted. Practitioners also have practical and ethical constraints under which they treat clients, therefore it is reasonable to establish a framework of these limitations for clients as well.

Developing goals

According to self-regulation theory (one of the dominant behavioral treatment approaches that focus on goals) people have both higher order goals that are tied to their sense of self as well as lower order goals that are constructed in support of the higher order goals. Both of these play an important role in treatment. For example, in treatment, goal structure is developed by exploring higher order life goals (e.g., wanting to lose 20 pounds) and tying health goals (e.g., increasing physical activity to lose weight) to these higher order goals. Then, discrepancy between current health behaviors (e.g., information on current levels of physical activity that is obtained often by the use of some self-monitoring technique) and what is needed to achieve higher order goals is examined. Goal setting (devising more specific, small goals about how to change behavior, e.g., increase physical activity to 50 minutes this week)—as well as action planning (details of where, when and how to do physical activity in order to achieve the goal) serve to better align current health behaviors with higher order goals. Finally, feedback with regard to goal benchmarks helps to revise and extend behaviors until goals are achieved.

In practice, many of the features of this approach to goal setting and implementation mirror our own approach. However, there are two key points where we diverge. First, self-regulation theory and other goal theories (e.g., achievement goal theory) do not distinguish between the relative autonomy of the goals being set. That is, in these other approaches, all goals are created equal and what matters most is the successful achievement of the goal. As SDT researchers have shown over the last 40 years, *what* goals people pursue (not just achieving a goal) matters to health and functioning, such that more autonomous goals are linked to greater persistence and well-being whereas extrinsic goals (e.g., pleasing others, improving physical appearance to get others to admire you) are associated with greater pressure, less persistence at behaviors over the long term, and ill health (see Ryan & Deci, 2017). So, within our approach we focus on helping clients to focus on these more autonomous reasons for behavior change.

Second, although self-regulation and achievement goal theories emphasize that interventions should help clients' form self-relevant goals, in practice these interventions have typically been adapted so that goals are set *for* clients rather than set together *with* clients. Again, this becomes quite problematic for several reasons. Clients each have a different starting point. Goals that are set for them will likely not match many clients very well. Thus, it sets up clients right from the start to feel like they have failed. Also, goals that are set *by* clients are meaningful to them and are more likely to be attended to because they have personal relevance. Thus, engaging in defining and setting the goal is just as important, if not more important, than achieving it. So, our focus is to have clients actively engaged in devising their personal goals.

Third, in many intervention approaches feedback about goal progress is thought of as the responsibility of the provider--that is, the provider gives the feedback. However, from the beginning we try to help clients learn to give themselves feedback using their own experience. What we have recognized is that many clients already know what is not working well for them, what their core challenges are, and what they might want to do to improve. Thus, they often don't need the infinite wisdom of practitioners to handle this task. More importantly, as one our core interests is in promoting the maintenance of behavior, clients who can provide self-relevant feedback will be better able to correct and sustain their behaviors long after treatment contact has ended. So, practicing this skill early on becomes a critical feature for self-sustaining behaviors. Below we discuss the core steps of goal setting, highlighting how these key features are integrated into this process.

Seeing health behavior in context in big picture life goals. Clients have complex lives that pull them in many different directions. Their own health often takes a back seat to other priorities. In fact, many clients focus their energy on helping others fulfill their goals and make sure that others needs are being met, sometimes even to the neglect of their own needs and their own goals (not just their health goals). Many clients worry that they are being selfish for wanting to focus energy on themselves and forget that being their best selves not only will benefit them but will also help them to be better supports for important others in their lives. This exercise to define big picture life goals explores ways that a healthy lifestyle might fit with other important autonomous values and goals (e.g., better able to play with kids/grandkids; being healthier will let me be around longer to be with my spouse). That is, this exercise helps client consider how a healthier lifestyle might help them to achieve other goals and support other priorities that are most important to them.

So, how do we actually help clients to prioritize themselves and incorporate health goals into their daily living? The first step is to have them take a moment to take stock of their big picture goals in various life domains, such as family (e.g., I want to be a good provider for my family), career (e.g., I want to run my own business), friendships (e.g., I want to spend quality, fun time with my closest friends), leisure (e.g., I want to travel), and other areas (e.g., I want to dedicate time to growing my spiritual life), as well as also articulate their overall goals for health (e.g., I want to get off blood pressure medications). Appendix L provides a worksheet that we often use with clients to help map these big picture goals. You may choose to use this exercise as

75

a guideline to shape the conversation with your clients rather than use the worksheet itself. Here's how we introduce this exercise.

People often have goals for family, work, friendships, leisure, and health, among other things—these are the things you are trying or would like to do, regardless of whether or not you are actually successful at them. We often find it helpful to understand the bigger picture of your life to better understand how making health changes can fit within that bigger picture. So to start, I'm wondering what some of your "big picture" goals and values are for different aspects of your life.

It's important to pay attention to goals that sound like they are for other people (not clients' own goals) and query about this. Remember that this exercise is about helping clients find their own voice and not simply continue to follow what they "should" or feel obligated to do.

The second step is to assess where clients' time and energy is going and evaluate whether their time is going towards their desired priorities. Here's how we might engage in a conversation about the balance of their priorities:

As you think about your "big picture" goals, I am wondering whether you are pursuing the things that are important to you? If not, what do you want to be your top priority?

Do you have the life balance that you want? If not, what is getting the most attention? What would you like to get more attention?

Beyond having a conversation, some clients find it is useful to further map out how much of their day or week or how much of their overall activity is dedicated to each life area. For those that want this visual exercise, our colleagues have had clients partition hours in the day, sections in a weekly calendar, or sections in a pie chart to represent how their time is allocated to each life domain or activity. Whether you end up talking about or visually seeing an illustration of their life balance, this step can help clients begin to think about how to put energy back into those things that are most important to them.

Because our work with clients is about behavior change, the focus is not just on their overall life goals but also closely examines clients' health goals and how they fit into the big picture of their priorities. First, it is important to understand the current state of affairs--what are their health goals and how do they fit into the overall picture right now.

> *So I wonder if I can hear more specifically about your health goals? How does your health fit into the big picture?*
>
> *Ideally, how would daily life look different if your health goals got more attention?*
>
> *How are other goals or aspects of life potentially derailing attention to your health?*

Next we want to help clients understand how their *current* health behaviors affect reaching important life goals and how health behavior *changes* might support reaching these life goals. Clients often isolate health goals as something that is separate from their other life priorities. However, health goals can often work in concert with other life goals and serve to enhance them as well. For example, if a top priority for a client is being a good parent (e.g., being able to be active with one's kids and set a good example for them), then being healthier (e.g., losing weight) can serve to help them keep up with their kids and show their kids about how to take good care of their bodies. Here's how providers can directly examine with clients how being healthier might serve their other important life goals.

> *Are there ways that improving your health can also benefit your other life goals and priorities that you highly value?*

You identified X and Y as some of your top priorities. I'm wondering how improving your health might also help you to better meet your goals in those areas?

It is important to pay attention to the quality of the goals that clients want to pursue. So, for example, if they want to look better so they can get a relationship, they are framing their goals in terms of externally controlling factors. Consider how they might be able to reframe their goals to support value for themselves rather than relying on others for such validation. For example, clients might reframe this goal to focus on developing feelings of self-confidence that can impact many aspects of their life, including relationships.

Not only do we want to talk about how goals may be integrated but we also want to help clients recognize that there are creative ways to give attention to multiple goals at once. Using the example again of wanting to be a good parent, a client might spend more quality time with their kids by going out for a walk or cooking a meal with them, thereby fostering both their parenting and health goals. If a client wants to make more connections at work, a potential way to do that is to see if others are interested in walking at lunchtime. Because clients often complain that time is one of the biggest barriers to making health behavior changes, this approach helps them to think more creatively.

Are you interested in seeing how we might be able serve both your health goals and some of your other important goals at the same time? Here's what I mean by that [insert example such as above]

Linking health to other important life goals serves a few purposes. First, health in itself is often not a primary motivator for many people. That is, the reason why people engage in health behaviors initially is not for health per se, but rather to serve other goals. So, explicitly focusing on health behavior change as a means to meet other priorities can help clients to see a purpose for their behaviors. Second, clients will experience challenges and setbacks (and for some, significant challenges and repeated setbacks) in their attempts to make behavior changes. For some of these clients the challenges and setbacks are experienced as failures and they have difficulty rallying to re-engage in behavioral changes. They simply don't want to experience failure repeatedly. So, helping clients to remind themselves of the purpose and meaning of continued engagement in behavior change--how health can enhance their "big picture" goals and priorities--can make it easier to find the energy to overcome these hurdles. Finally, linking health to other important life priorities that are already integrated into one's identity can also transform motivation for engaging in health behaviors such that there is less emphasis on controlled reasons (e.g., "I have to", "I should") and more integrated value and interest for health in itself (e.g., "It's important to me to take care of my health; "I have fun exercising"). Thus, health goals might be more readily internalized and integrated into clients' identity.

Macro-level health goals. Once you have examined the big picture goals, the next step is to discuss macro-level health goals. Clients have already formulated these in the initial session (e.g., I want to lose 20 pounds and I would prefer to do that by focusing mainly on changing my level of physical activity) but it is good to review these macro-level goals and see if there are any additions or edits. As always, it is important to reflect back clients answers and then provide structure for how you might go about tackling these goals.

> *So in our first meeting you said [insert information about the specific health goals they had for losing weight, improving diet and/or physical activity, or quitting smoking]. I am wondering whether these are the goals you want to focus on or whether there are any additional ones you want to add?*
>
> *Okay. So, you want to lose 20 pounds and you want our main focus to be on doing this through changing up your physical activity. That seems quite doable. There are lots of things we can do to change up your physical activity. We can begin by going over some information about physical activity and talk about some of the*

79

ways you might go about approaching this change or if you already have some specific ideas about how you might want to get started we can create a plan of action to experiment with. What do you think would be most helpful to you at this point?

These options allow clients to give you feedback about their starting point--do they need more educational information at the start in order to build their ideas for change or do they have a sense already about a path and approach they want to pursue so that your focus is on tailoring the next steps? For those who are raring to go, if you slow down the process to first "educate" them about physical activity you might be arresting the motivational momentum they have. Remember that educational materials can always be added to support a plan if the experiments that they do reveal that they need more information. On the flip side, if you start by jumping into a plan and clients feel ill-equipped to begin this discussion, you may inadvertently over-challenge them. So, be flexible to meet clients where they are.

Summary: Developing goals

Illuminating clients' goals and bringing into focus how big picture life goals can be reconciled with health goals begins to map the pathway for the internalization and integration of health behaviors. At the end of this conversation both you and your clients should have a better sense of the relative balance of their goals. Understanding this balance will help you to anticipate where some of the challenges may arise in the course of treatment as well as some of the points of shared values (e.g., wanting to be a good role model for kids and being healthy is part of that) that can be capitalized on and strengthened. After examining big picture goals and macro-level goals some clients may need more information to better formulate plans of action while others will be ready to jump in to begin experimenting with change. In the former case, it will be important to understand clients' knowledge base for the behaviors they are intending to change and assess with them what materials, information, or exercises might be helpful to support them. In the latter case, clients will be ready to move into developing micro-level goals. Developing micro-level goals--identifying specific problems to tackle, as well as the small, manageable changes to make to address these problems--is an iterative process that unfolds from problem solving exercises across sessions. We further describe the development of micro-level goals later in the section on creating a plan of action.

Gaining knowledge

Clients enter treatment with varied levels of knowledge about the health behaviors they are trying to change. At a basic level, information about the health benefits of making specific behavior changes can help clients anchor how their behaviors may have a broader impact on their overall health (e.g. eating healthier can lower your cholesterol and reduce your risk for cardiovascular disease). Educational content can also include specific information on the "how to's" of health behavior changes (e.g., how to read a nutrition label; how to accurately measure portions of food; how to take your pulse). Most interventions focus on developing appropriate content ("*what*" information to provide clients). Not surprisingly, our approach is concerned not only with "*what*" is being provided but "*how*" information is selected and delivered.

First, because clients have various starting points of knowledge it is important to ask them about what they need. Providing clients with a menu of options of resources allows them to inform you of what they might need so that you can collaboratively structure a curriculum that best matches their knowledge level. So, for example, a menu of options for changing one's diet might include handouts that explain key nutrients in foods, how to read nutrition labels, how to navigate making healthier purchases in the grocery store, and where to go for local farmers markets, as well as instructional videos on how to prepare healthier meals. Or, to change up one's physical activity routine, a menu of options could include information on local exercise facilities or classes and how to get free introductory classes or trial memberships, as well as instructional videos on how to complete stretching or strength training exercises at home.

Second, beyond providing a menu of options of resources, we also need to be aware that everyone learns differently and has different facility with language. We have found that providing information in a variety of modalities (e.g., paper based handouts, links to reputable websites, instructional videos that we have created) that are clearly presented in accessible language (both in terms of reading level and in everyday use of words rather than "scientific speak") and use relevant examples allows clients to also choose the tools that best fit their learning styles.

Third, clients are often bombarded with information (handouts, pamphlets, websites, etc.), and this information overload is often way more than they can absorb. For many, no sooner do they leave your office then the information gets thrown into the pile of things that they will get to later (and in actuality is never looked at again!) or the information immediately finds its way to the trashcan. Thus, the volume and timing of information is important for optimizing engagement in any resource materials. Further, to reiterate an earlier point, clients will differ in what information is challenging at different times in treatment. For example, reading food labels may be too challenging for clients at the beginning of treatment, as some simply want to get a handle on changing up quantity or general types of foods that they are eating. But, as they feel like they have mastered portion control and menu planning, then they can perhaps be more potentially discerning between products that they are choosing. For others, reading food labels is critical to the first steps of making a dietary change (e.g., to immediately lower their sugar intake), whereas other skills (e.g., learning how to cook diabetic friendly recipes) come at a later step in their behavioral change repertoire. The appropriateness of educational materials may also depend on first developing baseline skill sets. For example, strength training or trying more advanced exercises or activities may not be possible early on but instead may come later once clients have been able to gain more flexibility. So, educational materials are resources that should be accessed flexibly throughout treatment as skills are being honed, as new arenas are being explored, and as new skills are being developed.

Fourth, information is often just delivered to clients without a rationale for its utility and without explicit links to their relevant concerns. Therefore, educational materials become meaningless if they not are tied to clients' key goals or key skills they are interested in developing. For example, to simply provide guidelines (e.g., the ACSM recommends 150 min/week of moderate to vigorous physical activity) has little meaning for clients. Why is 150 min/week of moderate to vigorous physical activity the recommended level? To provide a rationale we need to know a little bit more about the benefits of this for cardiovascular health, mobility, longevity, or other health and quality of life factors. Practitioners need to be reading the guidelines to understanding their clinical utility. Further, treatment guidelines also need to be framed in terms of their relevance to clients. Part of translating the information into practical terms is that a particular level (e.g., 150 minutes/week) may have less meaning but being able to walk without being out of breath, being able to play with one's kids, or do other activities that previously were not possible when the client was more sedentary may instantly make more sense for the client. As practitioners we also need to be cognizant of the fact that there is some benefit for clients even if they don't reach the top benchmarks of the treatment guidelines. Will being more active and less sedentary benefit the person—of course it can! So, it is also important to help clients understand that not achieving the top recommended levels does not mean that there are no benefits.

Finally, we don't want to just know what information clients need but how we might be helpful in guiding the use of this information. For example, some clients need a more concrete translation of what it means to eat more servings of whole grains (What constitutes grains? How much is more? How do I do that?) while others can translate this information without need for much more detail or guidance. Remember the concept of optimal challenge--presenting information that is below or above clients' current skill level will not support their mastery. Thus, we want to be measured about matching the information to clients' needs for scaffolding. Here are some of the ways that we might address the issues above.

So we have a lot of materials on physical activity that you might want to take a look at. Let me go over what we have and then we can narrow down what might be most useful to you right now. **[presenting options of educational materials]**

We have a lot of materials on physical activity that might help you get some more ideas about how to make some changes. Given what you have told me about your starting point it seems that X, Y, and Z might be most helpful to begin with. But, you are welcome to look through any of the materials here on our website/our information library that might catch your interest. **[presenting options of educational materials; helping to narrow task so that the plethora of information is not overwhelming]**

Sometimes clients find information that looks interesting to them but they don't feel that right now it is something they feel really equipped to tackle. Let's make note of the things that are interesting to you and we'll build up later incorporate those strategies when you feel more ready. **[bookmarking strategies that will be incorporated later when other skills are grown and mastered]**

The guidelines suggest that adults get 150 minutes of physical activity per week to improve health and reduce risk for disease (such as diabetes, cardiovascular disease, and cancer). That amounts to about 30 minutes a day, 5 days a week. For some people that seems like a lot. One of the things to remember is that if your goal is to try to hit this benchmark we would work up to this gradually. But it's also worth noting that some people aim for a different benchmark, and that any physical activity is a good thing for health, even if you don't reach 150 minutes per week. **[providing rationale for guidelines and flexibility to clients' use of benchmarks]**

What I have found is that some clients will read this information and need more concrete details (e.g., What does it mean to eat more servings of whole grains? What constitutes grains? How much is more? How do I do that?) while others can translate this information without the need for much more detail or guidance. If you want more information or want me to clarify any of the materials, just let me know. I am happy to help you to navigate the information **[providing further support to clarify and refine information].**

Providing educational resources for foundational knowledge. So what informs the information we give our clients? In terms of treatment guidelines we follow the most up to date recommendations for weight loss, physical activity, nutrition, and smoking cessation. Recommendations for weight loss include the NHLBI practical guideline for the identification, evaluation, and treatment of overweight and obesity (2000) and the AHA/ACC/TOS Guideline for the Management of Overweight and Obesity in Adults (2013). Physical activity guidelines are also outlined in the ACSM's Physical Activity Guidelines for Americans (2011) and those for diet are in the USDA's Dietary Guidelines for Americans (2010). Recommendations for smoking cessation come from the U.S. Department of Health and Human Services (Treating Tobacco Use and Dependence, 2008).

We also try to build a library of practical resources. Our educational handouts that are focused on physical activity provide information as well as self-directed exercises so that clients may learn how to incorporate both structured activities (e.g., working out at the gym) as well as how to increase everyday activity (e.g., taking the stairs rather than the elevator). To help participants learn how to engage in stretching and strength training, we developed videos as well as companion instruction sets to demonstrate how to do each exercise (exercises demonstrated on the video by our ACSM certified exercise physiologist). We housed the instructional video on a

YouTube channel to make it readily available and more easily accessible for our clients but we also provided DVDs for those who preferred the videos in that form. Our educational handouts that focus on nutrition provide information on general nutrition (e.g., serving size, calories; importance of increasing fruit and vegetable intake) as well as specifics about the sources of fat, fiber, sodium, and sugar so that clients may learn how to create healthier, more balanced diets, reduce their overall consumption to be in more line with their caloric needs, and better monitor and make choices about the foods they consumed. Self-guided exercises also help them to develop specific skills to support these goals, including how to weigh and measure foods that they eat, how to read food labels, how to structure their meals (e.g., regular times for meals; snacks), and how to create nutritional balance within meals (e.g., MyPlate). Finally, our tools for smoking cessation come from the National Cancer Institute's Smokefree.gov website, which several SDT colleagues were involved in creating.

Further, because a typical challenge that participants often face is how to find low-cost or no-cost options for physical activity, resources for healthy eating, and programs that provide either no-cost access to nicotine replacement therapies or medications to assist in smoking cessation, we compile this information to assist them. For example, for physical activity we compile information on local recreation complexes and pools, local malls hours and walking groups within each, free meet-ups or other clubs (e.g., hiking) that promote physical activity, and different practices (e.g., yoga, dance, kickboxing) that people could try out for free around our area. This allows clients to explore different forms of movement to find what resonate most with their own interests and abilities without having to commit to a large financial cost. To assist in creating a healthier diet we offer a library of recipes that provide healthier options for everyday as well as traditional foods served during the year (e.g., barbeque) as well as provide links to our staffs' favorite healthy recipe websites. Worksheets on cooking conversions, guides to foods in season, information on local farmers markets, and a grocery store tour with guidelines and tips for healthier shopping are additional tools we offer for making a transition to healthier eating a bit more manageable. Finally, we provide information on how to obtain free or low-cost nicotine replacement treatments and medications to assist in smoking cessation from government agencies or pharmaceutical companies.

As professionals we recognize that we need not be the only source of education or information. In our practices we welcome suggestions from our clients regarding resources they find helpful. These organic functions allow clients to contribute to building support for other clients who come after them. To be sure, there is a lot of information out there that can actually be harmful to clients. However, inviting them to bring in information allows us to generate a discussion, critically evaluate the information together, and help clients be better consumers of the information out there in the general public.

Using behavior change tools to gain knowledge. Clients gain knowledge not just from instructional materials but also from their own behaviors. For example, many intervention approaches use self-monitoring to help clients' gather baseline information about their patterns of behaviors and track their behaviors over time. So, clients can learn about how often, when, and at what intensity they engage in physical activity; what they eat, how often they eat, and the nutritional balance of their day; and how much and when they smoke. Moreover, tracking can also provide insights into why they engage in a behavior (e.g., due to craving, stress, etc.), why they don't engage in a behavior (e.g., sat on the couch instead of working out), and how they feel about it. Importantly, framing self-monitoring as *information* helps clients to orient around gathering data as a way to gain some power over their behaviors rather than seeing this activity as way to evaluate them as a success or failure in their behavior change pursuits. In fact, in our practice we never use the phrase "monitoring" because it implies evaluation and most do not respond well to this concept.

There are many ways to track one's behaviors. For example, to track physical activity, clients can be offered a free pedometer as a way to get feedback about their activity levels. Innovative use of technology can also increase interest and participation. For example, if clients are interested we provide detailed written instructions and train them on how to use free online programs (e.g., My Fitness Pal, RunKeeper; smokefree.gov) or they can use their own personal wearable devices (e.g., FitBit, Jawbone, FuelBand, Apple Watch, etc.) to track their food intake and physical activity. Programs such as these provide breakdowns of the energy expended by engaging in various forms of physical activity, nutritional information for the foods they consume (e.g., calories, sodium, fat), as well as other benchmarks that clients can choose to monitor. Moreover programs often show the interplay of different health behaviors, such as diet and exercise, helping participants see how their calories burned by adding exercise can tip their overall energy balance for the day. For smokers, QuitGuide, quitSTART, and NCI QuitPal are all mobile programs from the National Cancer Institute's Smokefree.gov initiative that can help clients track cravings, moods, and slips, so they can better understand their smoking patterns and progress. For those not interested in using these technologies, we provide paper and pencil tracking options and guidance as to how to record information that is important to clients. In our experience many clients choose to use online programs, associated smartphone apps, and wearables as they find that the mobility helps them to be more accurate and timely in self-monitoring. But, most importantly, clients use whatever tool (if any) makes the most intuitive sense for them.

Like all other activities we have described in this manual, clients are always free to choose whether or not to use a given tool. Practitioners are often compelled by the literature that suggests that specific tools, such as self-monitoring, are quite useful for successful behavior change and thus actively "encourage" clients to use such techniques. But, some people adamantly do not want to engage in such tracking. So, when clients don't want to use it, they won't and no amount of "encouragement" will get them to. Remember, a tool is only as useful to the extent that it is willingly used. So, if it is not in their interest, don't sweat it. Many people have changed their behaviors without formal self-monitoring! The key is to work with clients to find what fits best with them. Here's how we introduce the use of such tools:

> **<u>Using self-monitoring for gathering baseline information.</u>** *Oftentimes clients find it useful to track their physical activity behaviors for a week so we can gather information about patterns, challenges, and things that work well. We can track this information in different ways—some people like to just keep a paper diary or notes about times during the week that they are physically active, others like to track this information using an app or online program like My Fitness Pal. Others prefer to wear a pedometer or some other wearable device during the week so we can get an overall sense of their activity each day. Do any of these options sound appealing to you to try out so we can gather some information?*

Once clients are using the tools it is important to regularly check in about their experience with these tools in regular intervals (e.g., after they have used it for the week; after a two week experiment with it; after a month).

> **<u>Asking about regularly using self-monitoring for gathering information.</u>** *You used [diary, My Fitness Pal, pedometer) to track your physical activity behaviors during the week. I'm wondering what you thought of using this strategy to help you learn more about your behaviors? Anything useful about it? Any down sides?* [Allow the client to respond and reflect back that you heard what they said].
>
> *Sometimes clients use tracking to help them stay on course with their weekly goals? What do you think about using this regularly for a few weeks to see if this is a helpful tool?*[If yes, come up with a time period that they will experiment

with this tool. It is usually good to check in and re-evaluate its utility after a few weeks]

Checking in after experimental period or longer term use. *So, you've been tracking your physical activity for the last month. I'm wondering how that is going? What's been useful about it? Any downsides or challenges with keeping track? What do you think about continuing to use this as we go forward?*

It's worth noting that self-monitoring can also be used more flexibly to provide information periodically. For example, if clients feel they have a good handle on their behavioral patterns and want to discontinue its use, you can always introduce the idea that tracking can be used at any point in time. In fact, clients may stop using it but find that at some point later they can use it for a week to check in about their behaviors or again use it regularly if they want to help them get back on track with their goals. Thus, teaching clients to see how to apply tools in a way that best matches their needs helps them to learn to use the tools in their tool belt more flexibly.

Creating a Plan of Action

Creating a plan of action encompasses identifying small, reasonable changes to health behaviors (micro-level goals), articulating the details of how to carry out the changes, anticipating some of the obstacles that may get in the way and brainstorming a way around them, and engaging important others in support of the plan. Planning does not end there, as clients experiment with their plans, use information that they gather about what works and what doesn't to feed back into revision of the plan, and continue this process until the behavior is refined. Importantly, even once a behavioral plan has been working well for clients, life events or other factors may introduce new challenges to their plans of action, requiring clients to revisit and revamp their behaviors yet again. Thus, creating a plan of action is not a one-time process but rather it is a set of skills--tools in the tool belt if you were--that will need to be employed flexibly throughout treatment and carried into the maintenance of health behaviors.

There are important nuances in the delivery of each step of the process, which we will detail in each section below. But there is an important point to remember for all tasks. Some clients will be able to navigate these tasks with relatively little guidance, while others will need much more help to handle them. At every opportunity, providers need to give clients choice about how they want to handle the tasks at hand, including the extent to which the bulk of the work of planning is done within the session or is left to clients to do on their own. For example, some clients experience the exercise of walking through specific, detailed plans with providers as belittling because they feel quite capable of planning on their own, and prefer instead to simply begin with an idea about what they want to do (without the nitty gritty details about how they are going to do it). Practitioners tend to want to control *how* clients go about making changes and want to prevent plans from failing, and thus can get caught up in wanting to be more detailed with clients to assure that plans are "right". To be sure, if not being more detailed backfires, then clients have information about what they need to do differently and can choose to use time with you to better hone this skill. The process itself thus becomes an important learning opportunity.

Problem solving. Clients have likely tried to problem solve how to change their health behaviors in the past so it is important to understand where they have gotten stuck in the past. For some, their plans get derailed because they don't feel that they have the skills or knowledge to make it work. Others may abandon their plans because they feel guilty about making time for themselves to work on their health. Identifying their unique challenges will help to be more aware of these pitfalls and will help to gauge where greater attention might need to be paid during treatment. Regardless of their unique challenges, it is important to acknowledge the

91

challenges they have faced in the past and recognize that there will be some in the future--thereby normalizing this as part of the behavior change process. It is also important though to also couple this message with the acknowledgment that together you will work to better manage these hurdles.

Behavioral interventions typically identify five main steps to problem solving--articulating the specific problem or challenge, brainstorming alternative options for behavior, selecting an option that is reasonable to try out, making an action plan to carry out new behavior, and trying it out, with review and revision to optimize its result. Although these approaches often address how others can help support the plan, we place greater emphasis on understanding how the social context impacts both how the behavior unfolds and how it can play a role in its change. Moreover, we pay particular attention to the feelings associated with the behaviors (leading up to, during, and following their engagement). Below we describe these core problem solving strategies in more detail and Appendix M contains worksheets that, if needed, can help guide this exercise. However, this process can be entirely conducted in conversation format. We caution that clients don't always need or want to use worksheets, so ask if these are useful to them before simply assigning them or pulling them out in session.

Describe the problem in detail. Because the behavior that clients are trying to change is usually integrated into all parts of their daily activities, it is often beneficial to first have clients describe in detail a recent day or part of their day that captures their experience of what leads to them engaging in the behavior they are interested in changing. Some programs refer to this process as identifying the links in the behavioral chain. This narrative provides context of the behavior.

So when we first met you told me a bit about how you eat throughout the day. For us to do a bit more planning about how to change up some of these patterns it's often helpful to walk through a recent example to help me understand your experience around eating and the main challenges you encounter when trying to eat differently. Can you tell me about your typical pattern of eating during your day?

If clients have difficulty identifying the features that are most difficult, practitioners might walk through the narrative with them to help them identify these specific features.

So your workplace sounds quite stressful—lots of meetings and too many tasks leave you little time if any to actually eat. You also have a lot to manage when you get home, with three kids demanding your attention right when you walk in the door. So, how does this affect your approach to eating each day?

Laying out the narrative of an event or day helps clients to identify specific features that might have contributed to smoking, eating poorly, or not being active. Practitioners want to be listening for the cues that make clients want to eat, be inactive, or smoke. Cues can take the form of environmental factors. For example, a client might identify that in his workplace sweets are readily available on people's desks and in the break room (environmental cue). Moreover, thoughts and feelings that clients experience around a particular event can also cue the behavior. So, for example, a client may reveal that he has regular run-ins with his boss throughout the day in which the quality of his work is publicly criticized (leaving him feeling ashamed, incompetent, and demoralized). The client may also be may be encouraged to eat foods he might not typically select because the workgroup has incorporated birthday celebrations into regular work meetings (giving in so as to avoid feeling guilty for transgressing the norm). Practitioners should explicitly listen for and attempt to help clients articulate the feelings and thoughts they have around a particular event and what other people did (or didn't to) to contribute to their behavior. Don't just assume you understand the experience, but rather dig a little deeper and query about the social dynamics and the feelings that emerge from these dynamics.

> *So, you said that you have a lot of run-ins with your boss about your work. I wonder how that criticism affects you in the moment? How does it make you feel about yourself? About your job? How do you imagine those feelings are connected to your eating?*

> *So you said you have to eat a piece of cake at work when the birthday celebrations happen. What happens if you refused or someone else in your group declines a piece of cake? What do others say or do? How does that make you feel in the moment?*

Reflecting back clients' experience and showing empathy in response to their disclosures is important here, as it helps clients to see their behavior in context and legitimizes their feelings. It is particularly important for clients who attribute their failure to engage in a healthier lifestyle as a personal downfall or shortcoming, as the reflections normalize their behaviors rather than isolate them as defects.

> *It seems pretty understandable that when your boss criticizes your work you feel pretty bad about yourself and eating helps you to soothe those bad feelings. But I also hear that it then backfires, because you then feel bad about eating things that you didn't intend to.*

> *It makes sense that when others give you a hard time for not eating the birthday cake you just want to make them stop nagging, so you eat the piece of cake. But I also hear that this brings up other bad feelings for you—that you feel like a failure for not sticking to your goals.*

Practitioners often have a tendency to want to jump in and identify the points of change for the client. However, it is important to ask clients about what *they* think is most difficult for them By having clients identify that which is most difficult for them, you get in their shoes, take their perspective, and show value for them knowing their own behavior best.

So it seems like there are a lot of things that might contribute to you having challenges around eating throughout the day. What do you think is the most difficult part for you?

Helping clients identify for themselves their biggest hurdles highlights the potentially biggest barriers to change. Hold onto this information as you go into action planning. Clients may or may not want to tackle these hurdles initially, as there may be other changes that feel more doable. However, if these barriers prove to be powerful, they may derail even the seemingly simpler changes. Thus, they may need to become the core focus of your work together or may warrant other treatment options (e.g., stress reduction, individual, couples, or family therapy, career counseling) to precede or supplement further work together.

Understanding the ideal scenario*.* In many programs the next step is to brainstorm some concrete steps to change their behavior. This brainstorming is treated largely as a cognitive exercise. However, we find that it is helpful for clients to first think about how they would like things to be different before brainstorming different concrete steps for change. This part of the exercise ignites the notion of what they would wish for--how would things be different if their basic needs and their goals were getting met. Oftentimes this allows for emotion, not just thoughts, to emerge. To proceed, practitioners should check in about each challenge that clients identify and have them articulate how they would like them each to be different.

So, if you woke up tomorrow and this was different, what would that look like? What would happen? How would you like this to be different?

The important part of this exercise is to be realistic (e.g. we all would likely benefit from having enough money to not work but it is unlikely that this will happen for most of us), but also don't worry too much about whether the wishes will actually come true. Defining what they want helps clients build a rationale for their behaviors, which will aid in being more concrete about what they need in terms of support from others.

Brainstorm other options. In this activity clients take each feature that they identified as a challenge and they come up with alternative options that better help them to meet their behavioral goals. The key here is to identify specific, small changes that clients might make to directly address each of the challenges they have identified.

> *So you said that one of the things that happens is that you get so busy during your work day that you often don't get up from your desk. That leaves you feeling sore and tired by the end of the day. You would like to have time to get up and move around each day so that doesn't happen. So I'm wondering if there are some small changes that you can make to your day that will help you to do that?*

Clients may need some help thinking creatively about some options here. Oftentimes they aren't making changes because they are getting stuck in how a change ideally should happen. So, for example, someone who wants more breaks to get up and move around during the day might be imagining this as a half hour several times a day. What would happen if they broke that up into 5 or 10 minute intervals? Brainstorming with them can help grease the wheels of this process.

> *So I'm wondering if there are some other creative ways that we can help you get more breaks during the day. What about X, Y, or Z?*

Pick one option to try. Through discussion we help clients identify those options they can have some control over and then weigh the pros and cons of each of those options. To pick an option they would like to try out we encourage clients to choose options that feel most capable of doing in order to maximize their chances of success—in essence we help them to select what they believe will be an optimal challenge that is not too easy but also not too difficult.

Of all of the options, what do you think is the most manageable to try out?

At times it is clear that clients feel that a quite complex and difficult challenge needs to be addressed because it stands in the way of executing other changes. In this case, providers can still work with clients to make this an optimal challenge by further breaking down the change into smaller, more manageable steps. For example, remember the woman who was trying to make dietary changes but was getting pushback from her husband and kids? Rather than simply making changes to the food in the house, where might be a good place to start? Perhaps the first step is to talk with her husband to get him on board and brainstorm with him about how to make the transition more palatable (literally and figuratively). And it may be that even before that it would be good to role play with the provider to practice how to approach this conversation. The key is to begin to take apart challenges with clients to see how far the challenges need to be broken down to be more manageable.

So I hear that you feel that to make some strides in changing your diet you need to get your family on board but that there has been a revolt when you try to make any changes. I'm wondering if we could brainstorm together about some smaller steps to gradually make this transition?

Make an action plan. Action plans are specific steps that one will take to engage in different behavior. In essence this is mapping out what are they going to do, how and when are they going to do it, what are the obstacles that might get in the way, who are the people that might help them with the plan, what do they need from them in terms of support, and how they ask for or enlist that support. Here's how practitioners might want to provide a rationale for this process.

> *We often find that clients find it useful to walk through a specific plan of action-- mapping out what you want to do, when you'll do it, and how to do it-- and talk through how to manage some of the obstacles you might encounter. Planning in advance is often helpful because in the moment generating options can become stressful and may not go as well as if you thought through some different options-- plans B, C, and D to fall back on when plan A doesn't go the way you might hope. Does creating a specific plan of action sound helpful to you?*
>
> *So, you want to do XYZ. How do you think you might want to go about doing that?*

Providers can use the worksheet in Appendix M as a guideline to creating a plan. One of the main things to recognize here is that there is a fine balance between working with clients collaboratively to devise a plan and falling into a banter where you pepper clients with questions and detail the minutia of how they will handle themselves. In the latter scenario, the exercise feels condescending—like a parent checking off an exhaustive list of "what ifs" to make sure their kid is totally prepared. They key is to treat your clients the way you would want to be treated--as a functioning adult. You also want to recognize that no matter how much planning is done, there will always be unanticipated obstacles or other surprises. There is always room for new insights to emerge after clients try out the plan. So, be thorough but be reasonable.

We also will want to understand if there are educational tools, behavioral techniques (e.g., self-monitoring), or other assistance that might be useful to support their plan. In terms of educational tools, the library of handouts and self-guided exercises that providers develop, as well as new m-health tools (e.g., Smokefree.gov) can be accessed to support clients' specific plans. Moreover, providers can work with clients to select behavioral techniques that best match their plan. For example, online tracking programs (e.g., MyFitnessPal) can help participants to create a daily caloric benchmark that should help them to lose 1 pound each week. When participants enter the foods they consume into the system, it allows them to monitor where their calories go each day so that they can be more choiceful about what they choose to eat and how much they eat each day. It also allows clients to be planful about their day so that if they knew they were going out for a special dinner they could input that meal and then preemptively adjust what they eat the rest of the day to better meet their overall goals.

Finally, providers can use session meetings to guide the development of specific skills. For example, clients who are trying to lose weight often fear that eating healthier means that all flavor and enjoyment of food will be lost. Providers might work with clients together on altering their own recipes or exploring some new foods to add to their diet so as to "healthify" their intake. Or, if clients want to incorporate stretching or strength training techniques into their repertoire, providers can spend time with them demonstrating some of the exercises and discussing how to engage in the exercise safely. If they are interested in more information or guidance, then providers can detail some of the different options, allowing clients to choose what they think will work best for them.

> *As we go through this plan, I wondering if you have any ideas about what information or tools might be useful to help you better tackle this plan? What do you think you need some extra help on?*

> *I have been thinking about some materials and tools that I have that might be useful to you and I also thought about some ways that we might use some of our time together to work on some parts of this plan. I'm wondering whether you would be interested in hearing more about some of these options?*

> *I wonder if scheduling time in your weekly calendar or setting some other reminders, like an alarm in your phone, might be useful to keep the plan on track?*

Identify roadblocks. The next step is to help clients generate list of potential roadblocks and solutions to how they might handle these obstacles. There are some common challenges that get in the way of many clients following through with their plans, such as carving out time and other unexpected demands (e.g., work, family) that derail their plans. In Appendix N we have listed some common things that people say create challenges for them, both across the spectrum of behavior change as well as particularly in each of the health arenas. Recognize that this is not an exhaustive list nor is it meant to pigeonhole clients' challenges. Rather, it can be filed away in your library of knowledge so that when you are engaging in this conversation with your clients you might be able to check in with them about some of these potential obstacles. However, we always first want to start with understanding the clients' perspective, so we ask about what they anticipate as obstacles and how they might address these.

> *Are there particular obstacles or hurdles you can think of that might make this plan more difficult to execute? How do you imagine you might cope with those challenges or better manage those challenges?*

> *Can you think of ways you may avoid, or minimize certain activities that trigger your smoking? Is there something else you could do at that time? Things you enjoy doing as an alternative to smoking?*

Some clients may have difficulty generating ways to manage their obstacles, as they may not have yet developed effective tools in their tool belt to draw from. Providers can offer up some potential options to explore whether clients would be willing to experiment with using different coping tools. Again, the key is to identify something they might consider trying out and then you can check back in the next time to see how well some of their coping strategies worked.

> *It sounds like there are a lot of cues in your work environment that make you want to eat more often than you like – the candy dish on your desk, the treats in the break room. I wonder if there are some ways for you to avoid or minimize these cues that trigger your desire to eat?*

When you feel the urge to eat candy or other sweets, is there something else you could do until that urge subsides? Like take a walk, drink some water, or munch on a healthier alternative that still will taste sweet--like fruit or raisins?

I'm wondering if there are things you can say to yourself in those moments to remind yourself of your bigger goals? (e.g., "I want to be healthy for me and my family.")

Gather support from close relationships. As we have already discussed, health behaviors, and by extension health behavior change, does not happen in a vacuum but rather is intricately tied to social dynamics. That is, others influence the extent to which healthy options are available (e.g., what food is available in the home or workplace; where friends meet for a meal), how norms are established (e.g., eating meals together at the table or in front of the TV; smoke breaks; whether employees actually get breaks at work), food traditions and cultural norms of what and how people behave (e.g., what are the written and unwritten rules for eating?), and how health behaviors fit into the broader goals of the social group (e.g., to what extent friends engage in physical activity when they get together; what they eat when together; whether my social group smokes when we go out). In an ideal world, important others provide support for behavioral changes. However, more often the "dark side" of the social environment-- pressures to smoke, drink, eat, and forgo exercise--can derail even the best laid plans. Thus, in our work, a critical feature of planning is to help clients identify those who are or can be need supportive around health behavior change (e.g., spouse, friends, etc.) and work on how to enlist the support of these important others in helping them to achieve their personal goals. Moreover, it is also important to understand who may derail plans and how to engage (or at times disengage) from such relationships in the service getting one's needs better supported. More about how to do this is contained in the next chapter. But, in short, the core tasks are to help clients identify potential supports, identify what behaviors seem supportive, and develop a language to ask for their needs to be responded to. Here is how to start this conversation, with more detailed queries found in the next chapter.

> *Is there anyone that you would find helpful in supporting your efforts to change your behaviors? Any family members, friends, or others?*
>
> *How can they help you? What kinds of things would you like them to do for you? What sounds supportive to you?*
>
> *Is there anyone that makes it more difficult for you to change your behaviors? What do they do that makes it more difficult?*

My clients are stuck in the planning process and I don't know what to do! If clients are getting stuck at any point in the action planning, it can be useful to understand how they handled problems in other aspects of their life. That is, what strategies or strengths can they borrow from other aspects of their life and employ in the service of changing their health behaviors? Sometimes simply stepping outside of the current problem can create a fresh perspective.

What about rewards? One of the core steps in action planning in other intervention models of behavior change is to have clients devise rewards to give themselves for the positive steps that they make. We *do not* do this as part of our treatment approach. Why? What's so bad about giving yourself a treat?

Well, there's nothing wrong with giving yourself a treat. However, as we noted at the beginning of this manual there are many ways in which rewards can undermine motivation. Reward structures are often set up such that receiving the reward is contingent on reaching some benchmark of success. So, for example, a client might make a bargain with herself that if she walks for 30 minutes each day during the week she can buy herself a magazine or treat herself to a movie at the end of the week. What happens if she doesn't make that goal? By setting up this reward contingency she deems anything less than meeting the benchmark a failure and withholding the positive treat in essence equates to self-punishment. People have a hard enough time making behavioral changes and they will experience setbacks, so why would we want to set them up to feel worse?

Further, focusing on the reward takes away from the inherent reward in mastery of the behavior itself. As we discussed earlier, external motives (such as rewards) are much more difficult to sustain in the long run. To optimally sustain behavior, we want to help clients adopt value for the behavior and even potentially enjoy the behavior itself---that is, become more autonomous in their actions. Thus, the reward is in engaging in the behavior itself or in the other valued activities that the behavior allows them to do (e.g., playing with one's kids).

If participants want to give themselves a treat for the hard work they have done, let it be just that—focused on the effort they put forth to change their behaviors, not on a particular outcome. Further, encourage them to think about treats that will feed back into their behaviors. So, for example, perhaps their treat can be to buy a new cookbook, get some new workout clothes, purchase a new piece of sports equipment or a new kitchen gadget, or take a class (e.g., cooking, fitness) that they have been interested in trying out. The idea is that clients should be thinking of how to take good care of themselves and this should not be contingent on achieving particular outcomes.

Skill building through experimentation

So, clients have devised a plan and have gone out into the world to try it out. Even the best laid plans are bound to need some tweaking. Thus, a key feature of our work with clients is to understand clients' experience of their experiments and try to help them revise their plans and re-engage in the behavior change again. Beyond revising the details of plans, we spend considerable time focused on assessing the emotional impact of trying to change on clients'

103

sense of self and on reframing experimentation as a learning exercise, working to develop clients' mastery in providing themselves with feedback from their own experience.

Why is this emphasis so important? First, behavioral change is rarely if ever simply about coming up with the right details for the plan. People eat to feel better, curl up on the couch to hide away from the world, and smoke to calm their nerves. Clearly, these are not the only reasons for these behaviors, but the point is that these health behaviors are often linked to emotional experience, so plans often get derailed in part because of clients' emotions. Moreover, changing health behaviors is also naturally going to rock clients' emotional landscape, as health behavior change challenges their long-relied on tools for coping and impacts their social interactions. Thus, attending to their emotional experiences is key to fully understanding the challenges of behavioral change.

Second, one of the key challenges for clients is to not treat experiments gone awry as failures, and more importantly, themselves as failures more globally. Our emphasis from the beginning of treatment is to take a mastery approach to behavior change, anticipating that change requires experimentation and learning from these experiences. So, even tools such as self-monitoring are reframed as information rather than evaluation. We explore these two emphases in more detail below.

Understanding clients' experience of the experiment. The first step is to have clients provide a brief narrative about how their experiments went. It is useful to have them describe specific examples during their week, highlighting both when the plan or parts of it worked well (if this occurred) and when it didn't work so well.

> *So, last time we me we talked about experimenting with getting more exercise this week. I wonder how your plan went overall?*

Were there times that parts of it worked well for you this week? Can you tell me about one of those times? What worked well? How do you feel about that?

Were there times that parts of it didn't work so well for you this week? Can you tell me about one of those times? What didn't work? Were there hurdles that you didn't anticipate? How do you feel about that?

It is important to follow up with the information that clients offer. Ask more questions to understand some of the details. Providers can also wonder about some features that clients may not have offered up (e.g., omitting some features of the plan that you had discussed in the prior week; feeling angry about not getting support for their plan). The key is to listen to what clients are saying but also what they may not be saying (e.g. having a friend hijack their efforts would make anyone angry but they don't seem to be acknowledging that), and be curious with them about these observations.

Fostering positive self-relevant feedback. Clients are the ones that tried out the experiment so it's important to get them to first reflect on their strengths, affirm small steps they took, and celebrate positive changes. Helping clients learn how to self-administer informational feedback that does not imply evaluation can be challenging at first, as most people are trained to first and foremost evaluate and criticize what they did wrong and what they need to do to improve. That is not to say that we don't want clients to give themselves critical feedback, but rather we want to turn this practice of feedback on its head and have them develop skills to first appreciate and prize their successes, no matter how big or how small.

What do you think you learned from your experience this week?
What kind of positive things do you think you did to try to tackle this change?

Some clients won't be able to generate a response to these questions. So, it is important for the provider to begin to cultivate the process of appreciating their efforts.

105

To me it seems like you actually did quite a few things that were pretty different than how you may have approached things in the past. For example, when your friend cancelled on you, instead of just not doing any exercise you caught up with another friend by phone while you went for a walk. Seems like a pretty clever solution.

This week got really busy and it felt pretty overwhelming to even attempt your plan. Awareness of how stress can easily derail the plan you made is actually an important step—now we can take some of that information and maybe revisit whether this plan might be too challenging given your current stressors.

It is important to reflect back to clients the things that you heard might be adjusted for the next time, and what might be further strengthened, and ask how they want to revise the plan for next time.

So, I heard you say that the schedule you tried to fit in your workouts didn't work so well because you often didn't have consistent childcare. But I also heard that on days that you had childcare the other parts of your plan worked pretty well. I'm wondering what you think might help to create some more consistency in your childcare? Are there other alternatives (like bringing your child to the gym or going for a walk with your child in the stroller instead of going to the gym) that you might do so that you can still get in your workout?

Reflecting back feelings that clients have about their experience and normalizing the experience of negative thoughts and feelings is important here, as it will help to minimize the global feelings of failure and serve to build and reinforce emotional coping strategies.

It is entirely normal, and even expected, that at some point all people trying to lose weight will have some negative thoughts and feelings regarding their weight loss efforts.

Having negative thoughts and feelings are normal. It is your response or reaction to these thoughts and feelings that are important—you can use your feelings to help you make different choices the next time.

On days that you didn't get to the gym it sounds like you got pretty down on yourself and felt like a "failure". When people change their behaviors there are bound to be bumps in the road and disappointments along the way. These bumps are actually important pieces of information--it helps us to learn what is working for you and what is not, so that we can make adjustments to your plans and make it work for you.

If clients are having difficulty with framing the experiment as information, providers may need to introduce emotion regulation strategies to help them be kind to themselves until this orientation sinks in.

I'm wondering if there are things that might help to get you out of that space of beating yourself up? Maybe someone you can call on or something you can do (e.g., play with your kid) to shake those feelings?

You might wonder why not work to correct their thoughts and feelings? Cognitive approaches suggest that clients have many maladaptive thoughts and these lead to negative feelings about the self. The strategy they employ is to have clients "talk back" to negative thoughts by replacing them with positive thoughts and more reasonable expectations of themselves. In principle, it is important to encourage clients to find their power and quiet their negative thoughts. However, the cognitive approach suggests that the thoughts need to be corrected. "Correcting thoughts" can be exhausting work and in reality no matter how much clients do they may never rid themselves of those negative thoughts or voices which are deeply entrenched. Moreover, too often when clients perceive that their thoughts are maladaptive or need to be corrected, the perception extends to their concept of self—that is, they are defective, they need to be corrected. Mindfulness-based approaches instead take the position that we want to cultivate awareness of present experiences and be receptive to those experiences, whatever they are. Thus, thoughts and feelings are not adaptive or maladaptive, but rather are to be noticed without judgment. In this case, negative thoughts and feelings are treated as *information* about experience, with the key being how clients respond to that information. So for example, many clients compare themselves to others (or to their former younger, healthier selves) and then blame themselves for not "measuring up" ("I'll never be as thin and attractive as Lisa...no wonder people like her better"). We cannot take these thoughts or feelings away from clients. Rather, we can help them recognize when they are making those comparisons and why (e.g., they want others to see them as attractive), and we can help them try to respond to themselves with greater compassion.

Revision of goals and strategies. By this point you should have a pretty good sense of how well the plan worked and what revisions would be useful to make it more effective. It is useful to present a summary of what you and the client have identified and check in with them about the accuracy of that summary. Then, similar to earlier action planning steps, collaborate with the client to specify how to change the plan, including how to manage any new roadblocks, employ new coping strategies, and enlist others for social support. It is worth noting that it is also possible that the experiment has made it clear that the goals initially set are not reasonably attainable at this time. So, before revising an action plan, the work of treatment is first to return to the goals and create optimal challenges that are better aligned with clients' skills and life circumstances.

Expansion of goals (beginning to do more challenging, interesting activities). As treatment progresses and as clients begin to solidify some of the behavioral changes, they may begin to feel bored with their routine and want to shake things up or they may simply feel ready to take on new challenges and grow budding interests. This process of keeping behavioral practices "fresh" is critically important for maintenance, as people will be more motivated to engage in behaviors that stretch their skills, capture their interest, and engender some joy and fun. So, when clients begin to find themselves wanting more, you can revisit their goals with them, help them to set new goals, and plan how to back these goals with action. It remains the same process as described before, yet for most it is more readily navigated because the motivation is to increase interest, pleasure, challenge, and learning. Thus, the obstacles are fewer and the energy to pursue the aims tends to be greater

Enlisting Social Support

Social support is a very important part of the behavior change process. Clients need supportive people to help them meet their goals. But, sometimes getting the support that is needed can be challenging. In some cases, clients hesitate to ask for support. Sometimes clients aren't sure who to turn to for support. And sometimes, even when clients are willing to ask for support and have people to turn to, the support doesn't turn out to be what they had hoped for. Below we address each of these challenges and provide some tips as to how to help clients tackle them (Appendix O). First, though, let's explore why clients may hesitate to tell others what they need.

What gets in the way of asking for support? Time and time again when we hear from clients about their concerns about asking for support several core themes emerge. First, clients do not want to perceived as "needy". Many clients are taught that they should just be able to handle things on their own and that asking for help means that they are weak or incompetent. Second, clients oftentimes worry that asking for help will just burden others and make others feel overwhelmed. They assume that others don't have the resources to be helpful. Third, some clients are taught that some things are just meant to be private—that no one should know what is really going on behind the scenes about their health (or anything deemed "personal" for that matter). Fourth, clients are often embarrassed about working on their health and some of the challenges they have and are worried that others will judge them (e.g., if others know how I really eat they will think badly of me). Fifth, clients are sometimes quite hesitant to tell others what they need or how they feel because they worry, perhaps, that others won't respond with care even when they express their needs and feelings. Certainly, the fact is that others don't always respond in the way clients hope or in the way they need them to. The first thing to find out is what keeps clients from asking for more support.

> *What has happened in the past when you've asked for support around making behavior changes?*

> *What things keep you from asking for support from others to help you make behavior changes?*

An important function of providers is to both empathize with normative concerns but also provide some alternative ways to challenge and test out these concerns. Below we explore some possible ways to respond to each concern.

> **Needy**: *Remember, we all have needs and sometimes others' support is necessary to get through life's challenges. Having needs doesn't equate to being needy. Do you feel others are being needy when they ask for your help? I wonder if you can extend yourself the same break and kindness that you afford to others.*

> **Burden.** *It seems like you are assuming that others don't have the resources to help out without getting overwhelmed themselves. Before you assume this, why not ask? Let others decide whether or not they have the resources and desire to help you. They may surprise you.*

> **Private.** *Remember, you can be selective about who you turn to. Choosing others who you trust to care for you is important. Are there certain people that you really trust in your life? [If no: Anyone you think you could maybe take a chance on?]*

> **Judged.** *Those who really care about you will not judge you, especially when you are struggling. Rather, they will try to understand and be helpful. I wonder who shows you real care, even when you are struggling?*

> **Others won't respond with care**: *I'm wondering if you are choosing the right person to get support? It's always possible that the person in a bad place themselves and do not have the resources to be helpful as they might be at other times? Perhaps there are some ways to improve on your approach to asking for some support?*

Choosing the right people to turn to for support. One of practitioners' goals is to assist clients in identifying strategies to build social support networks and identify who in their support network can help with specific tasks (e.g., meal preparation) and/or provide moral support. Clients' social supports can include family, friends, peers, co-workers, clergy, and therapists, among others. So, to begin with it is good to explore with clients who are the people that serve as their key social supports.

> *Relationships that are good for you will support you, not tear you down, especially at times when you are struggling to reach your goals or when you're not feeling so great about yourself...*
>
> *Who are the people that have been the sources of strength and support along the way? What makes them good supports? What do they do that is supportive?*
>
> *Who are the people that can help remind you of your strengths and join forces with you to fight challenges that come your way? What makes them good supports? What do they do that is supportive?*

Once you have a bit more of an understanding of their core support network, it is then important to understand who might be able to provide support for specific challenges. If clients have been using the worksheets in Appendix M to identify specific challenges, wishes for how things would be different, and small changes they would make to better meet these goals and needs, the remaining column guides them to think about who might be enlisted for help for each challenge and what might they do to be supportive. Why is it important to articulate who might be helpful for each challenge? Practically speaking, if a client wants to change up the family meal but is only getting support from friends about it, the client is likely going to run into some problems with their family. Moreover, different people might be better at tackling different challenges. So, for example, John might be the one to turn to for practical solutions to getting more out of an exercise routine but Roger might be better at providing the moral support needed

111

to get to the gym in the first place. Finally, some clients will have great supportive networks but these networks may not live in proximity to them (e.g., the client's brother is a great support but lives 400 miles away) or may not have the flexibility to be able to support them (e.g., friend can't afford to join the gym that the client belongs to). So, creative solutions for how to expand their network to meet specific challenges may need to be explored.

> *It seems like your friend is a real help to problem solve about how to change up your family meal, but it also seems important to also get your family on board before you make changes. I wonder what you would think about getting your spouse involved in the planning?*

> *Different people might help you to tackle different challenges. Who do you think would be most helpful for the particular challenges you are facing?*

> *It sounds like you have some really great supports but that they might not be available to help you navigate some of these challenges, like having someone to workout with at your gym. I am wondering if we might think creatively about some ways that you could potentially meet other people through your gym to workout with?*

Sometimes clients think that they "should" seek support from particular people, especially family and friends. But these folks may not be the best supports and/or they may be too invested in a particular outcome. So, it is perhaps useful to have clients consider more "neutral" others with whom they can grow support. Again, this usually requires some creative thinking on the part of both providers and clients. For example, many clients are hesitant to join a gym because they feel self-conscious and ill-equipped to engage in different forms of exercise. One solution is for clients to consider what they enjoy doing (walking in nature? dancing? swimming?) and find groups of people in the community that share those interests (e.g., meetup organizations or groups). Finding others with common interests can lessen the typical social pressures in a new social situation, as the client can focus on the activity of common interest, thereby garnering some support for staying engaged in the behavior.

Aside from answering "who" could be supportive (worksheets in Appendix O) it is also important to be specific about what others might do to be supportive. For example, some clients might just want someone to be available to talk with them, while others might want someone who will be an active participant in solving problems. Being specific will help clients better articulate their expectations of others, which in turn will allow others to provide feedback about whether they can provide such support.

What would you like them to do to be supportive of you?

What specifically could they do to help you out when challenges come up?

Asking others for support. Clients often assume that others know what to do to be supportive. Although others might have some ideas about how to be supportive, typically they need information--what clients are feeling, when they need support, and what specifically they can do to be supportive. Without knowing this information, others cannot be expected to adequately respond to clients' needs.

So, what are the key steps in asking for support? First, clients need to do some work on their own to understand their own feelings and needs before they talk to others. They actually have already done this work with you. The worksheet in Appendix M helps them to articulate what their specific challenges are, how they would like things to be different, and what others can do to be helpful.

Second, clients need to consider timing. At one time or another everyone has had the experience of being bombarded with questions or requests right as they walk in the door. Unless you are prepared, this approach can feel pretty overwhelming and the likelihood of you responding well is low. So, it is important for clients to make sure to let others know that they would like to talk and what they would like to talk about, and then set up an uninterrupted time to do so. Giving others a heads up gives them a chance to think about how they feel and what they need, and by setting aside some uninterrupted time both parties have a better chance of responding more thoughtfully to each other.

Third, clients need to remain focused on clearly communicating what has been challenging for *them*, how *they* are feeling, and how *they* hope things might be different. The worksheet in Appendix M can help them to clearly identify and express these features.

Fourth, clients need to communicate clearly what they want others to do to help. For example a client might say to their friend "*I need you to tell me I'm doing a good job keeping up my exercise routine and if I am having trouble getting motivated it would help if you could maybe join me in a walk to keep me company, okay? Can you do that for me?*" Or a wife might say to her spouse "*I need you to help me get dinner ready on two nights of the week. I was hoping that you could handle Tuesdays and Thursdays since those are my longest days at work? Do you think that is something you could do?*". Giving others some guidance as to how they can be helpful can make it easier for them to respond in the way that clients need them to. As a provider, you may need to help clients develop the language they use to express their needs. Role plays with feedback to clarify and modulate their language (soften or be more direct with a request) can be useful in this regard.

One the most important parts of any request that clients make is that they check in to see if what they are asking from others is manageable. You will notice this in the examples above. Others may have their own challenges and stressors, so they may not be able to be responsive in the way that clients had hoped. Thus, clients also need to anticipate that they may need to brainstorm with others about alternative ways they could manage to help. This requires them being open to hearing about what others might need as well. So, clients might ask *"Are there other ways that maybe you could help me out in making some changes?"*.

Finally, clients and the people they are enlisting for help will want to make a plan of action together and try it out. Just like what you do with them in session with their own plans, it is important for clients and their supports to decide on a time to check back in to see how the plan is working for each of them. In that way they can work on how to fix the things that aren't working well and strengthen the things that have worked for them.

Others who might undermine clients work. Sometimes important players--a spouse, close family, friends--are not identified by the client as being positive supports. Sometimes the people who have been most supportive to clients in the past may not be able to provide the support that clients need right now. Others, despite occupying an important role in a client's life, may simply not be a good support. Providers want to understand what makes these important players not good supports---are they simply absent or "checked out" or are they actively undermining clients' efforts for behavior change.

> *So I noticed that when I asked you who might be a good support you didn't mention your spouse. I'm wondering what is keeping them off that list? What do they do that gets in the way or what do they neglect to do that you need them to?*

> *So I wonder if there are people in your life that might make it difficult for you to change some of these behaviors? What do they do that gets in the way or what do they neglect to do that you need them to?*

Providers will want to assess whether clients want to engage these players to try to get them to be more supportive or whether clients want to disengage their energies from attempting to get support from these relationships.

115

We can work on a strategy to better communicate your needs to your spouse. Would that be something you would be interested in doing?

I'm wondering whether this person is someone you would like to talk with about the challenges they are creating for you so that you might be able to get them to at least stop creating obstacles and maybe even find some ways that they could support you?

For clients who want to disengage their energy from particular others, it is important to express empathy and help them to find ways to turn their energies back toward those who can provide support.

I'm sorry that your friends are making it difficult for you. Is there anything you can do reduce your exposure to them? Are there ways to focus more of your time on those people that you said are more supportive of you?

Sounds like you have asked for support many times, in many different ways, and have been disappointed over and over again. It makes sense that you wouldn't want to subject yourself to that anymore with this person. So, maybe it's better to focus your energy on those people that you know have been good supports.

It's certainly understandable that you just don't want to turn to certain people for support anymore because you just continue to get hurt. Are there consequences for spending less time with these folks?

For those who do want to turn towards these relationships and try to amend how they interact, many of the steps for asking for support are the same. However, there is one step in which clients often get into trouble. When clients feel that others are not doing enough to be supportive or are actively undermining their efforts, they can often get swept up in the negative emotions that emerge and become accusatory, critical, or blaming. Others will not be receptive if clients only focus on how others haven't been helpful in the past or what others are doing wrong. This will just raise others' defenses and lessen the chance that clients will be heard. Again, help clients to focus on what has been challenging for *them*, how *they* are feeling, and how *they* hope things might be different (again, Appendix M can help them articulate this). That doesn't mean that they can't point out others behaviors that are making life difficult. It just means that the tone is not critical but rather is linked to the clients' own experience. So, here's an example of how to transform a statement from other-focused into one that is self-focused:

> **Other focused:** *You never help me with preparing meals but then complain when I change things up to be just a little healthier. I need to make some changes to my diet but you are making it impossible for me to do that.*

> **Self-focused**: *I am trying to make meals a little healthier because I need to lose some weight and lower my cholesterol. Changing up what I am eating is really difficult because I am trying to find ways to make things still taste good but help me reach my goals. When you criticize the healthier meals that I cook I feel really defeated and want to give up. I really need you to not criticize me when I am trying to make some changes. What I really could use is your help in figuring out some ways to make meals that we all will like but will still help me to get healthier.*

As you notice, the emphasis on the self-focused response provides others with a rationale for why changes need to occur, gives concrete examples of what behaviors they are asking others to stop, and offers a potential solution for behaviors that would be supportive. This offers others a clear way to respond. Again, clients need to check in to see whether these things can be agreed upon with others or whether other solutions might emerge. Then, clients have to try out the plan and see whether others are more supportive and responsive to their needs.

Clearly, others may not get it right on the first try. So, it may be that clients will have to give gentle reminders about what they need for support. If their genuine efforts to approach others in a reasonable way continues to leave them wanting, it can be helpful to recognize with them that their efforts may be better directed towards those who can consistently provide them with the support they need.

> *If you don't get the support you are hoping for, use this as information. You may want to try talking with them again. But if you find that this continues to go*

117

nowhere after trying to ask for their support, perhaps this person isn't truly the best one to turn to for help with this challenge.

Working with clients around navigating social interactions happens throughout treatment. The examples we have given focused on how clients might navigate conversations with close others. However, clients will face new challenges with peers, co-workers, and others whom they may not be close to. The same principles of communication still apply. Be cognizant that social support becomes one the key factors of maintenance so attention to building these skills will be important to helping clients sustain their behavioral changes long after treatment has ended.

Stress & coping

Clients experience stress both as a function of making health behavior changes as well as other life events. How significant of a problem is stress to successful health behavior change? First, nearly half of all people in the U.S. report using food to cope with stress. Greater stress is associated with greater preferences for more palatable, higher fat, energy dense foods, greater binge or comfort eating, as well as greater disinhibited eating and more ineffective attempts to control eating. Stress is also associated with reduced physical activity and increased sedentary behaviors. Finally, people often cope with stress by smoking. Clearly, stress can sabotage health through its impact on clients' health behaviors (Adam & Epel, 2007; Brisson et al., 2000; Elfag & Rössner, 2005; Groesz et al., 2012; Mouchacca, Abbott, & Ball, 2013; Ng & Jeffrey, 2003; Wing & Phelan, 2005).

Second, at a basic biological level, regular stress can increase risk for disease, raise heart rate and blood pressure, increase atherosclerosis (a precursor to heart disease), raise blood sugar, and increase abdominal fat. These physical changes, coupled with clients' behavioral responses to their stressors, may make it that much more difficult for lifestyle behaviors to have an impact.

For example, clients who have consistent stress may gain weight simply as a function of stress and may exacerbate this weight gain by eating more to manage their feelings of stress. If they want to lose weight they are working against the basic biological effects of stress on their weight as well as their tendency to eat to feel better. Thus losing weight may be slower and more challenging. Anecdotal evidence from clients in our health behavior change programs suggests that most clients view stress as a contributor to their current issues (e.g., overweight/obesity, smoking).

Third, an important consideration for providers is that clients' stress often sabotages their continued participation in treatment and maintenance of health behavior changes. For example, in our own programs, the vast majority of those who dropped out of programs cited that they did so not because they weren't motivated to participate or didn't want to change their behaviors but rather because real, significant life stressors got in the way. Moreover, an inability to effectively manage stress has been shown to be a significant factor in why clients are not able to maintain health behavior changes over the long term.

Thus, clearly understanding the landscape of clients' stressors provides further context for some of the challenges of behavioral change. The first goal is to increase awareness of the emotion-to-behavior connections--helping clients get to know how their feelings relate to their eating, drinking, physical activity, and smoking behaviors as well as how their own life stressors directly affect their health behaviors. The second goal is to understand how their experiences are tied to their basic needs. That is, people are often unhappy with different aspects of their lives either because their basic physical needs (e.g., food, shelter, safety) or their basic psychological needs (autonomy, competence, relatedness) are not getting met in some key ways. By learning more about what needs are not being fulfilled, clients can develop a rationale for their feelings (*why* they feel stressed), which in turn allows them the opportunity to identify potential choice points for how to address their feelings. The final goal then is to provide a menu of tools to help clients more readily manage their emotions, including referrals to other providers if this is outside of your scope of practice.

Again, it is important to remember that clients come into treatment with varying abilities to manage their stressors. Some clients have very few tools in their tool belts from which to draw on and may need more basic guidance on coping, others will have tools that just need to be dusted off, and others will be well equipped to manage the challenges that come their way. Thus, the strategies that we will discuss below should be flexibly adapted to the needs and skills of individual clients. But first, let's explore how this approach differs from other dominant approaches to stress management in the context of behavioral change.

The philosophy of cognitive-behavioral approaches is that changing perceptions or evaluations about life events and the responses to these perceptions is the key to stress reduction. These approaches tend to be problem-focused and imply that changing how you *think* about your situations will lead to better coping. Typically most of the effort within the context of these behavioral change programs (programs that are focused on another set of behaviors such as weight loss, diet, physical activity, or smoking cessation rather than stress management per se) is dedicated to helping clients stop and correct negative thoughts that come up as a result of their experience around the behavior targeted for change. So, for example, when a client relays his experience around eating and weight loss (e.g., I am working very hard to eat healthy, balanced meals, yet my weekly weigh-in showed no weight loss.), the thoughts that emerge (e.g., "I want to just give up", "I failed", "I'll never lose the weight!") as well as the expectations that underlie those thoughts (e.g., I expect to lose a pound *every* week) are explored. Then, clients are taught how to stop the thoughts (at times literally even saying "stop") and restructure them by creating more realistic expectations of themselves (e.g., Losing weight is going to take time. I did really well sticking to my eating plan so that was a big accomplishment). Overall stress reduction from other life events receives relatively little attention other than brief behavioral coping strategies (e.g. take a break, get some physical activity).

More recently, mindfulness-based approaches have been garnering attention as an adjunctive treatment to health behavior change interventions. Mindfulness-based approaches emphasize the development of attention and awareness to physical sensations, emotional states, and cognitive processes, without judgment about the experiences that one is having. Further these approaches teach clients contemplative practices that involve sitting, movement, and dialogue with others to restore personal resources for managing stress and taking better care of themselves. So, for example, a mindfulness approach might help clients with the specific targeted behavior, such as focusing on more mindful eating--being choiceful about what they eat as well as slowing down, drawing attention to taste and experience of food, as well as listening to cues that one is full or finished. Moreover, mindfulness approaches might also teach clients overall strategies to be more aware of their thoughts and feelings when they are stressed, how these thoughts and feelings spark targeted health behaviors (e.g., eating, physical activity, smoking), and use techniques to directly regulate the emotions that emerge through centering practices (e.g., meditation, relaxation) rather than engage in attempts to change thoughts or the targeted behaviors per se.

In our view, there are a few pitfalls in these approaches. First, with regard to cognitive-behavioral approaches, thought stopping (saying "stop" to oneself when a negative emotion comes up) as an emotion regulation strategy may indeed pause clients from entering into a spiral of negative thoughts but in our opinion it comes at a cost. Thought stopping implies a judgment about the thoughts that are emerging (and associated feelings that go along with them)--that they are inherently wrong. Indeed, cognitive-behavioral approaches call the thoughts that emerge "maladaptive" and the strategy for management, at its core, is about correcting the thoughts. We contend that the *emotions* that emerge (and the thoughts that follow from them) may be signaling some real and potentially substantial challenges that are going on for clients that require a change to life circumstances, not simply how one thinks about them. Relatedly, both the cognitive-behavioral and mindfulness based approaches focus on how clients respond to life events but do not systematically address how to address the practical challenges that give rise to those feelings. So, for example, the reason why clients turn to eating when they feel bad might be because they are regularly interacting with people who are poor social supports. Thus, the intervention that might serve clients best is to have them consider how to better approach interactions with these unsupportive others or alternatively withdraw from engaging with them. In essence it is helping the client to stop sticking their hand over the fence that says "beware of dog" and getting bit rather than helping the client to rethink or otherwise regulate their reactions to getting bit. Our approach shares elements of both the cognitive-behavioral and mindfulness based approaches and works to remedy the gaps in each.

Addressing emotions associated with targeted behaviors. People may eat poorly or eat more in response to feeling good (e.g., at celebrations) as well as in response to feeling bad (e.g., after a fight). They might be physically active both as a response to positive events (e.g., having a great day with the kids) and negative events (e.g., to relieve stress from work), or alternatively they might be physically inactive as a response to those same positive events (e.g., having a great day relaxing with the kids) and negative events (e.g., relieving stress from an awful work day).

Similarly they may smoke more in response to both positive events (e.g., hanging out with friends) or negative events (e.g., financial woes). So, to first understand the landscape of their experience, we explore with clients the different ways that their health behaviors (eating, physical activity, and smoking) are tied to their emotions.

> *People often eat in response to both good and bad things that happen to them. I'm wondering if you notice that there are times recently when you do this too? Can you tell me about those times?*

Clients will often spontaneously identify feelings that emerge in different events. But if they don't, it is important to ask about the feelings that they have during those times.

> *So, I hear that you often eat more after fights with your spouse. I'm wondering what feelings are going on for you during and after the fights that lead you to eat more?*

Importantly, the emotions that emerge often don't end there, but new emotions emerge after clients engage in the behavior. For example, a client might feel really angry and sad after a fight with his spouse but then shift to guilt and shame in response to eating the big bowl of ice cream to make himself feel better. So, it is not often simply a single emotion that emerges but rather a complex pattern of emotional responses.

> *So you feel angry and sad after a fight with your spouse and often eat a bowl of ice cream to feel better. How do you feel after you eat the bowl of ice cream?*

A step that is often missed here is that articulating the pattern is not the only function of this exercise. Rather, a key piece of this exercise is to help clients develop understanding and empathy for themselves and their behavior. The provider can aid in this process by offering reflective statements that capture this empathic stance. Empathic statements by providers convey a very simple point—that the emotional reaction is a valid and reasonable experience (not maladaptive!), and that allows clients to be more focused on changing how they respond to those feelings.

> *After a fight with your spouse you eat ice cream so that maybe you won't feel so bad about yourself and your relationship, but eating ice cream backfires because then you feel awful about eating it. Wanting to feel better when you feel upset with your spouse makes a lot of sense to me. Nobody likes to feel that way.*

Developing awareness of clients' common emotional reactions and empathy for them is the first step before any change to these behaviors will likely occur. Why? People often have difficulty "in the moment" recognizing what they feel and how their feelings fuel their behaviors. And, they frequently punish themselves for their feelings and behaviors (even without any prompting from anyone else!). So, articulating the pattern of behaviors and having them attend to these moments as a keen observer helps them to create self-knowledge and cultivate mindful, non-judgmental awareness.

Because the intensity of people's feelings in the moment often hijacks their positive coping strategies, it is also important to consider what coping tools clients have in their tool belts and what new strategies might be useful additions to their repertoire.

> *I wonder if we could consider ways to feel better after a fight, other than eating, that won't make you feel worse later on. What kinds of things might you do that could help you to not go from feeling bad directly to ice cream?*

As you notice we first turn to clients to generate their own strategies but we can also offer them a menu of tools. For example, talking to others (e.g., friends, family, counselor), eating a healthier alternative, doing some physical activity, getting sleep, engaging in self-soothing (e.g., hot tea, bath, read, listen to music), using holistic practices (e.g., yoga, meditation), turning to faith or spirituality, and doing activities that capture interest and bring joy or pleasure are some common strategies that we discuss with clients.

Above we have talked about how food, drink, physical activity, and smoking behaviors emerge in response to life events. Sometimes stress can be related directly to clients' attempts at making behavioral changes (e.g., feeling discouraged and disappointed when they don't lose as much weight as they expected to; feeling self-critical when they smoke). To address these issues we follow similar to the steps outlined above—we help clients to identify the events that stimulate an emotional reaction and the emotional pattern that follows, develop empathy for their reactions, and explore tools that might help them better manage their emotions. However, we also often focus on two other things.

First, when clients have negative feelings emerge about behavioral changes it may signal that how they are going about making behavioral changes does not feel volitional, they feel over-challenged, or behavior change is creating significant ripples in their social interactions. Thus, they are feeling that their autonomy, competence, and relatedness needs are being challenged. To address autonomy, providers may want to explore whether the behavioral changes that clients are making are ones that they are willingly doing. Oftentimes clients are operating out of "shoulds" or "should nots" ("I should work out", "I shouldn't eat sweets", "I shouldn't smoke") rather than seeing that their behaviors are always a choice. This can reflect all-or-none thinking ("I can never eat a brownie") and may be resolved by helping clients to think more flexibly about their behaviors ("I want to have a brownie tonight for dessert so I'll eat a little lighter to account for this"). When providers hear clients feeling obligated or pressured, it may be worthwhile to acknowledge just how tough behavior change is (*"Resisting eating a cookie when the yummy smells are wafting through the house is hard to do."*) and then also re-visit with clients their goals for behavioral change (e.g., "*And at the same time, you have a long term goal to be healthier so that you can be around longer for your partner*"). At times, reaffirming macro-level health goals coupled with developing more flexibility around how clients engage their health behaviors can address these concerns. However, when their feelings reflect a genuine shift in their behavioral goals (potentially away from changing behaviors) then providers should offer understanding and empathy and offer follow up contact if needed (see initial session strategies for working with clients who do not want to change behaviors at this time).

Negative feelings (especially anger, sadness, failure, and defeat) often emerge when clients feel over-challenged by the behavioral changes they are making. Providers can readily address these issues by helping clients articulate the challenges and work to rescale the scope of the changes they are making. We have discussed this in depth in the action planning section of this book and recommend revisiting this section to review these strategies.

Finally, negative feelings quite often emerge when clients try to change their health behaviors in the context of their social environments. For example, food is an integral part of many of our social interactions. Clients have their own traditions for everyday meals with family, friends, or other groups (e.g. co-workers) as well as special occasions (e.g., holidays, celebrations). These traditions are further influenced by culture. The stated and sometimes unstated rules dictated by these traditions and cultural norms (e.g., "clean your plate"; eat everything so you don't offend the host) influence what clients eat and how they eat. Thus, all of these norms can pose significant challenges to maintaining a healthier lifestyle.

When clients initiate health behavior changes they will inevitably encounter some resistance to changing the norm. One of the important things to help clients do here is to remember why they are engaged in making behavioral changes (e.g., both macro-level health goals and macro-level life goals) and be choiceful in the behaviors that they are changing (e.g., being selective about keeping traditions that are important to them but altering others that might be less important) so that they can provide others with a rationale for their behavior. Moreover, providers will also want to recognize with clients that their behavior change is not happening in a vacuum and thereby encourage clients to have conversations with important others so that they can garner the support that they need (or withdraw energy from those individuals or groups that are not able to adequately provide support). We refer you to the earlier section in this chapter on cultivating need support to revisit how to navigate this with clients.

Building vitality and resilience. Beyond stress prevention, we focus on building greater vitality so as to increase personal resources, which can also be used toward behavioral change. Building vitality occurs through two key processes--cultivating connections to important others and engaging in activities that are personally meaningful. So to help foster vitality we ask clients about who are the important people that provide them joy and energy and we have them think about how to cultivate those connections. For many, their daily lives get filled up with other tasks and they can go without making contact with people who are most important to them. So, clients are asked to think about how to make contact--whether that is a phone call, sending a text, or actually carving out face-to-face time to spend with those who are important--both in the immediate (so, what can you do today or this week) as well as long term (how do you make time with those who are important to you a priority, even when they are at a distance). Sometimes that takes some creative thinking, but what most clients realize is that it is well worth the effort.

We also ask clients about what they do for themselves to cultivate their own interests. For some people, they no longer know what their interests are because it's been too long since they gave themselves any time. Again, in most people's lives their interests get pushed to the bottom of the list, the thing they will do later if they have some extra time. What we suggest is that putting activities back in your life that make you learn, grow, and enjoy life actually works to increase positive mood and recharge your energy for other life tasks. We ask clients to think about what they would like to do--hobbies, interests, leisure time activities--and if they aren't sure about these they can first begin by doing some exploration of available possibilities (e.g. searching the internet, accessing community activity bulletins and newspapers). Then we help them develop some creative ways to cultivate their interests. This may mean that they want to take a class (e.g., gardening) but don't have time, so instead they create smaller ways to develop these interests (e.g., start by taking time out in the evenings to read gardening magazine or take a trip on the weekend to a local gardening center). The main idea is to begin to reintroduce these sources of joy and interest back in their lives in small ways. Once that flame is sparked it is oftentimes enough to begin the process of building their interests.

As you will note, actively building vitality is about cultivating clients' basic psychological needs—getting connected to important others (relatedness) and cultivating one's personal interests towards growth and development (autonomy and competence). Not only does this have direct benefits to psychological well-being but it also provides a store of energy to draw from to support behavioral change.

When the stress is too much. For some, engaging in stress reduction and getting other things in line might need to happen first before they try to make concerted efforts toward behavioral change. Why? Consider thinking of your life as a bucket. You fill it up with activities and events (positive and negative) and at some point you reach capacity---your bucket is full. There's no way to add anything else without the bucket overflowing, without something spilling out. So, when life demands that you add one more thing to the bucket, you can feel really overwhelmed--or in other words *stressed*--and it can be difficult to manage all that you have in your bucket. In fact, the bucket overflows. Sometimes, the work of providers is to help clients give themselves permission to put some health behavior changes on hold (or at least largely on the back burner) to give more energy to other parts of life that need attention. We have created a brief stress reduction program (La Guardia, 2014) that may be used first to work on these issues explicitly and then once clients feel that they have a little more room in their bucket, they proceed to tackling other health behaviors.

Preparing for maintenance

Maintenance is a process that poses its own unique challenges (e.g., how to grow and transform behavior changes when they get boring; how to manage behaviors when injury or new health challenges emerge) and clients often wonder how they will sustain their health behaviors once the structure of treatment and the guidance and support of the provider and/or others (e.g., group members) is not regularly present. In clinical and research terms maintenance refers to the period in which clients are trying to sustain health behavior changes once a behavioral goal has been achieved (e.g., quit smoking; lost 10% of body weight; achieved 150 minutes of physical activity per week; increased fruits and vegetables; decrease calories and fat to recommended levels). However, in reality, because clients often have limited healthcare coverage or treatment services are time-limited, many have not fully achieved their goals and the period after treatment is marked by attempts to both maintain their behavioral gains *and* continue to grow them on their own. With such a burden on clients to pick up the baton and run with it even when they are just getting their legs under them, we believe that treatment fundamentally needs to address maintenance as part of the process of helping clients know how to continue to grow their skills to

129

sustain their behaviors over the long term. Thus, maintenance is not just simply something that happens once people are done with the "main" treatment but rather is a process that begins as a core part of the later sessions of treatment.

So what are the fundamental issues to address in preparing for this transition? From our perspective there are six core tasks: 1) revisiting motivation for behavior, 2) developing plans to integrate health behaviors with other life goals, 3) developing new goals or challenges, 4) revisiting the role of life stress and links to health behaviors as well as anticipating upcoming challenges that may up-end health behavior maintenance, 5) solidifying social support to continue behavior, and finally 6) developing strategies for relapse prevention. We address each of these in turn below, but first, we would suggest that providers set the frame for the shift in treatment to a focus on maintenance and future growth.

> *We have been working together for some time and we are nearing the end of treatment. One of the things that is often helpful is to give some thought to what we want to tackle in the time remaining together--what are some of the challenges that you are still having--but we also want to spend some time doing some planning about how you can sustain and even grow with some of the changes you have made after we are done with treatment. How does that sound to you?*

Revisiting motives and goals. To start this process it is useful to revisit clients' motivations for behavior change and their goals so that together you can get a sense of the current state of affairs. At the beginning of treatment, providers talk with clients about their reasons for behavioral change (and for not changing behaviors). Over the course of treatment these reasons may or may not have changed, but in our experience, there is often a shift. So, the first task is to revisit clients' early motivations for behavioral change and have them assess if, and how, these may have shifted over the course of treatment.

So, when we started treatment you had a lot of different reasons for wanting to make behavior changes. I remember that you said x, y, z. I wonder if you have noticed if these reasons have changed for you at all since the beginning of treatment? Any new reasons for trying to lose weight and keep it off?

So, when we started treatment you had a lot of different reasons for wanting to make behavior changes. I wonder what keeps you going with the changes that you have made? What do you think will keep you going after we have finished treatment?

Do you think you have changed how you think about your diet and physical activity since you started treatment? (if yes: How are you different? What motivates you to keep up with the changes to your diet and gets you physically active?)

Do you think you have changed how you think about smoking since you started treatment? (if yes: How are you different? What motivates you to keep up with the changes you have made?)

Often what follows from this conversation is that clients have naturally linked their health goals to other important values or goals. In this case, you can readily draw attention to this link.

So, eating right and being active is important to you because it has let you be more engaged with your kids and it also lets you set a good example for them so they'll grow up healthier. Is that right? So reminding yourself of just how important this is to you and your kids helps to keep you going with these changes, even when it gets tough to.

So, smoking less made you feel better, more energetic, and that helped you start doing more things that are important to you.

However, if they don't make these explicit links then you can query about how their behavior change goals fit with their other current big picture goals. You will have already discussed this with them at the beginning of treatment so this isn't a new conversation. Rather, you are again revisiting what they said earlier and allowing for opportunities to revise and update these big picture goals.

I remember that at the beginning of treatment you really weren't feeling well when we started treatment but it sounds like you have felt your energy and mood improve since you made some behavior changes. So, it seems like one of the most important things for you is to feel good and keeping up with these behaviors helps you to do that. So not feeling so good might be a good signal to you that you need to get back to working on some of these health behaviors.

One of the other things you will notice in the statements above is that you further draw attention to how clients can utilize their big picture goals to remind themselves of why they are making behavioral changes when it becomes challenging to keep up with them. These reminders help clients to counteract those feelings of failure and refocus on their purpose, thereby serving as a tool to build their sense of competence.

In essence, for people to maintain a behavior over the long haul they have to integrate it into who they are---their identity. Mind you this doesn't have to be the defining feature of who they are, but it has to be a part of it. Why? The behaviors that people are trying to change are intimately tied to many parts of their lives and without value for their behaviors they will get pushed aside in the service of other goals, pressures, or concerns.

Developing new goals. Once clients have a basic handle on some of their behaviors they will want to create new goals and find more optimal challenges. Together you may have already tackled some of this with clients who progressed in their behavioral changes during treatment. For others, thinking about ways to challenge themselves and continue to develop their skills is a new task. Wherever their starting point, the main issue is to help clients recognize that behavioral change does not end once treatment ends but that the same process that you have honed during treatment can be revisited to create new and exciting challenges in the future. It is also good to let clients know that it is normal for them to get bored with their behaviors and need to change things up. So, for example, at some point the zumba class that was oh-so-much-fun six months ago now bores the client to tears. Or walking on the treadmill-to-nowhere no longer holds their interest. Maybe it's time to try a new class. Maybe training with a group to do a 5K becomes a new goal they set and a new scene for them to continue their behavior. The point is that the role of providers is to help clients recognize that reinventing their behaviors is important to cultivating their intrinsic motivation--the enjoyment, interest, and pleasure in their activities--as it has its own power in fueling their behavior.

Revisiting stress. Clients may deeply value and integrate health behaviors into their lives. However, even the most valued priorities that they have can be derailed by life stressors. Indeed, as we have talked about earlier, health behaviors are often the first things to go when people get stressed. So, as a provider it is important to revisit the role of life stress on clients' health behaviors and review their strategies for coping. Moreover, in preparing for maintenance, it is important to talk with clients about anticipating upcoming challenges that are looming—these can be big (e.g., declining health of a parent may lead to a greater caregiving role) or they can feel big (e.g., winter is coming and the client will be less active outside). As with other challenges, together you and your clients can strategize how to employ coping skills and consider new supports or resources they will need to enlist when the time comes.

Fortifying support. It is clear that people can value behavioral change but it is hard to sustain their motivation without the support of others. That is, it should be clear by now that there are times when it is tough to maintain behavioral changes. Others can help lift up clients when they don't feel they have the confidence or energy to do so. It should also be clear that others can actively sabotage behavioral change or create obstacles to maintaining change over the long term. So for example, others might be tolerant of a client's behavior changes while they are trying to lose weight, but once they perceive that the person has reached their goal others

133

may expect that things can "go back to normal". Further, during treatment, clients may not run into all of the social challenges that might come up for them. For example, clients often have trouble navigating big holidays (e.g. Thanksgiving, New Year's, etc.), as these are times when it is normative for people to engage in behaviors to excess (e.g., overeating, drinking, smoking, being sedentary). You have worked extensively with your clients to develop their social support network outside of treatment. The task here is about helping clients to strategize about how to maintain the support from that network, anticipate and plan for any changes that might occur to that network or that might create new challenges for support, and brainstorm ways to cope with any lapses.

It is also important to recognize that for many clients ending treatment with you will be an important loss. They have counted on you for guidance and support. Together you have navigated some behavioral changes with them that they may have not previously been able to realize on their own. For many, sustaining their behavioral changes without regular contact with you feels like a daunting task. So, it is important to make some time available for them to give voice to what they appreciated about the work you did together and their concerns about moving forward without this relationship. This serves not only an important point of closure for the work you have done together but it also can be an opportunity to highlight a few other important points. First, your relationship illustrates what need support really is about, so it can be used an exemplar of what they can ask for from other relationships. Second, having this conversation gives you the opportunity to invite clients back to treatment if they find they are relapsing, an important point we talk more about in the prevention section below. Finally, having a good relationship with you also sets an example for how treatment can be useful when navigating tasks that are difficult on one's own. This encourages clients to think of health professionals as a potential resource for when they are struggling and may translate to the next time they need to seek treatment--reducing hesitancies to try treatment again in this setting and other healthcare realms.

Relapse prevention. All of these conversations serve to teach an important skill---relapse prevention. That is, people don't have to wait for fires to erupt but rather they can be somewhat planful to try to avoid a full-fledged crisis. Relapse prevention involves recognizing "red flags"--those signals that warn the client that things are not going so well with maintaining their behaviors (e.g., pants are getting tighter, can't walk up the stairs as easily). It also involves having a plan to employ a menu of strategies to get back on track with behaviors, problem solve and revise plans when they don't work, and pull in others who can provide supports when needed. Another important part of relapse prevention is to identify steps to re-engage treatment in some capacity (e.g., single visit to a doctor; monthly booster sessions; intensive program) if clients are feeling like the slide backwards has momentum. Thus, relapse prevention is about refocusing on getting autonomy, competence, and relatedness needs met.

In summary, preparing for maintenance is a core part of the main treatment. From our perspective revisiting motivation for behavior, integrating health behaviors with other life goals, developing new goals or challenges, revisiting the role of life stress, solidifying social supports, and developing strategies for relapse prevention are the core tasks to be addressed. In attending to these features, clients will be better prepared to sustain behavior changes and also revisit treatment if needed to bolster the work you have done together. By doing so, you set up clients to solidify the tools in their toolbox before they leave treatment.

Section Summary: Individual Treatment

To understand how to put SDT into practice it is necessary to think not only about the structure and content of the intervention but also the processes that guide interactions within the intervention. The roadmap for individual treatment shows that different content is covered when initiating treatment versus in the extended work with clients. Initiation involves deeply understanding clients' experiences, history, motivations, and goals; helping clients to clarify options for changing or not changing their behaviors; and providing opportunities to make autonomous decisions about their path. If they decide to change their behaviors, treatment not only focuses on the nuts and bolts of skill building, but it helps clients develop the roadmap for their personal journey, decide who they want to bring along to support their travels, and learn how to effectively manage stressors and other detours that reroute their path. Notably, no matter what content is being addressed, the process--providing support for clients' basic psychological needs--remains the same. If the content is the roadmap, the process is the lens through which clients see the landscape along their journey. Let's now examine how these same principles apply to different modalities of delivery.

CHAPTER 10.

Group-based Interventions

One of the great challenges of healthcare delivery is finding ways to reach a larger audience, in cost effective ways, without diluting or losing the power of an intervention. Many have addressed this issue by delivering programs to groups rather than individuals (e.g., Silva, Markland, Minderico, Vieira, et al., 2008; La Guardia, Cook, Stanford, Potter, & Povec, 2015). Intervention techniques for individuals that we have described throughout this book can be employed within groups as well. Groups can offer opportunities for need support that cannot be afforded by individual treatment. Groups can also pose their own unique challenges for delivering a person-centered, optimally need supportive approach. In this chapter we review both the additional challenges and benefits of group-based delivery.

Challenges of translating need support into the group format

One of the first challenges in designing a group intervention is determining how to set up the framework of treatment so that clients still feel that the activities of treatment speak to their individual concerns, the tasks are at their skill level, and providers are being individually responsive. Again, when we think about how to structure groups we begin by thinking about how we can be optimally supportive of clients' basic needs for autonomy, competence, and relatedness.

Relatedness is fostered by providing ample opportunities for individual contact with the group leader but also opportunities to build supports with other members of the group. Autonomy is fostered by creating both individual and group-based opportunities for choice about how treatment will unfold—what topics will be covered, what goals will be pursued, and how participants will go about pursuing them. Finally, competence is fostered by creating opportunities to personally tailor individual exercises within the structure of modules or lessons so that it best matches clients' skill levels and provides optimal challenges for each individual to stretch and grow. Moreover, competence is developed through feedback, which within a group can also come from other group members. Let's discuss how we achieve each of these within the context of a group.

Fostering Relatedness

Building connections to the group leader. Individual treatment affords opportunities to grow and develop connections to clients over time, but within a group the individual can quickly get lost. Structurally, we create opportunities to connect with the group leader through an initial individual intake session as well as through regular individual check-ins (e.g., monthly, beginning of each group session). These meetings, however short they may be, are critical for getting to know clients--their unique strengths and challenges around the behaviors they are attempting to change --but also who they are personally beyond the particulars of behavioral change. They are often also critical points of contact for keeping clients engaged in treatment, as relying only on group meetings as points of contact can often obscure the challenges clients are experiencing and the subtle (or not so subtle) shifts in clients' engagement that may be festering behind the scenes.

To combat this challenge of losing touch with the pulse of individual clients, group sessions can also be structured to provide some opportunities for individual time as well. Some providers check in briefly with each client as they arrive at the group session or before they leave. Others provide "open time" just before and just after each group so that clients know that that there will always be time available if needed.

More subtly, individual attention is fostered within group sessions by responding to clients' questions and comments with thoughtful, empathic responses. Clients will often make personal disclosures and engage in self-criticism in the context of group discussions. Providers are often uncomfortable when this occurs, wanting to address these disclosures with clients personally outside of the group context. Providers can also feel pressed for time, recognizing they "have a lot to cover" before the session ends, and worry that stopping to address such personal concerns will derail the group. We argue that these opportunities to model empathic, thoughtful responses are precisely part of the work of group treatment, as they are not only responsive to the individual's needs but also vicariously provide need support to others in the group for whom these same concerns or feelings have gone unspoken. Even brief moments of attention can foster personal connections and provide clients with a sense that they are noticed and are important, not just another face in the crowd.

We further foster relatedness by providing follow up if there is not sufficient time for issues raised. Providers can also bookmark clients' concerns so that these can be addressed in depth after session or within individual meeting times. We recognize that going above and beyond--being available to clients outside of groups, working collaboratively with our extended team to tackle challenges that cannot be easily be addressed by a single provider, and working with PCPs or other health providers to address other health challenges--is an important part of treatment. Thus, within reasonable limits, good care may require a bit of our time outside of the prescribed group hours.

139

Building connections to the group. Groups have many different personalities in them. When groups get large, providers often fall back on didactic instruction as the default. However, we design each session around experiential exercises and discussions that allow participants to interact and connect around their shared plight (e.g., to lose weight, change their diet, increase their physical activity, quit smoking). In this way we try to capitalize on the support of other group participants by building opportunities for interacting and connecting within sessions. We also encourage participants to gather organically (e.g., forming walking groups with other participants of the program who have share work locations and convenient time of day) so as to further capitalize on and build social supports. This is one of the most potent ways that groups can afford greater need support than any one individual provider can offer.

Developing the interpersonal climate of the group. Participants are used to having their health-related behaviors judged by others. And, within group sessions these judgments can leak out, either through self-judgments that clients disclose to the group (e.g., "I am a total failure") or comments that they make to each other (e.g., "You should just try to be more positive.") . It is important to not simply ignore these comments and move on. Rather, these are teachable moments to help participants be gentler to themselves, have greater acceptance when disappointments arise, and be gentler to each other. For the provider and the group to create this supportive climate, providers often must first model non-judgment by recognizing with clients when their self-critical voices are speaking loudly and offer them an alternative to treat themselves with empathy, understanding, and kindness. In other words, the function of your words is to take the whip out of clients' hands and stop them from flogging themselves repeatedly.

It sounds like it is hard not to judge yourself negatively when things don't go as planned. Behavior changes are really hard to make, so it is expected that things are not going to go perfectly. Each time you try out a plan it provides us with more information about what is working and what is not working. Rather than beat yourself up about not reaching your goal, let's see if we can learn something from your experience.

Providers can bring the group into these discussions by having the group as a whole reflect on the impact of judgments and criticisms on their feelings about themselves and their behaviors.

I'm wondering if other people have had the experience of judging themselves when they don't meet their goals? How does that feel? How does that impact you wanting to return back to try making changes again?

Moreover, the group can brainstorm about what they actually need in those moments when they are feeling self-critical or are subject to others criticisms.

When you are feeling more self-critical who are the people that can offer you support, help you to find your empathy, understanding, and compassion for yourself and what you are struggling with?

What we often find is that through these conversations the group can begin to offer ways to work toward being more understanding and supportive of one another, thereby beginning a group norm to provide need support.

Fostering Autonomy

Providing choice to the group overall. Typically, manualized group treatments have a set of packaged modules or sessions with specific educational content and exercises that are delivered in a particular order. This structure is useful in that it packages knowledge into discrete chunks. However, we like to think of these modules as the menu from which the program can be structured, with flexibility on how and when these chunks are delivered based on the needs and

141

interests of the group. So, to begin with, we try to understand the greater interests of the group by engaging in an assessment. That is, we discuss with the group what challenges are most pressing for them as a whole and what they are interested in getting out of the group so that we can arrange sessions in such a way as to be optimally responsive. Moreover, we provide as many opportunities for the group to select activities within modules that are most interesting to them. So, for example, if we include opportunities to try out new forms of exercise, we make possible those activities that are of greatest interest to the group.

Certainly, in a group you are often trying to balance potentially competing interests and needs of 10, 15, or 20 or more people. To be sure, it can be a daunting and sometimes a nearly impossible task to perfectly satisfy everyone at once. Moreover, for many providers new to the idea of tailoring group treatment, rearranging modules to fit groups' interests and needs may feel overwhelming. If this is the case, providers can still deliver the modules in a set order and use individual sessions with clients to address specific skills or issues that might be pressing in advance of the group sessions. In this way, you are still tailoring treatment to individual needs. We contend that allowing as much opportunity for the group to have influence on how they approach treatment, while still maintaining structure, help clients to feel greater authorship over their treatment. And, as we have discussed before, greater ownership (autonomy) is associated with greater engagement and persistence.

Providing choice to individuals. Within sessions or lessons there is also great opportunity to allow individual clients to tailor treatment in the way that makes most sense to them personally. For example, there are many ways to begin to approach changing ones diet--- starting with portion control, daily dietary balance of food groups, tracking nutritional content (e.g., fat, sodium, sugar), cooking new recipes, and the list goes on. Most programs prescribe steps for the client in a particular order, assign homework, and ask clients to continue to add each step to their repertoire, without a true opportunity for choice about when and if they add each of the tools.

The way we have managed to address different interests and concerns is that we use group sessions to introduce basic tools for engaging in several different strategies so that they can experiment with different approaches to making behavioral changes and then through our individual sessions with clients we collaboratively tailor strategies and goals to hone the requisite skills to meet those goals. Thus, we can then help clients choose small changes that make the most sense to them individually while still providing opportunities to be exposed to new information within the group context and incorporate new information if the client so chooses. Here's how we introduce this approach within the group.

> In our sessions we are going to learn about many different tools to help you address weight loss. We will be working within group to provide you with information about these different options and provide opportunities for you to test out some of these tools so that you can see how they work for you. Not all of these tools will necessarily appeal to you. Some tools seem might seem interesting but might be more difficult to incorporate until you have mastered other tools, so you might put them on the shelf until a later time. Our main goal is to expose you to different options in our group meetings and then help you individually build your own tool belt, incorporating those things that work best for you at a pace that is manageable. So, as we go through the options in sessions and try out some of these tools, consider whether they are something you want to add to your tool belt right now and we will work together to help you both inside and outside of sessions to master those tools.

Developing personal goals and strategies for achieving goals. Although people might share common broad health goals (e.g., lose weight, quit smoking, eat healthier, be more active), it should be clear by the discussions throughout this book that the personal meaning of these goals can differ substantially and the way that clients move toward fulfilling those broad goals

143

can differ quite widely as well. The work of developing goals and strategies for meeting these goals does not have to occur simply within individual sessions. All group exercises are structured to guide participants through the steps of tackling particular tasks (e.g., goal setting) but they also allow each client to develop their individual narrative within the exercises. Thus, the experiential exercises within group sessions are delivered *en mass* but are designed help clients to personalize their treatment.

Fostering Competence

Managing differing levels of guidance that people need. Within any group you will likely have a wide range of knowledge and capabilities. So, how do you speak both to the most basic levels of knowledge and to those who are ready for a greater challenge? First, we structure sessions so that didactic time is relatively short and experiential activities consume more time. Moreover, we aim to have any didactic experience be interactive so that information is actively engaged rather than passively engaged, a strategy important to deeper learning. Experiential activities are constructed such that participants work individually on guided tasks and then reactions and responses to these activities become part of paired or small group discussions and are also then brought back to the full group for discussion. The pair or small group work gives participants the chance to work at their own pace through exercises and additionally work through personal issues without having to necessarily disclose these within the full group. Even when they do not disclose, clients can actually learn from each other through the group discussion, a potent learning tool that is not afforded by individual treatment.

We often find that beginning with a rationale for how sessions will proceed can go a long way to helping address the differences in knowledge and ability. Moreover, providing different ways for participants to engage the materials--including interactive learning with the group leader facilitating, group activities in which group members engage each other to learn, and self-directed exercises--provides an opportunity for all levels of knowledge and abilities to be engaged. Finally, within each activity (whatever the format) there should be tiered challenges, such that some tasks will be easier and others will get progressively more difficult. In that way, all clients can calibrate their engagement in the task to their current level of knowledge and ability, thereby experiencing optimal challenges. Thus, clients can expect that basic learning tools will always be a part of the session but that there will also be opportunities for people to attend to their own personal goals and skills within each session. As such, the structure addresses the needs of those who have less knowledge or ability in a particular area as well as provides opportunities for those who already have foundational knowledge and skills to expand these through more challenging self-directed exercises. Here's how we might address the group to highlight these features:

> *We are going to talk about a lot of topics in our time together in group and we will do a lot of activities. Some of the information might be things that you already know and some of it may be new to you. Because everyone in this group comes with a different set of knowledge, experience, and skills we are going to do our best to address these different starting points. We will review some basic knowledge as well as do activities to help solidify skills in each session. But we will also do some activities in each session that might challenge each of you in different ways. I encourage you to approach each task as a way to learn more about yourself—learn where you feel you have some solid tools in your tool belt and discover areas where you might want to get more practice mastering the use of the tool or even get some more detailed guidance (kind of like an instruction manual). We'll use this knowledge to help develop your own personal plan of action for changing your behaviors.*

Creating opportunities for individual and group feedback. As we have discussed above, each exercise is designed so that participants can work through a given strategy (e.g., how to problem solve a change in behavior) and develop personalized responses. While clients are

145

doing this, it is important for providers to go around and see how clients are doing navigating the exercises. Learning about where clients are struggling can help them to get unstuck in the moment, but these observations can also be important information to share with the larger group. As always, it is important to call upon the group to talk about their reactions to each exercise. What was challenging? How did they work through the challenge? Are there alternatives that others in the group might be able to offer? An important role of the provider is to moderate this discussion. This includes having the group generate ideas but also actively drawing their attention to how some of these ideas might potentially backfire. In this way, it is not the provider that is simply doling out advice but rather the provider is facilitating the process of learning how to self-regulate behaviors.

Summary of group applications

Groups can offer unique opportunities for need support. Relatedness is fostered not only through connections to the group leader but also by building connections to other group members—those who share the behavior change process. The group can exercise their autonomy by making choices about the timing of what and when content is delivered, and individuals within the group can also make choices about how they utilize content to construct their own personalized treatment plans. Finally competence can be supported not only through graded exercises that allow group members to optimally challenge themselves, but they are also able to work with and learn from each other by example and through feedback. Thus, key principles of the SDT intervention approach can be readily applied and even enhanced in group treatment.

CHAPTER 11.

Leveraging Technology:
Mobile health (m-health) applications

Today, the use of technology is pervasive. Young and old regularly use the internet to access health information and interact with their health providers. The increased flexibility and sophistication of smartphones and the proliferation of wearable devices also creates dynamic opportunities to track and intervene with health behaviors. In fact, consumers are beginning to expect that interventions leverage technology to better manage care.

There are several ways that providers utilize technology to support their intervention efforts. First, the internet is a vast repository of information, albeit some helpful and some misguided. At a basic level, practitioners can provide clients with select, reputable sites to help clients learn more about their health and obtain additional guidance for making health behavior changes. Practitioners also now create their own websites to serve the programs they offer. These sites are commonly used to provide information, links to self-directed exercises, and post instructional videos to guide clients through specific behavioral techniques or activities.

Perhaps the biggest change in the use of technology over the last 10 years is the explosion of the use of m-health interventions supported by mobile devices, such as mobile phones, monitoring devices, personal digital assistants (PDAs), and the like (NIH, 2015) . Mobile optimized web sites, phone apps, text messaging (SMS) programs, social media sites, and wearables are just some of the ways that psychological and physiological health is now monitored and engaged.

M-health technology can be used as stand-alone interventions or as a component of an intensive treatment program. Each day it seems that there's another app or device that touts its ability to help you manage your health. Many companies have built programs and devices, guided (sometimes loosely) by health sciences, to be used as stand-alone interventions. For example, MyFitnessPal and similar programs allow people to track the foods they are eating and the physical activity they get throughout the day, thereby giving them instantaneous feedback about how well they are meeting their caloric and fitness goals to achieve weight loss. Moreover, wearables such as Jawbone, FitBit, and the AppleWatch provide momentary information on fitness (e.g., steps taken, heart rate) but also are used to prompt behavior (e.g., signalling the person to get up and move around). Because many people are reluctant to step into a health providers' office, whether because of cost or other factors, these m-health applications allow people to try to change their behaviors on their own.

Increasingly, traditional intervention programs are leveraging technology to further enhance individual or group-based interventions, using m-health programs and devices as tools to supplement the work being done face-to-face. For example, rather than relying on paper and pencil diaries to self-monitor caloric intake, physical activity, or tobacco use, practitioners have clients use apps or wearables to engage in the tracking process. This often not only increases clients accuracy and completion rate of such diaries, but it also provides clients with a set of tools that they can rely on long after formal treatment ceases. From this perspective, m-health is not seen as a replacement for face-to-face contact, but rather as a useful tool in the toolbox to help foster initial behavioral change and then successfully maintain it.

Benefits and Drawbacks

There are great benefits to leveraging technology to support client health. Technology can exponentially grow the reach of health interventions. That is, although there are still disparities in access to healthcare and access to technology because of people's socioeconomic status and location (e.g., rural), among other factors, many more people who might not be able to access regular face-to-face intervention services can access the web and/or have smartphones to employ m-health applications. Thus, through these portals practitioners have an opportunity to make people's first contact with behavior change (and potentially for some their only point of regular contact) a good experience.

Technology can also serve as the gateway for those that are not yet committed to making behavioral changes. That is, m-health can provide a way for people to access information at their own pace, in a self-directed way so that they can focus on the facets that most interest them and/or are most doable for them. Thus, people are able to dip their toes into the behavior change waters without necessarily committing to intensive treatment.

Technology can also provide a plethora of health information to clients that previously were only available to them if they went to their practitioners' office. For example, wearables can track heart rate, blood pressure, sleep, steps, and up-time (essentially how long one is sitting/lying down vs. standing), among other information, and clients can receive analytics to summarize their patterns of behavior. And, this information is not just passively delivered anymore. Many devices provide "coaching", offering personalized tips and reminders that are driven by the users' own data.

149

Finally, companies are now building platforms in which raw health data and data analytics (e.g., graphs, alerts regarding particular behaviors or thresholds surpassed) can be uploaded to practitioners in real time. These platforms also often have 2-way communication with practitioners built in so that practitioners can offer clients feedback based on data received. Thus, practitioners have greater ability to help guide clients manage behavioral change as it is unfolding.

Of course, there are also potentially significant drawbacks of current m-health applications. One of the biggest downsides to the explosion of this technology is that the technology is often not guided by research evidence, and even if it is, it rarely considers the evidence around motivation. For example, some app developers have tried to stand out in the vast sea of available apps by using gamification--capitalizing on making their programs fun and interesting so as to engage users and make behavior change more palatable. The problem with many of these programs is that they use incentives, such as points or prizes, to attract their users, and they try to keep users hooked by engaging them in direct competition with others. That is, the main goal of behavioral change is to gain rewards or incentives rather than to develop value for and interest in the health behaviors themselves. Further, rather than framing health achievements as informational feedback so that people can learn and improve from information about their own behaviors, competitions put success or failure always on the line. Not surprisingly, users often disengage from these programs either because the rewards stop being all that interesting or rewarding or because they don't like losing competitions (who would?!?!). The result is that people leave discouraged rather than motivated to further pursue behavioral change.

A second critique of current m-health interventions is that most do not address important aspects of behavior change. For example, as we have discussed throughout this book, much of health behavior change is not simply about health behaviors themselves--it involves changing significant social dynamics and emotion regulation tools of the users. Most m-health interventions do not address these components at all. Therefore, although apps or wearables might be able to prompt people to walk more, put down the cookie, or nix the cigarette, they don't help with the emotional and social dynamics that led people to do the behavior in the first place and keep them engaged in the behaviors--key factors that need to be addressed to not only change behaviors but maintain these changes over time.

Third, providing users with more information or data does not equate to supporting their competence. For example, most people have trouble with the translation of numbers, graphs, or other information into action. Applications try to ameliorate this translational challenge by providing self-referent information to users ("You have 1800 calories today, you've already used 1268, so you have 532 left!"). But, what they don't necessarily do well is to help people to translate what people can do in order to meet their goals. Often users are offered generic prescriptions rather than personally driven, nuanced solutions that take into account people's unique interests, goals, situations, and challenges. Thus, people need guidance on how to use data (and go beyond it) to improve their health, and current m-health programs lack these personalized options.

Fourth, m-health interventions do not often help people deal with the many, sometimes complex, factors that influence success at reaching their desired behavioral outcomes. For example, in part because of complexities associated with age-related hormonal shifts, some perimenopausal and menopausal women will not reach weight loss goals even with changes to their diet and level of physical activity. Such efforts many require creative, coordinated solutions with various health professionals rather than the simple calories-in/calories-out approach used by many m-health programs. Further, some people will have physical limitations or mental health conditions (e.g., anxiety, depression) that make basic m-health data inadequate for safe and effective management of their health. Thus, without considering the complexity of health of the whole person there is a ceiling on the utility of current m-health interventions.

Finally, although such technologies provide opportunities to connect with others who are also engaged in similar behavioral changes through online communities and the like, there is something to be said for engaging "live" practitioners and "live" others in your own community (e.g., group members; family, friends) to help foster behavioral change. Practitioners can see the "big picture" and help people to not only see their health behaviors in context but adjust changes accordingly. Further, others are needed to change the actual context in which users are making their behavioral changes. Beyond this instrumental support, there is also nothing so comforting and so uplifting as being next to (or in even in actual contact with!) someone who understands and emotionally supports you. Simply put, we need other people, and technology can't always fully fulfill that. Although we cannot solve this "live" experience through m-health, we can exploit technology to further foster those "live" need supportive connections that people require in their behavioral change journey.

The question then is how to shape the next generation of m-health interventions. How can we use our knowledge of the science of motivation to leverage technology to create a need supportive experience for users? It should not come as a surprise that we use the same core intervention content and employ the process components that we have described throughout this book, albeit scaled in such a way as to adapt to the technology interface and expected attention span of users for the given interface. The techniques we discuss below apply to m-health applications that members of the SDT community have been involved in creating, including programs helping people manage their weight, improve their diet, increase their physical activity and decrease sedentary time, and reduce their tobacco use (see Appendix P for a select list programs and their descriptions).

Need supportive m-health

Before building any tool, we first identify the m-health medium we will use, the content we can reasonably address for that particular area of behavior change, and the desired functionality of the application (which essentially defines the capabilities of the program to engage users in particular ways; e.g., use of health data collected to craft personalized feedback and optimal challenges). It is important to recognize that different m-health mediums may be selected for different purposes. For example, a text messaging (SMS) program might explicitly focus on helping people pursue specific physical activity goals, assess reactions to experimentation around these goals, and encourage continued engagement, whereas the scope and activities covered by a physical activity app might be broader, including exercises to initially develop physical activity goals, provide education about different forms of physical activity, and offer tutorials on how to engage in stretches and strength training. Thus, setting a clear roadmap of desired parameters and selecting the appropriate medium is incredibly important to ensure that the tool serves the intended goal of the intervention.

Once the parameters of the tool are defined and the medium is selected, we use what we know about how basic psychological needs are supported in the environment (as well as the common ways that psychological needs get undermined) to build the core components of our tools. Below we review the core components that we have incorporated into various m-health interventions and provide specific examples of these applications.

First, an important consideration for any tool that we develop is to make sure that we leverage the capabilities of the technology itself to be need supportive. For example, many tools have built in ways to prod user behavior through alerts (e.g., buzzing a device to remind people to get up and walk) and "motivational" messages ("Monica hasn't logged in for a week. She might need some encouragement."), among other strategies. These prods can be annoying at the very least (e.g., getting buzzed 4 times during a meeting that you clearly can't leave or stand up in) and shaming at their worst ("Liz is that you? We haven't seen you in 28 days!"). So, when building an m-health tool, we allow users to choose how (e.g., email, text alerts, vibrate alerts), when (e.g., as information comes in, twice per day, end of day, weekly), and how much information (e.g., momentary feedback, digest of daily/weekly information) they receive while using the tool.

With that accomplished, we then develop substantive ways to address support for each of the three needs. First, let's address autonomy. We help users develop greater autonomy by facilitating exploration of their own motivations for wanting to make health behavior changes and by providing opportunities for them to reflect on how their specific goals for health behavior change can support their broader life goals and values. Another important part of autonomy support is to create opportunities for choice. Users select personally relevant, meaningful goals as well as how they want to pursue these goals from a menu of options. The flexibility and depth in which each of these functions is explored depends on the user interface. To illustrate these differences we draw from two examples of work we did for the National Cancer Institute--a mobile optimized website (http://women.smokefree.gov/) and a text messaging (SMS) program (http://smokefree.gov/healthyyou-about). Text messaging (SMS) programs allow only 160 characters to be pushed in a single message. So, the menu of options from which users select a goal (e.g., move more, sit less or a mix of both?) and the prompt to offer potential ways to meet the goal (e.g., How about adding 10 minutes of cardio activity 1-2 days this week walking, biking, or doing some other activity?) are going to be quite brief. Moreover, in text messaging (SMS) programs, considering how health fits into bigger picture life goals may simply come in the form of a prompt suggesting that the user think about and write down this information and post it in their home to remind them of their goals. In contrast, programs that operate through mobile apps or mobile optimized websites can use drop-down menus to offer more options for what goals are pursued and how they are pursued, and they can also offer opportunities for open-text entries to allow for greater user input into these menus (see Smokefree Women setting physical activity goals). Furthermore, a more nuanced picture of how health can fit with other life goals and values can be explored through engaging exercises or exchanges in this medium (see Smokefree Women weight loss expectations and goals).

Clearly, because mobile apps and mobile optimized websites have broader platforms and capabilities to interface with users, they also more naturally allow for the translation of other aspects of need support as well. For example, providing more detailed information about potential behavioral change options and a meaningful rationale for engaging in them (autonomy) as well as providing exercises to develop knowledge and skills at different ability levels (competence) is more readily accomplished using mobile apps and mobile optimized websites. However, it is worth noting that these communications are still relatively brief---often taking the format of short articles (similar to the length of what people read on mobile news sites) or frequently asked questions and answers (FAQs). Thus, m-health interventions are relatively

155

streamlined and pithy. Although the information contained on such sites may not exhaustively account for all challenges and questions that clients might bring our way, they are informed by our knowledge of the main concerns and challenging dynamics that clients typically raise in practice, and as such, attempt to anticipate and be responsive to basic psychological needs.

Across all m-health modalities one important way that we support users' psychological needs is through the creative use of iterative, 2-way communication and feedback. As in many m-health programs, clients get real-time, self-referent feedback on their progress vis-à-vis their goals (e.g., daily step counts, up time, caloric intake, or cigarettes smoked as compared to their desired daily goal). This provides informational feedback about their effectiveness at reaching a desired outcome and thereby supports competence. However, we take it a step further to check in on user experiences of behavioral change and provide tailored, supportive feedback. For example, users are asked a question about their experience of testing out a behavior change experiment they tried (e.g., You've spent the week learning more about your activity patterns. How do you feel about what you've learned?). They are then given relatively simple reply options so that we can better understand the overall tone of their thoughts and feelings about their experience (e.g., "good", "ok", "bad"). The follow-up response that they receive is customized to acknowledge their perspective, reflect empathy for their experience, and provide encouragement to bolster continued engagement--similar to what practitioners' do in face-to-face conversations (if "good": "Knowledge is power! Knowing your patterns will help you choose your goals."; if "ok": "Learning about your patterns can feel good and bad, but it also gives you the power to make new choices."; if "bad": "Try not to be too hard on yourself. Learning about your patterns gives you the power to make new choices."). Follow-up responses may also help users consider how to restructure their goals, capitalize on successes, or address barriers they may have run into. So for example, they might be asked "How's it going with adding 10 minutes of cardio activity 1-2 days this week?". If users respond "easy", then the follow-up reply focuses on building on this experience ("If increasing cardio by 10 minutes has been super easy for you, challenge yourself! Go for 15 minutes, 30 minutes or more!"), whereas if they respond "hard", then the follow-up reply focuses on helping the user develop optimal challenges---smaller, more reasonable goals to build efficacy ("Cardio can be intense. Increasing cardio time can be hard. If 10 minutes is too much for now, consider starting with 5 minutes & work your way up"). Finally, responses also draw attention to the sometimes high expectations that users often have for themselves. We help users be more empathic with themselves by offering a kinder, gentler, normative set of expectations for change so that they don't get discouraged (e.g., "Your weight loss isn't quite where you might like it to be. Sometimes other things in life, such as work stress or family demands, take priority over any weight loss goals. Remember that change is a journey. If this week allows, try to refocus your attention on making healthy eating and exercise choices"). We also remind them to identify and appreciate even small improvements ("It's worthwhile reflecting for a moment on what you have been doing to be successful and use this information to continue doing those things in the days ahead."). By focusing on clients' *experience* of behavioral change, and not simply the objective data on performance, we better capture the way that practitioners and clients typically interact and we more fully respond to the whole person. Thus, through these exchanges we not only try to support the developing competence of users but we try to understand the perspective of users (support for autonomy) and empathically reflect on their experience (support for relatedness).

Finally, throughout this book we have emphasized the importance of the social context in supporting behavioral change. As just described, our m-health programs provide relatedness

157

support by modelling empathy and acceptance--important components of unconditional regard. Relatedness to others is also supported in our m-health programs by two key functions. First, users are encouraged to actively think about who provides them with need support and to enlist these supportive others in their journey. For example, in SmokeFree Teen (http://teen.smokefree.gov/yourDecision.aspx) we help teens consider how to make life decisions, including decisions about their health behaviors, by using the metaphor of going on a road trip. Exercises help empower teens to not only make decisions about the tools they want to pack (competence) and route a map of where they want to go (autonomy), but also decide who they want to take on this journey (relatedness). Specifically, with regard to relatedness, we help teens articulate the qualities of a need supportive partner so that they can then better choose who will best help them get to where they want to go. Thus, we use the tool to help people to build their support networks.

A second way that we support relatedness to others is to provide opportunities for those using our programs to have a community space where they can learn from each other, offer each other encouragement, and organically develop opportunities for face-to-face contact. We have created this forum through social media communities (e.g., Facebook page) but we have also built it within our programs (e.g., chat rooms, text messaging). Similar to when we run groups, we provide a rationale for the mission of these community forums and set up need supportive norms (e.g. provide support, understanding, encouragement to each other). However, unlike our group programs, these forums are not regularly moderated by practitioners. Rather, the users determine the level of enthusiasm and activity on the forum as well as keep each other in line. Forums such as these have launched not only an incredibly far reaching network of others to rely on for emotional support but they have also provided new and exciting ways for members to extend and enhance their behavioral changes through face-to-face contact (e.g., doing a 5K, going to a local class, and raising charitable donations for health-related organizations together). Thus, we promote virtual support but we also help to transform virtual contact into actual contact.

New directions

There are a number of ways that we can use the science of motivation to inform the development and integration of m-health tools into our health care interventions of the future. First, we need to begin by reshaping the industry's mindset about what engages users. As we mentioned earlier in this chapter, m-health tools often use competitions or reward systems (e.g., gold stars, points, etc.) to "encourage" behaviors that program developers deem desirable. Rather than focusing on such high stakes competitions or fleetingly attractive external rewards we want m-health programs to focus on providing users opportunities to learn, engage in optimal challenges that increase interest, value, and fun, and if incentives are used, make them meaningful incentives that feed back into supporting targeted behaviors.

Some industry leaders and new start-ups are beginning to follow these principles, but this focus still remains relatively rare in the mainstream pool of m-health practice. However, members of the SDT community have been involved in putting these ideas into practice and help shape this movement. For example, in the EuroFIT trial (www.eurofitfp7.eu), men participate in an intervention through their local football clubs to increase their physical activity and reduce their sedentary time. These men already have a strong affiliation to their clubs and develop affiliations to other men like them within the intervention teams. Through the use of innovative technology, men's daily steps contribute to their team's score, which are then translated into weekly online football matches against teams from other football clubs. What's different about these competitions is that team members collectively contribute steps to the team total and it is this team total that determines the match outcome. Men still get informational feedback about their own daily step counts in relation to their own goals for the week and their step count from the prior week. Thus, rather than having their self-worth on the line, their focus is on learning from their own behaviors and challenging themselves individually as well as on working collectively toward a team goal.

Numerous SDT colleagues have also been working on how to shape m-health incentives to support rather than undermine psychological needs. For example, m-health programs that tie incentives to user engagement rather than to achieving specific outcomes (e.g., 5% weight loss) promote a learning focus rather than an outcome focus, a distinction that has important consequences for depth of conceptual knowledge as well as persistence. Further, when incentives promote health behaviors directly (e.g., discounts on gym memberships) they become part of the scaffolding for promoting competence rather than become the outcome itself. These task-relevant incentives are therefore more likely to contribute to developing value for sustaining goal pursuits rather than undermining them. Finally, offering choice of task-relevant incentives allows users to select those that are most personally meaningful and useful to them, thereby affording users greater control of their healthcare.

A second major focus of attention for future m-health inventions needs to be on leveraging technology to better approximate the need supportive, responsive care that clients get in face-to-face interactions with practitioners. Platforms are becoming increasingly more flexible in their use of 2-way communication between users and the user interface, such that data on health behaviors are not simply pushed to users but there is a greater iterative exchange with users about their experiences around health behavior change. The challenge we find is that many of these m-health communications are set up as "coaching" models, which essentially translates into telling users what to do and how to do it or simply functions as cheerleaders. Instead we advocate for asking about users' experience. As we described earlier, we have the knowledge about what clients typically struggle with and we know how to show empathy for their experiences. By the relatively simple gesture of asking clients to reflect on their experience, clients can not only learn more about their own thoughts and feelings but they can feel understood and cared for-- they are not the only person who has ever struggled, they are not alone on the behavior change journey.

Rapid improvements in technology mean that we will have the opportunity to extend and refine our interventions in the future, including developing more personalized ways to support users' basic psychological needs. For example, geotracking on smartphones can identify the location of the user, and if coupled with geosensing (contexts that users define as important to a personal goal), m-health programs can be tailored by users to push text messages, alerts, photos, or other prompts that will help remind them of their bigger picture goals and remind them to stay on track in the given situation or context[5]. For example, smokers could use this feature to tag places where they typically go to buy cigarettes, so that when they approach those places a picture of their child or a prompt to try out another one of their coping tools will appear on their phone. Those trying to lose weight could get alerted when parks or farmers markets are nearby. In essence the goal is to make technology functionally personalized.

Finally, aside from making the tools themselves "smarter" in terms of need support, we also need to work at better integrating m-health with our face-to-face interventions. This is particularly important in our efforts to promote behavioral change maintenance, as our current healthcare system cannot support this lifelong journey. At present, many of our m-health platforms are still relatively clunky--limited in the scope of behaviors assessed by any given program, limited in how data is culled into meaningful information about client behaviors and concerns, and limited in how this information is then practically translated to inform treatment. Moreover, traditional health care practice and m-health are still relatively siloed. That is, innovative m-health is developed largely in the domain of for-profit industry whereas most of the traditional face-to-face interventions are born within the context of academic medicine. As a consequence, practitioners often don't really know how to effectively integrate m-health into their current care models. Both users and practitioners need to develop greater m-health literacy so that they can more flexible use m-health as core tools in their health management tool belt. With collaborations between health researchers and industry growing, we will hopefully develop structures to support the integration and utilization of m-health and thereby further enhance client-centered care.

Summary: Motivation and M-health

There has been a veritable explosion of m-health interventions for health behavior change. Most are not particularly savvy regarding motivation science, and thus fall short of optimally supporting users' basic psychological needs. However, we have outlined a number of ways that psychological needs can be better supported through m-health platforms so that users are poised to successfully initiate and sustain desired behavioral changes. Clients will be increasingly interested in using m-health applications in the management of their health. Whether or not you build such programs now or in the future, being a good consumer will help you to be selective of programs that will best advocate for your clients' psychological needs.

SECTION IV

Cultivating a Need Supportive Practice

CHAPTER 12.

Where do healthcare providers often get themselves in trouble?

There are a number of common practices within healthcare that, although often well-intended, backfire by undermining clients basic psychological needs or by pitting needs against one another (making clients choose between getting one need met while sacrificing the other). Moreover, some practices aim at jump starting behavior change, with little regard for the potential downstream consequences on long-term motivation to sustain behavior. Below we review the top ways that healthcare practitioners tend to undermine client motivation and offer some solutions for how to shift these practices to be more need supportive.

1.   Incentivizing health behaviors

When healthcare organizations and employers have tried to move people into action, they have typically turned toward incentives as a motivator. These often take the form of paying people money for completing a health program, offering money for meeting specific goal (e.g., losing 10% body weight; changing fruit and vegetable intake; increasing physical activity to >150 minutes/week; passing a cotinine test to confirm they are no longer smoking) or awarding prizes for winning a health competition (e.g., being the "biggest loser" of weight). However, significant evidence shows that incentives <u>don't</u> solve the issue of motivation (see Moller, Ryan, & Deci, 2006). That is, often there isn't enough money, prizes, or other rewards to get people to change their behaviors and/or to maintain them over the long term.

In fact, incentives actually interfere with people maintaining changes (Moller, Buscemi, McFadden, Hedeker, & Spring, 2013; Moller, McFadden, Hedeker, & Spring, 2012). Why? Because once an incentive is offered, getting the incentive becomes a primary goal of behavior.

And, once a person receives the incentive, that motivator is gone. Organizations then have to create new incentives in order to continue to encourage behavior. Most organizations cannot afford to keep offering incentives. And, even if they can, incentives tend to lose their appeal over time such that organizations either need to introduce new incentives or continually increase the value of existing incentives in order to maintain the rewards' appeal. If other motivations (e.g. value for and enjoyment of the behavior itself) have not also been fostered, then behavior will likely cease.

Research on incentives also suggests that when incentives are offered people have a tendency to take the shortest path to the desired outcome. So for example, if receiving $100 is contingent on losing 20 pounds, a person might engage in more extreme weight loss behaviors to achieve the outcome. So, even though people may reach the endpoint outcome, in the process they may not learn sustainable ways to keep weight off and have a healthier lifestyle. Thus, although an incentive might get people moving initially, it will not likely sustain the behavior, which is the outcome that organizations (and clients!) are ultimately aiming to achieve.

One of the biggest challenges with the incentive approach is that the incentive is often tied to performance. So, getting a reward is dependent on meeting a set benchmark (e.g., losing 10% of body weight, quitting smoking). This contingency most clearly ties the reward to the health behavior. As we mentioned above, this has the greatest potential for undermining sustained motivation because once the incentive ends so does its motivational energy. However, receiving an incentive that is task contingent (e.g., get $100 for completing a health risk assessment or completing a 10-week program) does not have the same undermining effect because the incentive is received for <u>engagement</u>. That is, participation and effort is what is being promoted. So, an alternative to performance-based incentives is to instead use task-based incentives that promote engagement.

Another challenge with the incentive approach is that the incentive itself (most often money) does not have direct relevance to the health behavior. An alternative is to have choice around incentives, including incentives that feed directly back into promoting the health behavior itself. For example, rather than offer cash for the completion of programs, an organization might offer reduced membership to the gym, discounts on healthy food options, or vouchers to attend classes that grow skills to build a healthier lifestyle (e.g., cooking lessons; mindfulness instruction; yoga or dance).

2.   Focusing solely on clients' health behavior, not the whole client

People are more that the behaviors they are seeking treatment for. Sometimes practitioners get so focused on clients' health behaviors that they miss connecting with their clients, they miss the big picture. As we have said repeatedly, clients are more likely to trust and stay engaged when they feel a connection to their provider and they believe that their provider cares about them. Moreover, because health behaviors are intimately tied to clients' social dynamics as well as their cultural traditions and personal identity, behavioral change will need to attend to these factors. Don't miss the forest by focusing on the tree. Get to know and care for the whole person.

3.   Not taking time upfront to understand clients motivation

"I don't have enough time" is the phrase we hear most often when practitioners don't assess motivation upfront. This entire book is centered around the idea that understanding clients' motivations is an essential step to clarifying how you will approach your work with your clients. For example, a client who is well grounded in more autonomous motives will need to foster and grow these motivations, whereas those who are more steeped in controlled motives will need more active and consistent cultivation of their own value and interest in engaging in health behavior changes as well as a quieting of those controlled motives. Moreover, continuing to assess the evolution of clients' motivations throughout treatment will provide opportunities to grow new interests and develop optimal challenges as well as directly address those obstacles that threaten clients' feelings of confidence and persistence.

4.   Missing opportunities to explore clients' feelings about behavior change and responding with empathy

Clients continually grapple with various reactions to their behavior change efforts. When clients openly share disappointments and triumphs, it is easy to understand how to respond with need support. However, many of their reactions can often go under the radar and even defy practitioners own reactions. For example, although a client might lose 1 lb in a week (which is often objectively thought of as a success in weight loss treatment), the client might be disappointed in the return given how hard they worked to achieve it. Similarly, the fact that a client maintains their weight might feel like a real triumph during a week that posed extremely difficult challenges. Assuming clients' reactions to their behavior outcomes misses an opportunity to learn more about clients' experience and help them cultivate opportunities for self-compassion and self-appreciation. Thus, being mindful of and taking interest in clients' emotional reactions and providing empathic responses to these reactions importantly models need support and promotes sustainable self-regulation in clients.

5.   Not appreciating social and cultural traditions

You cannot separate the person from their social-cultural history. We use the term culture broadly and inclusively, not to just refer to race or ethnicity, but to acknowledge the various factors that make up clients' life experiences as they define it, as not all cultural factors and identities that are personally important to clients are visible or apparent. Taking interest in clients' experience of how their social-cultural history has influenced the development of their current health behaviors as well as being curious about their concerns about how changing these health behaviors may impact their relationship to this history (e.g., often feelings of loss abound) and their current social dynamics (e.g., how am I going to manage to not offend my mother when she cooks for me) becomes critical to making interventions client-centered. Although the potential permutations of social-cultural factors may feel overwhelming, paying attention to how the three needs are impacted can explain the commonalities in social-cultural dynamics. For example, food is an important part of social interactions and celebrations. It is used to convey love and care, cultivate kinship, and provides memories of important moments wherein people connected to important others. Food is thus relational, and to change how, when, and what one eats can therefore shake up this social contract. So, before even entertaining a behavioral change to diet, it will be critical to understand the important traditions around eating meals with family, friends, and acquaintances; how culture influences when and how a client eats; and how holidays or other special events affect their eating. All of these social-cultural dynamics come with stated or sometimes unstated rules about norms, and can challenge clients efforts to change health behaviors and maintain a healthier lifestyle. A client-centered approach helps clients choose what traditions to preserve intact, what to modify without losing meaning or food memories (e.g., smaller portions, "lightened up" recipe), and what they might opt to drop altogether, as

168

well as how to negotiate getting support from others to better align their chosen lifestyle goals with culturally meaningful traditions.

6.   Using controlling language

Whether they realize it or not, health care providers can pressure their clients through the words that they use. For example words such as "should" (you should lose 20 pounds), "have to" (you have to stop smoking), or "must" (you must cut back on junk foods) are directives for clients to change their behavior.

Some practitioners may argue that some of their clients need to hear the message loud and clear and that this language helps emphasize the gravity of their message. This "tough love" approach often backfires for several reasons. First, clients usually already know that they need to change their behavior. Using controlling language can feel shaming, and shame often breeds defensiveness and reactivity rather than collaboration. Second, controlling language sets up an expectation for clients to comply with the prescribed behavior (or else!). Thus, controlling language fosters feelings of conditional regard—they will only be "good clients" if they live up to your expectations. As we know, behavior change is a challenging road. So, when clients inevitably fail to meet goals, they may be less likely to turn to you if they have experienced such conditional regard.

An alternative is to use neutral language (e.g., "may", "could") to convey information that clients need without directing them to follow a particular course of action. For example, to convey the need to lose weight, a health care provider might say *"Losing 20 pounds could offer a number of benefits to your health and make your daily living a bit easier. Would you be*

169

interested in talking more about some of the possible ways to do this?". This neutral language offers information but also invites a dialogue and maximizes client choice.

7.   Providing treatment recommendations as "the law"

On the surface the noble motive to help others achieve greater health and well-being may seem uncontestably good for clients. However, healthcare providers sometimes have challenges in translating this noble motive into practice without being controlling. For example, each profession has guidelines for "best practices"-- principles about what the field says are the best treatments and the recommended behaviors for people to be healthier (e.g., number of servings of veggies per day; number of minutes of physical activity per week). Professionals are taught that it is their ethical responsibility to provide these recommendations to their clients. To be sure, guidelines *can* provide clients with very useful information and benchmarks to help clients regulate their behaviors. However, professionals don't often realize that *how* and *when* these guidelines are presented to clients makes a difference to whether they are well received and experienced as information or whether they are experienced as demands and standards that clients are expected to follow.

So how does the translation of treatment guidelines break down in communication? In many healthcare settings recommendations are often presented as a routine part of a treatment visit and are simply prescribed to the client. For example, a middle aged man who is obese might be told that he needs to lose 30 pounds, eat more fruits and vegetables, reduce his carb and fat intake, and get at least 150 minutes of physical activity each week. Although this information is well-intended, many clients report that they are not given adequate opportunities to express their thoughts, feelings, and perspectives about the recommendations prescribed, and they often receive little feedback on how to reach the recommendations provided. Without a roadmap for how to potentially go about making changes as well as a collaborative conversation to discuss if, when, and how a behavior change might be approached, clients often feel ill-equipped to make an informed decision and feel disenfranchised from managing their own health. In contrast, creating a collaborative process--giving clients options about how and when they receive treatment recommendations and how they use this information to guide decision-making--helps clients make informed choices about their behaviors and also fulfills providers' motives to help.

8.   Providing clients with ready-made goals and plans

Many health behavior change programs have been designed with a specific set of goals for clients and a pre-set series of modules to reach those goals. For example, weight loss programs typically set a target goal for clients to lose 5 to 10% of their body weight, with activities designed to achieve these goals through a combination of changing diet (what they eat as well as total calories) and increasing physical activity to ≥ 150 minutes per week. These programs are based on treatment recommendations of "best practices" that lead to weight loss and improve health.

The challenge we find with setting up goals and ready-made plans for clients is that they are often not flexible enough to accommodate the variation in clients, their desires, and their personal goals. Specifically, they do not help clients learn how to create *self-relevant* goals and they do not readily accommodate differences in how clients want to go about making health behavior changes. For example, clients can change their diet and eat healthier by addressing portion size, nutritional balance, meal planning, and food preparation. Oftentimes they are asked to make all of these changes as part of a program rather than given these as options, with the

171

freedom to choose whether they incorporate any or all of these strategies. Further, opportunities to create self-relevant goals (e.g., I want to walk a 5K) allows clients to create meaningful targets for their behavior. Thus, adopting a client-centered approach focuses on helping clients to develop personal goals and a unique roadmap for behavioral change, a practice that promotes sustained interest and value for their behaviors.

9.   Offering choice, but not true choice

Oftentimes what looks on the surface to be opportunities for choice is not experienced by clients as "true choice". For example, practitioners may say that they are interested in what clients want to do regarding their health behaviors, but in reality, clients are steered toward a particular path. This takes the form of coercing the client to comply, either subtly ("It would be good for you to try to quit smoking") or not so subtly ("You're going to die unless you quit smoking"). It also is manifest when providers give praise and positive feedback to those who follow their recommendations and show disappointment or frustration with those who don't.

Another way that practitioners undermine true choice is by forcing decision making ("We need to know that you are ready to change in order for you to join our program") or by creating deadlines or other pressures for clients to change ("Unless you start to exercise and reach the weight loss goals we won't be able to keep you in the program").

Finally, providers may also make choosing a seemingly impossible task. For example, giving clients an excessive number of options to sort through does not create optimal circumstances for making a true choice. In fact, too many options can feel overwhelming and can over-challenge clients' competence. More options, therefore, is not necessarily better.

If clients are not provided true choice, three potential reactions will likely result. At best, they might be somewhat compliant (e.g. showing up, but inconsistently; not fully following your prescribed recommendations; or "there" but disengaged). They may reactively resist treatment activities (what some have called "controlled defiance"; Haerens, Aelterman, Vansteenkiste, & Van Petegem, 2014). Or, they may simply drop out of treatment altogether. Devising options collaboratively *with* clients and respecting clients' decisions, even if they don't jibe with your preferences as a provider, provides true choice.

10.   Taking over when clients don't follow recommendations or plans of action

When clients don't follow health recommendations or don't follow them in the way that healthcare providers conceive that they "should", providers often jump in and take over. For example, healthcare providers often have a natural urgency to want to get clients to stop behaviors (e.g., smoking) or to start behaviors (e.g., exercise, improve diet) so that clients reduce their health risk. So, they may have difficulty allowing room for clients to struggle or falter. But, just like learning to ride a bike, clients are going to fall, scrape their knees, and still need opportunities to get up and try again. The job of the practitioner is to be there to steady the seat and run alongside them until they can peddle on their own.

Health care professionals' own values may also influence *how* they want clients to change, not just that they *do* change. For example, if a practitioner values the "healthiness" of a client's food intake while the client values simply reducing their total caloric intake to achieve weight loss, the client and the practitioner can easily be at odds. True need support is client-centered, not provider-centered. Thus, true support creates room for choice, including choosing to not follow recommendations at all or follow them in some limited way, even if the

173

consequences are potentially detrimental to clients' health and not the preferred path of the provider.

11.   Responding with judgment

All practitioners have had moments in which a client says or does something that shocks or baffles them. Like Billy Crystal's therapist character in the movie *Analyze This* the internal dialogue of the practitioner can quickly bounce from disbelief (How could they think *that* was a good idea?) to wanting to shake some sense into their client (What on earth are you doing?!? Noooo!). Although the client's behavior initially may make absolutely no sense to the practitioner, this is the moment to be even more curious and try to get into the client's shoes. For example, your client has been coming to a weight loss program for some time in which the principles of healthy eating and the perils of fad dieting have been discussed frequently. However, in your next meeting, your client reveals that for the next two weeks they are going to go on an extreme diet, which involves alternating between days of significant caloric restriction and cheat days. Simply responding to this client with admonishment of "you shouldn't do that" does not help to understand the motivation (the "why") behind their choice. It also immediately shuts down the dialogue with the client and increases the likelihood that the client will not share this sort of information again. However, if the practitioner is curious and asks the client more about what prompted them to try this out now, a dialogue can be started so that the practitioner can talk openly about what the client is trying to get out of this behavior. An open dialogue such as this also allows practitioners to raise some of their genuine concerns that they may have about the effects of the client's behavior on the client's health. Engaging in a conversation to understand their reasons for wanting to adopt these new strategies does not mean that as a practitioner you endorse the client's approach. Rather, it engages the client in a process to consider multiple perspectives. Ultimately, the client's behavior is the client's decision. Remember that sustained client engagement and a continued dialogue is always preferable to shutting it down. Otherwise the client may continue their behavior without the guidance that you can offer to advocate for their health.

12. Having a mismatch in expectations

What constitutes significant change or movement in your eyes? How does that align with your clients' perceptions? The scope of the goals and expectations that providers have for their clients doesn't always match their clients' own goals and expectations. On one end of the spectrum you have clients who have very high and rather unreasonable expectations of themselves (e.g. reclaim their body so it's like they are 18 years old again; quit smoking cold turkey without any consequences) while you might have more modest expectations. At the other end of the spectrum you may expect your clients to achieve more or change their behaviors in particular ways, whereas your clients have more modest goals or may want to change some but not all of the behaviors you envision.

If clients have unreasonably high expectations of themselves, it is easy to burst their motivational bubble by dismissing their goals as unrealistic. With such clients, it is particularly important to appreciate their desires for such outcomes and help them shape their journey with proximal, rescaled goals and expectations to maximize success (e.g., *I hear how important it is for you to reach your ultimate goal of losing 50 lbs. This might take a bit of time, so it is often helpful to have some short term goals--smaller steps to shoot for--to help you keep up momentum in this journey.*).

175

If practitioners have greater expectations of what clients can or want to achieve, this can get in the way of meeting clients where they are. That is, you might move faster than what your clients may be ready for or are able to achieve right now. For these clients, you may need to provide more guidance and structure and then work toward your clients taking over those functions as they establish greater self-regulation capacities. And, it is possible that you may still not achieve the outcomes that you envisioned. Thus, it requires practitioners to recalibrate their expectations to match their clients' vision and abilities. Remember, if a client has an experience with you where they feel supported through the process, regardless of the sum total of the scope of the work you do together, they will be more likely to see treatment as useful and will be more likely to re-engage it again along their behavior change journey.

13.   Pushing new tasks before mastery of others is achieved

In their eagerness to move along change, providers will often introduce new skills or push new or more difficult experiments on their clients without waiting for clients to first master prior challenges. This can be a symptom of the program structure (e.g., a prescribed sequence of new modules each week) or mismatched expectations between providers and clients, as previously described. It can also happen more subtly through the experiments that practitioners and their clients design. For example, for smokers who are ambivalent about stopping and highly doubt their ability to do so, a 2-day experiment to abstain from smoking and instead use nicotine replacement therapy (NRT) may initially be too long and exceed their level of optimal challenge. Alternatively, a half-day of abstinence coupled with NRT to manage symptoms may give them the opportunity to begin to build their sense of mastery. Most clients already start with the hope (secretly or not so secretly) that making behavior changes will happen faster and more smoothly than it typically goes. They want the endpoint desired outcome now. And in some ways, so do practitioners. Modelling patience--letting the process of behavior change unfold at a pace that is manageable--is actually an incredibly valuable skill for clients to learn and will help them to modulate their approach to behavioral change long after formal treatment has ended.

14.   Setting up competitions vs. others

What's wrong with a little competition? People will argue that it promotes motivation, as it gets people engaged and goal-directed. But, as mentioned earlier in the m-health chapter, competitions are typically set up so that you are either the "winner" (and rewarded with incentives such as points, prizes, or praise) or you are the "loser" (typically paired with some sort of shaming to "do better the next time"). Thus, competitions inherently put success or failure always on the line. Those who are trying to make health behavior changes have often tried changing their health behaviors before and are back at it again because they either did not achieve their desired goals or they were not able to maintain their behavioral changes. They typically encode previous attempts as failures, and oftentimes globalize themselves as failures. So, you can understand why having those predisposed to feeling like failures engage in a competition where they will likely "lose" at some point may not be the best way to start. Many clients tend to avoid competitions or quickly disengage rather than poke at that wound, and for those that do engage, they often leave more discouraged rather than motivated to engage in the health behaviors that the competition intended to promote.

What about team-based competitions? Again, to the extent that they are set up as a zero sum game (some team wins whereas the other loses), it tends to undermine motivation. Team-based competitions that are designed with need support in mind however can serve the important role of solidifying a community (e.g., family unit, friend group, workgroup) around shared goals (e.g., get the office team to get more steps this week than last) as well as create a space in which they can learn from each other and offer each other encouragement to achieve lifestyle changes. The mission is to focus on creating need support within the team itself (e.g. provide support, understanding, encouragement to each other rather than a space to pressure others into compliance) and this is achieved by focusing less on competitors and more on group-relevant accomplishments. To this end, it remains important to frame achievements as group-relevant informational feedback (e.g., how did our team improve or change from week to week), to provide mechanisms for individual members to learn and improve from information about their own behaviors without the risk of being called out in the group, and to have any incentives be tied to the groups' own relative achievements (e.g., surpassing a goal they set for themselves) rather than wins or losses.

15.   Setting limits

Inevitably there will be times when you don't like your clients' behaviors. Practitioners often get themselves in trouble by subtly or not so subtly judging these behaviors (e.g., "you've got to stop doing that") and/or by cutting off or simply avoiding discussions about the behaviors for fear that even discussing them implies their endorsement of them. We return again to the important distinction made earlier between *endorsing a behavior* and *accepting the person*. Practitioners can genuinely accept and empathize with the feelings and motives that might underlie a client's behavior *as well as* express care and genuine concern about the client's behaviors and set limits on the behaviors that they will help the client to engage in. Having an open dialogue to understand clients' perspectives and respecting their decisions about their own behaviors, even one's you don't agree with, shows support for their autonomy, and perhaps more importantly, it serves to preserve the connection to your relationship. Again, the integrity of the client-practitioner relationship is critical to the journey of behavior change, as clients rarely decide their behavioral trajectory in a moment but rather tend to repeatedly revisit and revise decisions about their behaviors. Need supportive practitioners can serve to shore up clients in these sometimes rough waters of their journey.

16. Focusing on outcomes rather than the process

What are the appropriate and important outcomes to measure the success of lifestyle behavior change? Scientists, policymakers, and organizations (and practitioners by virtue of the standards set for them by these players) are typically focused on the bottom line--the efficiency and cost effectiveness of interventions (e.g., doctor visits, medications needed)--and objective gold standards (e.g., total weight loss, total minutes of physical activity and sedentary time, intake of fruits and vegetables, tobacco quit time) to quantify success. To be sure, these are desirable and reasonable metrics to measure. However, they are not the only ones to signal important and significant change. And frankly, they tend to be less meaningful for clients.

Let's use the example of weight loss. Clients and practitioners are concerned with moving the numbers on the scale. Although weight is one important marker of change, it can be motivationally problematic, as a multitude of factors can prevent its movement even when significant lifestyle changes occur on the part of the client. Focusing on weight loss alone will quickly get clients discouraged, and therefore a more differentiated view of success is warranted.

For many clients, noticeable improvements in their quality of life occur long before any significant weight loss—they feel more energy, they can walk up the stairs without losing their breath, their clothes fit a bit better, their mood improves, they find activities they enjoy. These outcomes are motivating in themselves. Thus from the beginning of treatment, helping clients to

179

focus on engaging in meaningful personal goals that enhance their quality of life serves to direct and sustain motivation.

For all clients, but especially for those for whom the scale doesn't move, it becomes particularly important to consider other meaningful health outcomes to focus on besides weight loss. For example, many people show a trend toward progressive weight gain from year to year, and as such, one important metric of successful lifestyle behavior change might be to slow or halt the trajectory of weight gain. Further, even when weight loss does not occur, significant health benefits of lifestyle behavior change can still be witnessed. For example, clients can observe changes to their health status (e.g., pre-diabetic to no longer at risk), changes to the severity of their chronic conditions (e.g., less medications to manage high blood pressure), and changes to their overall well-being (e.g., less depression, anxiety; greater vitality, purpose). Thus, differentiating health outcomes can also serve to provide meaningful markers for clients to work towards.

Summary: Typical pitfalls in supporting clients' needs

Even with the best intentions, practitioners can sometimes undermine clients' needs. By reviewing the top ways that healthcare practitioners tend to do this we hope to create greater awareness of these pitfalls so that practitioners and healthcare groups can better recognize and discontinue these practices. But good practice is not simply about making amends for the things that have gone awry. Rather, it is about building a culture that promotes a healthier environment for practitioner-client collaboration to flourish. In the next chapter we outline systematic ways to proactively assess the extent to which both clients' and practitioners' needs are being met so as to create an optimally enriched treatment environment.

CHAPTER 13:

Incorporating SDT in organizational structures:
Creating a culture of need support

One of key questions we are often asked is how to begin to integrate the SDT concepts into ones' practice. Most practitioners these days feel that their practices are stretched to their limits and they worry that the time it takes to be truly need supportive of their clients is simply not possible given their current demands. However, we suggest that this is precisely why attending to need satisfaction, not just clients' needs but one's own, is a critical endeavor. In this chapter we first discuss different ways that practitioners can begin to assess how well they are supporting their clients' needs. Then, we explore the broader work context in which providers are embedded and discuss the importance of understanding and taking care of one's own needs to not only to better take care of clients but to also cultivate a healthy professional life.

Assessing Your Support for Clients' Needs

Clients' presenting problems are complex. This is the norm, not the exception. Given this complexity it is almost inevitable that each client will challenge practitioners in different ways. Why? Even the best providers can get stumped by the layers of complexity---competing motives, complicated social dynamics, thorny physical health issues---that clients bring their way. Moreover, practitioners (even seasoned ones!) are going to get hooked by their own goals or agendas from time to time. Together these issues may get in the way of being truly need supportive of clients.

Whether providers have been practicing for awhile or are new to the profession, they all want to be seen as competent. Practitioners are often reluctant to expose their work to others, as such scrutiny can feel unnerving and potentially even scary. But, actively and regularly assessing one's work is essential to being a need supportive provider. The benefit of making self-assessment a normal part of one's practice is that it increases awareness of your dynamic with your clients and provides opportunities for growth. That is, it allows you as practitioners to not only better recognize with your clients when you have not been need supportive and reboot the connection, but it also allows you to build on the strengths of your partnership and capitalize on what is working well for you together.

How do practitioners recognize their own blind spots and challenges in being need supportive? How do they recognize what is going well? There are three main ways that we have helped providers structure such opportunities to grow their awareness. These include self-assessment, 1-to-1 supervision, and peer-group supervision. Below we describe the central features of each.

Individual self-assessment. One of the keys to being a good provider is to increase awareness of one's strengths and challenges in being supportive of each client. Each client has a different personality and has different wants from you as a provider. Some clients will push your buttons--leaving you frustrated, exasperated, and wanting to kick them out of your office--while others might make you want to swoop in and take control. You as a provider also bring your own needs to each session. Perhaps you have pressures to get clients in and out the door quickly or pressures to have clients make greater gains in their health progress. The dynamic that is created between you and your clients will set the tone of your work together.

We take a two-pronged approach to assessment. The first component involves an honest appraisal of how you think and feel about your client. The second component addresses how your current needs are being met and how this is affecting your work with your client.

Attitudes toward clients. First, let's examine how you think and feel about your clients. We created a set of questions as a guideline for considering your relationship to your clients (Appendix Q). Notice that these questions map on to your attitudes toward supporting each client's autonomy, competence, and relatedness needs.

We will start with relatedness. Remember that the need for relatedness is fulfilled by expressing warmth, genuineness, and empathy for one's client, or in other words, unconditional positive regard. So, to know whether you are poised to support this need we want to know: Do you like your client? How connected do you feel to your client? Are there things that they are doing that you disapprove of or frustrate you? Do you feel genuine when you are engaging with your client?

Next, examine autonomy. Remember that the need for autonomy is about feeling that one's perspective and goals are understood and valued and that one has meaningful choices about how to engage in health behaviors. So, to know how well you are supporting this need we want to know: What do you think of your client's personal goals? What or whom do you think is driving your clients' behaviors and choices? Is your client directing their own behaviors or does it feel like they are following someone else's agenda (including your own)? How do you feel when your client hasn't worked on what they said they were going to do?

Finally, examine competence. Remember that the need for competence is met by providing structure, meeting clients at their skill and ability level, creating optimal challenges to try out behaviors, and navigating behavioral feedback to improve and extend behavioral repertoires. So, to know how well you are supporting this need we want to know: Do you/your workplace have adequate structural supports and resources to provide what this client needs to be successful? What are *your client's* expectations about their own goals and what are *your* expectations about your client's goals? Is there a mismatch? What are *your client's* expectations about their own progress and what are *your* expectations about your client's progress? Is there a mismatch? What is your sense about how difficult will it be for this client when they review their progress?

Notice that the first step is to simply reflect on and write down your reactions to these questions. It's not about problem solving just yet. The second step is to recognize how your reactions can impact your connection to your client. So for example, if your answers to the relatedness questions are not very positive, then there are likely some significant risks for being less than optimally supportive with this client. Does not liking something they say make you want to tune out rather than fully listen to them? Do their mannerisms evoke strong emotions or reactions in you? Write down what your feelings toward your client make you want to do (or not do). This isn't always obvious. So if it isn't, just file it away as something to pay attention to as you interact with your client the next time.

Although these formalized questions provide a guideline for considering your relationship to your client, one of the skills that we cultivate in our work is to learn to pay attention to and take interest in our own reactions to our clients. We like to refer to these as the red flags---the warning signals that suggest that there is already a disconnect or a risk for a potential disconnect in your relationship with your client. Here are some of the typical red flags.

1) Dreading your client coming in. If you dread your client coming in, there is clearly going to be distance in this relationship and your client will feel it. Take a moment to ask yourself: What do you dislike about your interactions with this client? What makes you not want to get close? Are they overly anxious? Highly self-critical? Curmudgeonly? Identifying why you want to distance yourself from your client helps to determine where to turn your attention.

To change up the dynamic between you and your client, focus on finding your empathy. What must it be like to walk in their shoes? Imagine how the world feels to them. Is change scary? Do they feel helpless? Have most people that they've relied on for support disappointed them? Sometimes revisiting a discussion with your client about their experience of behavior change will help you to better understand the lens with which they see the world. This often helps to quiet your reactions to them and help you again walk the path with them. Mind you, this isn't a one-off occurrence. Empathy takes practice, and on some days it is going to be hard to be patient.

Here are two other things to consider. First, if you are dreading all of your clients coming in, it's probably a good clue that your own needs might warrant some attention! Complete your own needs assessment (see the section later in this chapter) and seek consultation to discuss how to give back balance to yourself. Second, if your reactions to your client are so strong that you shut down or try to minimally engage your client to avoid confrontation, seek consultation as well. Such a breech suggests that you and your client will need to have a frank conversation about how to proceed moving forward so that your client experiences support but that you also feel that you are in a mutually respectful relationship. Navigating this will clearly take some finesse, so gather more input to figure out the best solution.

2) Lack of interest in your client. Practitioners disengage for a reason. Lack of interest in a client often happens when the client has a disconnect between their thinking and feelings. Your conversations stay on the surface---discussing details, planning, and strategizing--but how they are feeling seems to be missing. To address this issue, you will want to revisit the process of exploring your client's experience, explicitly asking them about their feelings or "wondering" with them about potential feelings that accompany their experiences so as to draw a greater connection between the cognitive and affective components of their narrative.

3) Over-functioning for your client. Sometimes practitioners feel that they are working hard, maybe even harder than their clients. This typically occurs for one of two reasons. First, the things that practitioners are asking their clients to do are overchallenging for them at their current skill level. So when clients inevitably falter, the practitioner swoops in to do the work for them. The other time that practitioners often over-function for their clients is when they are asking clients to do something that clients don't actually want to do. In this case, practitioners feel like they have to do a sell job--trying to convince their clients to adopt a strategy or new behaviors.

In either case, it is important for the practitioner to step away from problem solving and "doing" for the client and re-examine the process of treatment. Are you creating tasks that are overchallenging? Are you pushing an agenda, being instructive, or wanting clients to change in a specific way? Do you detect yourself saying "should", "must", or making value judgments ("it would be good/bad to")? Turn back to the client and ask what their experience of treatment is. Are they finding tasks overchallenging? Is the treatment path being crafted in the way they had hoped? By hitting the pause button, examining your own behavior, and checking in with your clients, you can reset the process.

4) Feeling frustrated with your client. Practitioners sometimes feel like they are hitting their head against a wall or that every avenue they pursue just isn't quite right according to their client. When practitioners feel stuck in this way, it is useful to seek consultation to try to better understand the dynamics between you and your client and it is again time to check in with the client about the process of treatment. In fact, we often will say to clients *"I'm feeling a bit stuck and wondered if we could talk a bit about how we can improve our work together"* and then try to explore the pattern of challenges in collaborating. It is important to be specific and get clients' input on how they think you both could improve your interactions. The practitioner is normalizing the process of collaborating on solving not only treatment strategies but also interpersonal dynamics---an important model for the work that clients will also likely have to navigate outside of treatment with important others.

5) Driven by fear. Many clients who come in for treatment will have serious health issues that put them at high risk for disease and early mortality[6]. This can enliven practitioners' sense of urgency--making them feel as if there is no time to be patient with clients' process of behavioral change. Clients might also enliven fears about health risk when they are engaged in behaviors that have the potential to set off a health crisis (e.g., drinking alcohol to get the majority of daily calories; fasting for days to lose weight). Practitioners' concerns are warranted in both cases, but often the urgency to get clients to stop their behaviors immediately makes practitioners more controlling and critical, and at times, even resort to scaring clients in order to ignite behavioral change.

To be sure, some clients will need to immediately make changes to some of their health behaviors. However, the vast majority are not in such a crisis. When practitioners feel a sense of urgency it's useful to seek consultation. Talking with others will often help you to regulate your reactivity to fear and channel your concern for your client into constructive ways to help clients take control of their health. Oftentimes, this requires thinking creatively about how a healthcare team (e.g., primary care, mental health professionals, etc.) might provide clients with options to create high impact but doable changes. Being measured and thoughtful in your approach will convey to your clients your concern and will invite them to be engaged, even when potentially high risks and/or thorny challenges are being considered.

6) Being fake/not being genuine with your client. When practitioners are not being genuine with their clients it is often because they have an unfavorable opinion or judgment about their clients' behavior. Let's face it--you are not always going to like what your clients do. In these moments it's helpful to remember that it is your client's life and their choice about how they behave. Your judgment is about how you would make choices for yourself. So, how can you be more genuine? Again, we return to finding empathy. Consider these questions: How do their choices make sense for them, for their lives? How did they come to their decisions? In what ways can I help support them in their chosen path? By stepping away from your perspective and trying on theirs it can help you to be more in touch with genuinely supporting your clients.

In summary, although this may not be an exhaustive list of reactions that practitioners might have with their clients, the point is that your reactions are information. It can tell you a lot about where to direct your attention, how to better support your clients' needs, how to change the process of treatment, and sometimes when to attend to your own needs as well. Also, how you react to your clients can also tell you something about your clients' dynamics around behavioral change with important others in their lives. This will also help to inform how you guide them through communicating their needs to important others.

Assessing your own motivations and need satisfaction. Practitioners provide an important social context in which clients' needs may be met or alternatively thwarted. While many behavioral change interventions make considerable efforts to make sure that practitioners are optimally supportive of clients, they miss out on opportunities to help practitioners understand their own needs and their own motives and how these factors may influence their behaviors with their clients. Thus, the second component of assessment is to evaluate your motivations for working with your clients, how well your own needs are being met within your work environment currently, and how these factors are impacting your work with your clients overall.

Practitioners' motivation. Health care professionals have a variety of motivations that can influence their interactions with clients. As we discussed earlier, some of these motivations will come from practitioners own value for health and embody their desire to help others achieve better physical and/or emotional health. Other motivations will be driven by external pressures to produce client outcomes or profits as well as internal pressures to achieve and be lauded by others. Still, other practitioners will find themselves feeling completely disengaged from their work. The first step is to assess where on the spectrum your motivation is falling.

A relatively simplistic way to do this is to ask yourself the following question: "Overall do I mostly feel disengaged, pressured, or willingly engaged and interested in my work?" In other words this question seeks to understand if you feel more amotivated, controlled, or autonomous in general.

If this is too abstract, you can use Appendix R to help you better understand your motivations. In this table you will find some of the common ways that practitioners experience different motivational pulls around their work. First, read through the descriptions. See which statements best match your experiences. See if there are any other experiences you want to add. Then, see if you can locate where the relative balance of your motivation lies. That is, overall which column seems to be the "loudest" for you right now? It is worthwhile to note that even if your motivational balance is tipped more so in one direction (e.g., autonomous), you can still have one or more strong pulls in other columns (e.g. amotivated, controlled) that you may want to examine and turn some attention to.

So, how can you better understand the extent to which your environment is supporting or undermining your motivation for working with clients? If you are not feeling particularly autonomous, how can you get reinvigorated? Let's now turn to the assessment of your own need satisfaction.

Practitioners' own need satisfaction. Just like clients, practitioners have their own needs for autonomy, competence, and relatedness. We don't look to our clients to fulfill our needs. Rather, we need our workplace and our other life domains to be supportive so that we can function at our best. When we don't have these supports, some of our energy gets occupied. And, when there is less energy to go around, it can affect the extent to which we are present, engaged, and optimally supportive of our clients.

To practice at their best, we encourage practitioners to regularly check in on how well their own needs are being satisfied. Our assessment follows what we call the "CARE" model (Appendix S), and is a derivative of work that we have done to help practitioners and researchers in the biomedical sciences better advocate for their own need support (La Guardia, Sharp, & Ryan, 2015). Practitioners assess the extent to which they feel their three basic psychological needs (Competence, Autonomy, Relatedness) are being supported as well as the extent to which their organization provides essentials (Equity) to aid in getting these needs met. Two other sections in the assessment specifically address appreciation of diversity (e.g., gender, ethnicity, race, sexual orientation, disability, SES) and work-life balance (the extent to which you feel that you have achieved your desired allocation of time and energy on professional and other personal goals, such as family, friends, and health). These issues are considered separately because they can impact each component of CARE, they significantly affect how present and engaged you are at your job, and because they are frankly often ignored, despite being incredibly important. Thus, we explicitly attend to these issues in the context of the assessment.

To complete the assessment the first step is to write down initial thoughts and feelings in response to each component. What would we expect to see in this assessment if you have a need supportive environment? In a need supportive environment, you will feel genuinely welcomed and you will have a sense that others take interest in you--you have a sense of belonging. Your perspectives are inquired about and valued, you have an opportunity to express your own interests and goals, and you are given opportunities to pursue them. Further there are opportunities to stretch your skills without feeling completely overwhelmed and there are opportunities for informational feedback so that you can learn how to improve and develop your skills. In a supportive workplace your organization will provide adequate and equitable extrinsic supports (e.g., time, money, space, and resources for training or re-training) to do the work you are poised to do. And, you will experience a sense of fairness in in how these resources are distributed. Moreover, your diversity is prized and treated as an asset to the learning and growth of your organization. Finally, the environment is flexible and works to honor your desires around work-life balance.

191

In contrast, when practitioners do not have some or all of their needs are supported, we would expect a very different set of responses. When relatedness is undermined you will not feel valued or a part of the team. You may even feel isolated or alone. When autonomy is threatened you will feel like you have no voice or ownership over the type of work you do, you will feel pressured to perform, and you will experience colleagues as controlling or rigid. When competence needs are not being met, you will likely feel over-challenged, or alternatively, feel bored because your activities are not well-matched to your skills (e.g., over or below your skill sets, respectively). Further you may receive little feedback or the feedback that is given is critical rather than constructive. Expectations or rules that dictate the workplace culture will be unclear, disorganized, or inflexible. Resources that are needed to be successful are not adequate or simply not available, and as a result, it will be challenging for you to do your job well. When diversity is not recognized and appreciated it can create barriers to feeling welcome, included, and valued. And when there is lack of equity or sense of fairness, it will be hard to trust in others and invest in the mission of your workplace. Finally, when the desired balance of work and personal life is not respected, you will likely feel that one or multiple aspects of your life are being robbed of your attention and energy and the quality of your efforts will be less than you want.

So what does your assessment look like? If your responses suggest that there is some room for improvement in the support you are getting, the second step is to write down some ideas about how you would like things to be different so that you feel more supported. Being realistic is important, but don't foreclose ideas too quickly. What can you realistically do to take greater control? When? Are there other things you need to do to make this plan work? Essentially you are brainstorming a potential action plan.

Finally, to make workplace changes, you will likely need to turn to others to make this happen. So, this last step helps you to identify who might be able to help you exact change. Talking through issues with others often provides greater clarity, and others might also be able to offer useful perspectives. More importantly, for many changes, you need advocates to help make things happen. So consider who can be a good support and how can you enlist their advocacy.

In summary, the self-assessment tool is designed to help practitioners better understand their own part in being need supportive to their clients in treatment. Further, it helps practitioners make sure that their own needs are being met. This is important for practitioners' own health and well-being but it is also essential for being optimally supportive of clients. By giving attention to yourself and getting the support you need, you can provide greater energy for you, and by extension, for your clients—a much needed commodity in traversing the landscape of behavioral change.

In our practices, we also employ 1-to-1 supervision and peer group collaboratives to further assess practitioners' supportiveness of clients and to get the much needed consultation required to effectively tackle the challenges that clients bring their way. We now turn to a description of these two other structures for creating a need supportive workplace.

1-to-1 supervision. In this format practitioners meet on a regular basis (usually once every week for at least 1 hour) with someone who has training in the SDT approach. The Center for Self-Determination Theory (info@selfdeterminationtheory.com) offers virtual training and supervision for those wanting to learn more about how to utilize this framework effectively. But to start, the self-assessment tool just described can be used to inform the activities of supervision.

The format of this supervision is collaboratively directed. That is, we practice in supervision what we do with our clients--it is a parallel process. Each meeting the supervisee brings a case to review, and if possible an audio or video recording of a session of them working with a client. The supervisee conducts an individual self-assessment about the session and their work with the client before supervision. At intake, the supervisee gives pertinent information about the client history, identifies the core challenges in making health behavior changes for this client, and identifies the ways in which the client challenges the supervisee in being need supportive. In this way the supervisee is identifying some things for the supervisor to watch or listen for when reviewing the session recording. The supervisee also identifies what they are hoping for from the supervisor. That is, they set an agenda for what they would like some help on. This can be as broad as "my client and I have tension and I can't figure out why I am having so much trouble" or as specific as "I don't know how to respond when my client said this". The agenda also needs to have some flexibility so that new issues that arise from reviewing the work can have a space to emerge and be thoughtfully considered.

Another important function of 1-to-1 supervision is to establish a place to discuss practitioners' own motivations and need satisfaction in the workplace. Establishing this facet of mentoring as a normal part of supervision conveys that practitioners' needs and motivations are important, and not only helps practitioners feel valued and cared for but it provides a person (the supervisor) who can serve as an advocate for support. Thus, if challenges occur, providers have a natural place to turn to rather than having to establish such a connection in the midst of challenges.

Peer-group collaborative. In this format practitioners meet in small groups on a regular basis (usually we meet once every week for at least 1 hour). One practitioner is typically given the full meeting time (if desired) and prepares similarly as they would for 1-to-1 supervision. One of the things to note with this sort of group supervision is that just like any other group there needs to be some ground rules. The ground rules again mimic what we ask of our own clients in groups--respect and support of each other, take interest in each other's needs and wants, and provide thoughtfully crafted guidance and feedback to help each person meet their goals. In other words, we establish norms that create a need supportive group.

It is also worth noting that groups do not have to consist of practitioners of only one discipline. In fact, when you are engaging clients in behavior change you are likely going to be interacting on teams with physicians, nurses, dietitians, exercise physiologists, and mental health professionals, among others. A multidisciplinary dialogue is incredibly useful for treating the whole person. But a word of caution--the group dynamic cannot be hierarchical, deferring only to certain professionals. So, having each member agree to the ground rules and actively work toward giving each group member a valid voice will need concerted attention.

Section Summary: Assessing practitioners' need supportiveness of clients

Setting the norm of self-reflection on one's own strengths and challenges, being proactive in seeking out inputs from others, and being open to receiving feedback is vital to being need supportive of clients and to continue to improve one's work. In our mind, another core part of providing good treatment is to make sure that we attend to the practitioners who are providing treatment. Attention to providers own needs and motivations helps to establish more satisfied and fulfilled practitioners, and it also serves to create a treatment environment that is optimally engaging, thoughtful, and caring environment for clients.

The big picture: Cultivating a need supportive healthcare culture

The goal of most healthcare organizations is to cultivate an organizational culture that nourishes not only clients but practitioners too. To be sure, some organizations are better at executing support for this mission than others. But, there are also challenges brought on by the current healthcare climate that can test even the best organizations.

For example, organizations are driven in part by costs and profits. Healthcare services are in high demand, yet many workplaces are trying to meet these demands while being extremely under-resourced (e.g., personnel). Oftentimes this results in limits on the quality of services offered (e.g., types of programs; length of service) as well as high levels of provider burnout.

Systemic healthcare norms can also undermine the effectiveness of practitioners working together as a team. Healthcare systems tend to be physician-centric and hierarchical, thereby clearly creating a tiered system of whose voice is valued. There are also often rigid boundaries between disciplines, diminishing providers' ability to consider the whole client in treatment.

Furthermore, historically in many professions the predominant philosophy of treatment follows a provider-as-expert model, which results in information- and advice-giving. Treatment has relatively little focus on clients' psychological needs and motivation. Therefore treatment is prescriptive rather than a collaborative process with clients.

Finally, although most organizations describe a team philosophy, there is relatively little focus on practitioners' functioning and well-being within organizations. At times, there is even blatant disregard for practitioners' functioning and well-being if the bottom line ($) is at stake. As a result, both clients' and practitioners' well-being is at stake.

Considering all of these challenges might lead one to despair. However, being aware of these challenges can help organizations or groups within organizations assess what is in their control and then target those areas in which they can exact change. For example, groups don't have to wait for top down orders to do an internal assessment of the need supportiveness of their group culture. Many of the same questions about need satisfaction in the self-assessment tool can be extrapolated to the group culture. For example, do people feel connected to each other in the group? Do they have each other's backs? Are there dynamics in the group that are causing tension or creating roadblocks to effective teamwork? Are there norms that need to be changed (e.g., protecting lunch or break time) to ensure that people have opportunities to re-group and take care of themselves? What does the group want to do to grow and stretch their skills and/or services? Are we in need of resources to do our jobs better? How do we show value for diversity? Do team members have their desired work-life balance? Having an open dialogue and working together to solve challenges that arise can empower the team. And, for those challenges that need outside assistance to have an impact, the team can coalesce around how they collectively want to approach a problem and advocate for support.

As we have already described, another way that groups can create structures and norms to better support each other's needs is to employ self-assessments, 1-to-1 mentoring, and/or peer collaboratives. By normalizing a process of reflection and regularly checking in on how well individuals and the group as a whole is functioning, your group can proactively build and improve structural supports rather than wait for dysfunction to disrupt practice or negatively impact providers' and/or clients' well-being.

Summary: Cultivating a need supportive healthcare culture

Providers are embedded within a system (e.g., community health, private practice, group practice, hospital) where there are structures and limits, some of which are out their control. Systems, and the norms that dictate behavior within these systems, differ in the extent to which they are flexible and responsive versus rigid and unchanging. Even without large organizational change, workgroups can assess their own needs and functioning and work to develop structures and norms that are that are more responsive to providers' needs. By doing so, not only can you create a healthier place to work but likely a healthier place for clients as well.

SECTION V

How the SDT approach differs from
other theoretical approaches to health behavior change

One of the questions we often get is how does SDT differ from other theoretical models or interventions for health behavior change? Many of you who read this book will have had training in one or more of the prominent models of health behavior change, such as the Health Belief Model, the Theory of Reasoned Action/Theory of Planned Behavior, the Transtheoretical Model, Social Cognitive approaches, Self-regulation approaches, Cognitive Behavioral Approaches, and/or Motivational Interviewing. As we have mentioned, and as you have probably noticed throughout this book, the SDT approach shares similarities with some of these other approaches. However, there are also clear differences between the SDT approach and these other approaches. In this chapter we review the core principles and concepts of each of the models cited above and contrast the main ways in which the SDT approach differs (summary can be found in Appendix T).

Health Belief Model

The Health Belief Model (HBM; Hochbaum, 1958; Rosenstock, 1960, 1974) was developed in the early 1950's by scientists at the U.S. Public Health Service to better understand why people engage or don't engage in screenings for disease prevention as well as why they adopt or alternatively reject health behaviors that would benefit them. HBM has its origins in behaviorism as well as expectancy-value cognitive theory. HBM posits that people move to action when there is a perceived threat. Threat is sparked when people feel susceptible to harm (the health issue and or health risk is relevant to them) and they believe the harm is sufficiently severe (they are likely to experience negative medical and or social consequences if they do not change their behavior). The threat is thought to cue action if people believe that behavior change has the potential to reduce the threat and yield significant benefit, and if they believe they have the self-efficacy to overcome any perceived barriers.

Differences between Health Belief Model and SDT. First, HBM is descriptive and was primarily created to explain behavior (or lack thereof). Its core emphasis is on cognitive processes--the beliefs that people have about perceptions of threat, benefit, and barriers--and specifically cognitive processes focused on competence (e.g., weighing the benefits and barriers to change, estimating one's self-efficacy to carry out behavioral change). As we have discussed throughout the book, SDT broadens the focus of treatment to include connections of emotion and emotion regulation to motivation and it highlights the importance of both autonomy and relatedness, in addition to competence.

Further, according to HBM, readiness to take action can only be sparked by threat cues to take action. That is, there must be a threat to the person and a perceived benefit to change. Clearly, not all motivation for behavior change is fueled by external rewards and punishments or even by fear. External prompts are powerful, to be sure, as rewards and punishments do move people to action. But, they also need to be consistently present and compelling in their incentive value, otherwise behaviors will extinguish. Moreover, fear-based action, although powerful, is short-lived. For example, new health events or a new disease diagnosis can induce fear, but for most people the intensity of this initial fear subsides and no longer serves as a primary motivator of action. And, for those whose fear remains intense and persistent long after an acute health event, it can actually be immobilizing, resulting in inaction rather than action. SDT has shown that motivation is more differentiated to include identified (e.g., value) and intrinsic motivations for behavior. Thus, people can also start a behavior because they find it interesting or enjoyable (e.g., dancing for exercise), or because they value it (e.g., cooking healthier meals because they want to have healthy kids), not just because there is a threat to spur on action. Further, external rewards and punishments, or even fear, are not good at explaining sustained behavior change. In fact, the preponderance of research suggests that it is developing more autonomous motivations for behavior that will carry behavior change over the long term.

Theory of Reasoned Action & Theory of Planned Behavior

The Theory of Reasoned Action (TRA; Fishbein, 1967; Fishbein & Ajzen, 1975) emerged out of social psychology research on attitudes. TRA asserts that the most important determinant of behavior is behavioral *intention*. Behavioral intentions are formed from a person's *attitude* toward performing the behavior and the perceived *subjective norm* about the behavior. Attitude is determined by the individual's beliefs about the positive versus negative consequences of engaging in a behavior. Perceptions of the subjective norm are developed as a function of judgments about whether important others approve or disapprove of performing the behavior and one's willingness to comply with those judgments. Ajzen and colleagues (Ajzen, 1991; Ajzen & Driver, 1991; Ajzen & Madden, 1986) later recognized that there are factors outside the individual that may also affect intentions and behaviors. To account for these factors they suggested that *perceived behavioral control*--the extent to which people believe they are capable and have the resources to perform a behavior given the circumstances that promote versus create barriers to their behavior--is another important factor in predicting behavior. The resulting theory--the Theory of Planned Behavior (TPB)--thereby suggests that perceived control plus intention will result in a greater likelihood to engage in a behavior. Hagger and Chatzisarantis (2007, 2009) explore the synergy of TRA/TPB with SDT.

Differences between TRA/TPB and SDT. In TRA/TPB, major weight is given to what others think the person should do (e.g., "Most people important to me think I should" perform the behavior), and according to TRA/TPB, believing that one should perform a behavior and feeling compelled to meet expectations of others yields a positive subjective norm that will add positively to behavioral intention. There is no doubt that others judgments weigh into people's motivations for making behavior change. However, SDT would not view these imperatives as positive, but rather they would be considered controlling. And, as research has shown, although these controlling motives may contribute to people deciding to initiate a change, engaging in the behavior feels pressured and as such people will be less likely to persist at it over the long term.

Further, according to TRA/TPB having an intention to engage in a behavior will lead to greater likelihood to engage in behavior. In fact, in TRA/TPB research, intention is regarded as the best predictor of engaging in a behavior. From this perspective, all motivations are created equal. That is, it doesn't matter *why* you are engaging in a behavior or the *types* of goals that you set. Just as long as you have the intention to engage in the behavior you will be more likely to do it. However, a large body of research from the SDT tradition clearly shows that when people approach behavior change from more controlled motives, not only is the experience of behavior change more negative but they are also less likely to persist at their behavioral changes over time. Relatedly, intrinsic goals are linked to greater persistence, interest, and enjoyment of one's experiences whereas extrinsic goals are associated with greater feelings of pressure and a higher likelihood of dropout.

Transtheoretical Model

The Transtheoretical Model (Prochaska & DiClemente, 1983) was derived from a comparative analysis of change behaviors demonstrated by those engaged in self-directed efforts to quit smoking as well as professional treatments for smoking cessation (DiClemente & Prochaska, 1982). The model suggests that behavioral change happens in stages over time, with each stage of change characterized by a person's readiness for action. For example, in "precontemplation" people do not intend on taking action in the near future, whereas in "preparation" they have action plans in place and intend on engaging in action soon. The differences in stages are also reflected in differences in the relative strengths of pros versus cons for behavioral change (what TTM calls "decisional balance shifts"). For example, in "precontemplation" the cons for change outweigh the pros for behavior change and thus the existing behaviors remain, whereas in "preparation" the pros outweigh the cons and therefore shifts in behavior toward change begin to occur. Finally, each stage is characterized by relatively different levels of self-efficacy, such that earlier stages (precontemplation and contemplation) are characterized by low levels of confidence in one's ability to make desired changes and refrain from temptations to engage in undesired behaviors, whereas later stages (preparation, action, and maintenance) are characterized by relatively higher levels of confidence to carry out desired behaviors and resist temptation. Although there is a progressive sequence of the stages from inaction to action (or in SDT terms amotivated to motivated behavior), TTM suggests that people may move fluidly back and forth as they engage in behavioral change and as new challenges or successes occur.

According to TTM, there are different "processes" that people need to engage in to successfully move through each stage of change. For example, "conscious raising" is an activity designed to increase awareness of information about the targeted health behavior (e.g., consequences of smoking, potential treatments to promote cessation) and is most appropriate at the pre-contemplation stage, whereas seeking and relying on support from others to encourage behavioral change is the focus of later stages (preparation, action, and maintenance) . Thus, because the processes for change differ by stage, the intervention focus and techniques are matched specifically to each stage (Prochaska, Norcross, & DiClemente, 1994).

Differences between TTM and SDT. TTM suggests that the best model of behavioral change is not a single theoretical model but rather an amalgam of ideas from major theories (thus the name "transtheoretical"). The TTM model was derived from a bottom up, exploratory analysis of behavioral data to see which theoretical constructs most prominently emerged. In contrast, SDT is a top down approach--the model was driven by a strong theory about the nature of human motivation, how the social environment can support or undermine motivation, and the expected consequences for well-being--and it was tested empirically to validate its tenets. Moreover, SDT was derived not just as a model exclusive to health behavior change but rather to illustrate basic principles of human functioning across different domains (e.g., education, workplace, parenting, relationships, etc.). In essence, the SDT model was derived from a hypothesis driven, confirmatory approach whereas the TTM model was derived from an exploratory, data driven approach.

Another difference is that the TTM model was originally derived from behavioral data on smoking cessation. This population continues to be the focus of the largest number of TTM intervention studies (Prochaska, Redding, & Evers, 2015). Smoking is not an essential life function and smoking cessation is inherently an avoidance behavior. But many behavioral changes involve essential life functions and are not simply avoidance-oriented. For example, eating and physical activity are essential for our bodies to function. People cannot just stop eating or stop being mobile without significant and catastrophic consequences to their bodies. People can however quit smoking without it resulting in death. Also, changing eating behaviors is often quite complex. For example, changing one's diet is not simply about avoiding high fat or high calorie foods, but it is about increasing intake of fruits, vegetables, and fiber. Similarly, changing physical activity behaviors is not simply about avoiding being sedentary but rather it is also about incorporating movement in daily life as well as adopting exercise behaviors. Thus, any model of behavior change needs to account for both avoidance-oriented and approach-oriented behaviors. Although the TTM model has been applied to behaviors such as changing diet and physical activity, the processes of TTM vary across different health behaviors (Adams & White, 2004). As mentioned previously, there is significant consistency in the principles of the SDT model across not only health behaviors, but also across life domains.

Another difference between SDT and TTM is that the meaning of "process" in TTM is quite different than in SDT. The process in TTM is what we would refer to as content---the behavioral problems of focus and the concrete ways for people to address these problems. What seems to be missing from TTM is not the "what" (content) of behavior change but the "why" (motivation). Why do people move successfully from one stage to the next? SDT would suggest that shifts toward more autonomous motivation would explain progress through behavioral change toward sustained maintenance. Further, the mechanism of the intervention that explains why this shift occurs is that the intervention creates a need supportive environment. Thus, SDT provides a process model for the mechanisms of behavior change.

Importantly, there are some techniques used by TTM that SDT just does not endorse. One of the starkest examples is one that TTM emphasizes in maintenance. TTM essentially endorses a strict behaviorist approach in maintenance---it encourages the use of counterconditioning, reinforcement management, and stimulus control techniques to maintain behavior. These are techniques that SDT simply does not use because not only are they inherently controlling but they require consistent application of reinforcements or punishments to sustain desired behaviors. SDT, in contrast, suggests that building greater autonomous motivation--identification, integration, and intrinsic motivation for behaviors--is the key to maintenance. This autonomous self-regulation is an explicit focus of the SDT intervention approach and is further supported by helping clients to recognize how to continue to promote autonomous motivation in themselves long after treatment is complete.

The final differences between TTM and SDT are best characterized by how the treatments are delivered in practice. First, we argue that how interventions are delivered within TTM has the potential for being controlling. For example, TTM suggests that feedback and confrontations are important awareness-raising techniques to use with those who are in "pre-contemplation" and "contemplation" stages of behavior change. However, unless the process of how to provide feedback or raise awareness about potentially conflicting behaviors or goals is defined, these techniques have the potential for being controlling. SDT is specific about when and how feedback is given---we focus first on understanding clients' feelings and reactions and ask if feedback is desired--and rather than confrontation we focus on collaborative discussion. Thus, no matter what technique is used, SDT interventionists are cognizant of the potential for being controlling and work to avoid this dynamic.

Second, although TTM suggests techniques to work with those at earlier stages of change and recognizes the need to match strategies for engaging this population (e.g., active vs. passive recruitment), in reality many intervention programs use participants' stage of change to weed out those who are not yet preparing or poised for action (anyone in the pre-contemplation and contemplation phases). Indeed, most intervention programs are designed explicitly around the idea that people are ready to move towards change. By contrast, SDT's initial intervention is geared toward understanding the underlying motivations for changing and not changing one's

207

behavior and helps clients find their voice around the next course of action---including choosing not to further explore change.

Social cognitive theory

Social cognitive theory (SCT) approaches were originally derived from the work of Bandura and colleagues (Bandura, 2004). According to SCT, although knowledge about health risks and benefits of health behaviors is an important determinant of behavioral change, it is the perception that one has the self-efficacy to carry out desired behaviors that is the fundamental motivator of change. Efficacy beliefs are thought to influence the goals one sets, one's commitment to them, and the expectations one has about the potential positive and negative physical, social, and self-evaluative consequences of behavioral change. Thus, the main focus of a SCT intervention is to increase perceived self-efficacy, or one's perceptions about being capable to carry out desired behaviors.

To create opportunities to experience self-efficacy, intervention strategies focus on helping participants create short-term, attainable goals that are in the service of achieving longer term, higher-order desired goals. Further, attention is given to recognizing and problem solving around the barriers to change, including employing social supports to help make behavioral changes. Finally, SCT approaches challenge the negative thoughts or expectations that clients have about engaging in a behavior and reframe them into positive, manageable actions. As such, the assumption is that changing expectations about one's ability and expected outcomes will change people's willingness to engage in and persist at the behavior.

Differences between SCT and SDT. First, similar to other approaches that we have reviewed, SCT is mainly focused on building competence whereas SDT is focused not only on competence support but also support for autonomy and relatedness.

There are plenty of health behaviors that one *can* engage in and be efficacious in carrying out. However, just because one can engage in a behavior does not mean that one will do it. Said differently, just because a person knows how to be physically active does not mean he or she will do it. SCT focuses on self-efficacy but does not help clients define what behaviors are meaningful to them. In practice, the agenda and the end goals are often dictated by SCT practitioners. That is, the health goals and agenda for the program are often set for clients.

According to SDT, there has to also be a meaningful reason to engage in and sustain health behaviors. Thus, SDT does not just emphasize self-efficacy (competence) but it also emphasizes finding value or interest in the behavior (autonomy). Moreover, the goals are collaboratively driven toward behaviors and outcomes that are meaningful to clients.

Self-Regulatory Approaches (SRAs)

One of the key challenges to TRA/TPB and SCT approaches to health behavior change has been the gap between intention and behavior. That is, intentions are only converted into behavior approximately half of time (Sheeran, 2002). As such, several intervention approaches have focused more explicit attention on the self-regulatory strategies that will more effectively translate intentions into action.

For example, Social Control Theory suggests that to change behavior we must attend to how people set and regulate their goals (Carver & Scheier, 1998, 1999). The function of goal setting is to enable people to organize their behavior, establish priorities, and select amongst

209

different behaviors or courses of action. Personal goals also set standards of performance such that people can evaluate their ongoing behaviors according to these standards of performance and change their behaviors in response to this feedback. Broadly speaking, SRAs are characterized by stepwise, iterative processed that begin with goal formation in which people are asked to identify higher order abstract goals and then discrepancy is created by eliciting the association between current behaviors and these higher-order goals. Goal setting involves the formulation of concrete goals through techniques such as goal ladders (small, progressive goals aimed toward larger goals) as well as implementation intentions [explicit if-then links between specific situational cues and a specific behavioral response; e.g., "If situation X is encountered, then I will perform response Y"] and action planning (detailing where, when, and how to achieve goal). Gollwitzer and colleagues (Gollwitzer, 1999; Gollwitzer & Sheeran, 2006; Heckhausen & Gollwitzer, 1987) particularly emphasize the importance of implementation intentions and action planning to formulate a concrete decision about action and thereby increase commitment to action. Finally, self-monitoring and other related feedback techniques are used to provide information about goal progress as well as to revise or revamp goals or strategies used to work toward goals. Behavior is thus goal-driven and feedback controlled.

Differences between SRAs and SDT. Although there are many theories and approaches that fall under the SRA umbrella, there are common ways that all of these approaches differ broadly from SDT. First, echoing a common theme throughout this chapter, SRAs are mainly focused on competence building whereas SDT is focused not only on competence support but also support for autonomy and relatedness.

Second, according to SRAs, the key focus of the intervention is to maximize success at the goals that are set. Thus, the type of goal does not matter, so long as the person can achieve it.

However, as we continue to argue, the type of goal matters as to whether behavior will persist, such that more autonomous goals will more likely be sustained over the long term.

Finally, similar to our critique of SCT, in practice the structure of the agenda and delivery of SRA interventions is often dictated by the practitioner. That is, the health goals and agenda for the program are often set *for* the client. Moreover, although in theory goal formation is an iterative process, in practice it is often treated as a one-time, outcome-oriented prescription for change. In contrast, the structure and delivery of SDT goal setting is a collaborative and dynamic process, changing with not only the phase of treatment (e.g., initiation, maintenance) but also with the interests and competencies of clients.

Cognitive Behavioral Theory Approaches

Cognitive Behavioral Theory approaches draw their influence from both classic behaviorist principles as well as cognitive theory (Beck, 2011). Health behaviors are thought to be conditioned in part by the environment, and as such, undesirable behaviors can be extinguished through systematic conditioning--removing behavioral triggers in the environment and introducing new behavioral responses. Clients develop self-control over their behaviors by first learning about their behavioral patterns through self-monitoring. For example, through tracking his behavior a smoker will learn how often and how many cigarettes he smokes in a day as well as his subjective experience around smoking (e.g., cravings). Clients can then develop new behavioral targets through goal setting and develop behavioral strategies to reinforce these goals. For example, the smoker can engage in stimulus control by avoiding places where he usually smokes (e.g., bar) or removing the ashtrays or other smoking paraphernalia from his home to rid his space of these cues. He can also develop reward structures to shape targeted behaviors and reinforce behavioral changes, such as buying himself something as a reward for reducing his tobacco use by 50% that week.

Undesirable health behaviors are also thought to be reinforced by dysfunctional thought patterns and the negative mood states that result from them. For example, the smoker may want to stop trying to make quit attempts because he had a stressful day, smoked more than he intended, and thought "I failed…I'm never going to be able to quit." According to CBT if the negative thoughts and feelings are not dealt with, the person will be likely to return to their prior behaviors. Thus, cognitive restructuring is used to talk back to negative thoughts with positive thoughts and set goals or expectations that are more realistic.

CBT clearly holds that idea that behavior change is learned. As such, CBT engages clients in practical skill building to modify the behavioral and cognitive mechanisms just described. For example, clients learn to identify personal barriers to behavioral change, engage in problem solving, develop routines for behavioral activation, develop strategies to prevent relapse, and develop assertiveness in social settings to advocate for themselves, among other skills.

Differences between CBT and SDT. SDT recognizes that many of the tools employed by CBT (e.g., self-monitoring; modifying situational cues) are useful for supporting behavioral changes. In fact, SDT interventions offer many of these as potential tools for clients to adopt into their behavioral repertoires. However, SDT and CBT clearly differ in their fundamental beliefs about the core mechanisms underlying behavior change and therefore the targets of the interventions differ (see also Ryan, Lynch, Vansteenkiste, & Deci, 2010).

First, although external contingencies, rewards, and punishments will indeed move behavior, they are not the only motivators of behavior. Moreover, relying on such methods requires that valued or powerful enough external motivators need to be ever-present in order to maintain behavior. SDT clearly has shown that people are also motivated by value, interest, and enjoyment, and in fact, these motives help to sustain health behaviors over the long term. Thus, external prompts and prods are not necessary to produce behavioral changes.

Second, according to CBT, one of the reasons why people are not engaging in desired behaviors is that their beliefs or appraisals are maladaptive. However, it is clear that people face real challenges in their environment that make it difficult to carry out desired behavioral changes--this is not an illusion of thought. As such, SDT does not suggest that there is a core problem with how people are thinking about their behaviors (maladaptive thoughts) but that there is likely at least some reality to their perceptions--that their social environment is not being as supportive as needed. Thus, SDT explicitly focuses on helping clients to enhance supportiveness of their social context as a way to promote their desired behavioral changes.

Finally, some techniques endorsed by CBT are not need supportive. For example, one technique used is thought stopping, wherein one attempts to halt negative thoughts, sometimes even by yelling "stop!" at oneself. This technique imposes a clear judgment about one's thoughts and emotions as "bad" or "wrong". SDT suggests that rather than judge thoughts and feelings that emerge, participants are encouraged to pay attention to these thoughts and feelings, as oftentimes these thoughts and feelings are instructive. Other techniques endorsed by CBT, such as devising reinforcements (rewards, punishments) to modify behavior, also undermine efforts to develop more autonomous forms of motivation, as they judge success or failure based on outcomes rather than prize the effort towards mastery.

213

Motivational Interviewing

Perhaps the interventional approach that is most closely aligned with SDT is Motivational Interviewing (MI; Miller & Rollnick, 2013). Similar to SDT, MI subscribes to Roger's humanistic philosophy such that clients are regarded as the experts of themselves and are believed to already have within them the motivation to change. Thus, the work of practitioners is to create the conditions that will nurture this motivation. Several colleagues have written reviews on the synergy of these two approaches (see Deci & Ryan, 2012; Markland, Ryan, Tobin, & Rollnick, 2005; Patrick & Williams, 2012; Ryan, Lynch, Vansteenkiste, & Deci, 2010; Vansteenkiste & Sheldon, 2006; Vansteenkiste, Williams, & Resnicow, 2012). Below we summarize their points and add important new critiques to this discussion.

The foundation of MI techniques, referred to as the "spirit" of MI, follows four principles--partnership, evocation, compassion, and acceptance. Practitioners uphold these principles in practice by taking interest in clients' perspectives; exploring their values and goals; actively collaborating with clients to formulate manageable goals and a pathway for behavior change that builds on prior skills and develops new skills; evoking clients' strengths and acknowledging their efforts toward change; and showing them unconditional positive regard. Although MI claims to be expressedly atheoretical, it should be clear that this overall approach, as well as the specific tools used in MI, are client-centered (Rogerian) and seem to fundamentally support the basic psychological needs outlined by SDT. With regard to the latter, one of the core techniques explicitly espoused by MI is support for client autonomy, and many of the other techniques endorsed by MI (e.g., affirming general worth of client; exploring personal values and goals; building manageable action plans for behavioral change) further support relatedness and competence needs, respectively.

Despite the fact that these core principles and many of the techniques of SDT and MI share the same genetic roots, there are clear ways that SDT and MI diverge in their philosophy and process. These differences are evident in four key areas.

Differences between MI and SDT. First, as we have mentioned repeated throughout this book, the *quality of motivation*--or in other words, the reasons that fuel motivation--are important. MI emphasizes that its goal is to explore and elicit clients' own reasons for change. Yet, the core emphasis of MI practice is to concertedly move clients toward change talk, without regard for the quality of the reasons behind change (pressured versus volitional). In essence, in the MI approach all movement toward change is created equal just as long at the endpoint is change. This may become particularly problematic given that the behaviors that are focus of change may be inherently more complex with regard to the underlying motives to change. That is, people's reasons for trying to lose weight, changing their diet, physical activity, and/or smoking behaviors are often driven initially by pressures or external demands. Thus, particular MI techniques such as change talk may not result in long-term change if quality of motivation is not attended to initially.

Second, ambivalence about behavior change--grappling with both wanting to change and not wanting to change one's behaviors--is one of the most common places for people to get stuck. According to MI, its counseling style is particularly poised for addressing ambivalence. However, "MI is about influencing choice" specifically in the direction of change (Miller & Rollnick, 2013, p. 231). As such, there is a fundamental contradiction between the philosophy of the MI approach (the "spirit" of MI) and its techniques in practice (e.g., focus on change talk). For example, although MI suggests that ignoring "sustain" talk (desire to not change behavior) would violate the spirit of acceptance, "there is an intentional arranging of conversation to evoke and explore change talk in particular" (Miller & Rollnick, 2013, p. 168). Moreover, MI defines fairly narrow boundary conditions where neutrality is appropriate--when the practitioner has no opinion yet about the direction that is best for the client or when the practitioner does not think that they should influence choice even though they do have an opinion (e.g., exceptional cases such as adoption, donating a kidney). These exceptions are not applied to the everyday health behavior changes (e.g., weight loss, diet, physical activity, smoking cessation) for which people are seeking treatment. From the SDT perspective it is incongruent to both want to have a person-centered, autonomy-supportive focus of treatment while saying that change is the clear goal. *Not changing* has to be considered a valid choice that clients can autonomously endorse, and as such, moving toward what MI calls "sustain" talk to explore the possibility of not changing one's behavior has to be a fundamental component of treatment. Also, as we just mentioned above, moving toward change does not mean it will be autonomous, and in fact, an explicit focus on change by practitioners can potentially be another added source of pressure for clients and convey conditional regard (e.g., change is what is acceptable). Thus, MI's movement toward change talk would seem to have the potential to undermine rather than support basic psychological needs.

Third, the explicit focus of MI is on the *initiation* of change. Although Miller and Rollnick (2012) suggest that many practitioners may continue to employ MI techniques beyond initiation and MI can be valuable during a treatment because motivational issues can remain a concern throughout the course of treatment (Arkowitz et al., 2008; Gourlan et al, 2013), there currently is not a push toward using this approach beyond initiating commitment to behavior change. However, we contend that committing to change is not the same as engaging in it and maintaining it. As witnessed across numerous interventions, when the immediate intervention ceases, motivation for change and actual behavioral change often falls apart. Maintenance is where the SDT framework adds some unique contributions. Energization for change naturally waxes and wanes as a function of which side of the motivational balance (pressure vs. value and interest) is a stronger focus. Because the SDT approach attends to all motives from the start, clients and practitioners can more readily work collaboratively toward reducing controlled motives (e.g., reducing social and internal pressures) and increasing autonomous motives (e.g., envisioning how goals complement other core values throughout treatment).

Furthermore, just because clients are committing to change does not mean that they have the competencies or adequate relational supports to achieve their desired goals in the short or long term. A significant feature of SDT is its' focus on the social-contextual factors that support versus undermine motivation and optimal well-being. As we have discussed, the social context (e.g., close relationships with friends, family, romantic partners, health care practitioners, etc.) can have a strong influence on the extent to which clients initiate and maintain health behaviors. Explicit attention to the social context within SDT interventions helps to provide information about the origin of clients' motives as well as an understanding of who will support versus create real and substantial challenges for clients in the initiation and maintenance of behavior changes. Knowing the social landscape in which clients' behaviors are embedded allows them to become more choiceful about behaviors that they value rather than simply being pushed by external or internal pressures. Moreover, a core function of intervention can be aimed at how to enhance supportive social contexts outside of the behavioral counseling office to better maintain behaviors long after formal treatment ceases. Most interventions, not just MI, are still largely focused on clients only, with little consideration for the complex relationships in which clients exists outside the care setting. That is, they do not have an explicit focus on either the relationships that are supportive or those that might undermine clients' behaviors. As a consequence, many individually-based interventions may not achieve long-term maintenance because they fail to address the fact that individuals live in enduring family and relational contexts that may support or impede behavior change efforts (La Guardia & Patrick, 2014). As such, without attending to competence and relatedness needs simultaneously, clients may not have all of the tools they need to initiate and sustain the changes they intend. The SDT approach, with its attention to all three needs, has a strong impact on maintenance of health behavior change over the long term (Williams, Niemiec et al., 2009; Silva, et al 2008 & 2010; West et al, 2010), an outcome that is rare for lifestyle interventions.

Finally, according to MI, once change has been committed to then other counseling approaches or therapies (e.g., CBT) may be applied or perhaps no further intervention may be needed. As we have reviewed earlier in this chapter, some of these other treatment approaches are derived from theoretical models that are either silent about clients' motivation or do not entirely share the same beliefs about the principles of treatment as reflected in the spirit of MI. This is an important point. To have a coherent model of treatment and truly embody a humanistic, person-centered approach MI cannot then simply add motivational techniques onto other forms of treatment that do not share the same core foundations about the locus of behavioral change (e.g., the person vs. the environment) and intervene in a way that is inconsistent with its core philosophies (e.g., setting behavioral contingencies or righting irrational thoughts). By contrast, SDT provides a coherent theoretical approach that addresses both the initiation and maintenance of behavioral change.

Summary: SDT vs. other intervention approaches

Most health interventions focus almost exclusively on building clients' competence. Some techniques used in these approaches are inherently controlling (e.g., rewards) or may be delivered in a controlling way. Further, there is relatively little focus on the interpersonal dynamics of behavior change--the real ways that the social context has consequences for clients' health behaviors.

SDT is fundamentally concerned with how information and techniques are delivered. The SDT approach is client-centered and focuses on constructing client-authored pathways toward change. In this way SDT is not prescriptive, but rather strives to create an informed dialogue so that clients are fully aware of their options and have real choice about the goals that they set. Moreover, SDT provides client-matched optimal challenges to grow skills for carrying out behavioral change. And perhaps most importantly, SDT interventions help clients recognize how their behaviors are tied to their social context and provide guidance as to how to garner support for their basic psychological needs from important others.

SECTION VI: CONCLUSIONS

The question of how to initiate and sustain health behavior change is one of motivation. This book provides a comprehensive look into how to apply what we know from the science of motivation to the practice of health interventions. Specifically our approach is guided by Self-determination Theory, a humanistic, person-centered approach to motivation. We hope that this philosophy and "way of being" with clients will help you to use your intervention tools flexibly to work collaboratively with clients as they make their desired health behavior changes (e.g., improve diet, increase physical activity, lose weight, reduce and/or stop smoking).

The SDT approach described in this book is a product of over 40 years of compelling research and clinical practice conducted by SDT colleagues all over the world. These thoughtful, innovative practitioners and researchers continue to blaze the trail--translating this approach into new individual, group, and mobile health applications as well as integrating the SDT philosophy into how we do business in healthcare, not just for clients but for practitioners too. As we move forward we hope to transform the dialogue around how we deliver healthcare to firmly focus on adopting a motivational lens to our practices. Please join us at www.selfdeterminationtheory.org and help us grow this movement.

ACKNOWLEDGEMENTS

As an undergrad at the University of Rochester I was introduced to SDT by its creators, Rich Ryan and Ed Deci. From the very moment I read their work I found that it resonated with my sensibilities about how I wanted to be as a scientist and a practitioner. Over 25 years later, SDT still fundamentally guides the way I see the world and how I practice my craft. My intention in writing this book is to help continue the legacy of this theory in practice. I hope that the book serves as a useful beginning roadmap for delivering healthcare in a thoughtful, person-centered, need supportive way.

You may have thought it odd that I used the collective "we" when writing about the intervention methods in this book. Although I did write this book, it would be a great disservice to not have written "we", as the development and implementation of SDT-based interventions is a product of a large community of scholars who have brought this approach to life. To this group I owe a great deal of appreciation and credit for the hard work that they do each day.

I want to also express my deepest gratitude to those who directly contributed to this book coming to life.

Thanks to Shannon Robertson Cerasoli who is the backbone that keeps the SDT global community connected and moving in a good direction. Few truly understand the scope of your knowledge and contributions to SDT. I know I would not have finished this book (and kept my sanity) without your encouragement and support. For that I will be forever grateful.

Thanks to Heather Patrick whose prose helped to develop Chapters 1 and 2 of this book. I truly appreciate our lively conversations and shared passion for this work, as it has helped me to challenge and grow my own perspective and envision new possibilities for affecting healthcare policy and practice. Onward toward GPHD.

Finally, my sincere thanks to Richard Ryan and Daryl Sharp for reviewing early versions of this book. Your thoughtful comments, words of encouragement, and validation have always been greatly valued and appreciated.

AUTHOR'S NOTE

I purposely chose to use the term "they" throughout this book both when referring to a client (singular) or clients (plural). Although this may raise the hackles of the grammar police, I sincerely believe in respecting clients' gender identities and the use of non-binary, inclusive language is important to this practice. I encourage practitioners to be mindful of asking clients about and honoring important features of their identities in order to cultivate true support for relatedness.

FOOTNOTES

[1] Credit to Heather Patrick, Ph.D. for coining this term in one of her conference talks.

[2] Perhaps one of the most common ways that clients struggle with motivational pulls is that clients are often told by family and doctors that they have to change their health behaviors. Oftentimes these prompts are not subtle and can instead breed defiance (think: the obstinate teenager still in all of us). It is important to shift the balance of the dialogue away from what others want to focus on clients' own interests (e.g., I want to be around for my kids, I want to be healthier so that I can do more, etc.).

[3] Clients are often motivated by wanting others to find them more attractive or desirable. Clients have been taught that their physical appearance is the vehicle for getting love, care, or admiration, and as a result they rely on others' approval to shore up their sense of self-worth. As bodies age and change, it will be harder to live up to that ideal of younger, healthier self. Staying focused on others' approval or an ideal standard sets the client up for failure, as inevitably they will not measure up at some point. So, an important transition in treatment is to help clients learn how to appreciate what their body allows them to do (e.g. be active, travel, etc.) and appreciate what they like about their body. For those whom this motive is strong, this is not going to be an easy transition. In fact, those voices may never entirely quiet. However, helping clients to focus on their autonomous personal motives will begin to give them the opportunity to make different choices in response to those pressured voices.

[4] Credit to Heather Patrick, PhD for offering this example.

[5] Credit to Erik Augustson, PhD, MPH, Program Director of Tobacco Control Research Branch, National Cancer Institute, for sharing his wisdom about the new frontiers of geotagging and geotracking in mobile health applications.

[6] Clients are often changing health behaviors out of fear--they get a diagnosis (e.g., diabetes, CVD) and are facing illness and mortality for the first time. Fear is a temporary motive in that it gets people moving initially quite quickly but as the intensity of fear wanes so does the push that comes along with that. For example, after a cardiac event patients say that they engage in health behavior changes simply out of fear, but as they get further from the event this fear is still there but it is no longer the main motivator of their behavior. Other wants or desires start creeping back in so unless they have developed some other reasons for maintaining their health behavior changes (e.g., I want to be around longer to spend time with my wife and kids) the health behaviors often start to slip (e.g., eat donuts, stop exercising, smoke). The key is to start to have conversations with clients to cultivate other reasons for engaging in lifestyle behaviors before this emotional shift starts to happen.

REFERENCES

Adam, T.C., & Epel, E.S. (2007). Stress, eating and the reward system. *Physiological Behavior*, 91(4):449–458.

Adams, J. & White, M. (2004). Why don't stage-based activity promotion interventions work? *Health Educ. Res.*, 20 (2): 237-243. doi: 10.1093/her/cyg105

AHA/ACC/TOS Guideline for the Management of Overweight and Obesity in Adults (2013). A Report of the American College of Cardiology/American Heart Association Task Force on Practice Guidelines and The Obesity Society. *Circulation*, 1-70.

Ajzen, I. (1991). The Theory of Planned Behavior. *Organizational Behavior and Human Decision Processes*, 50, 179–211.

Ajzen, I., &, Driver, B. L. (1991). Prediction of leisure participation from behavioral, normative, and control beliefs: An application of the Theory of Planned Behavior. *Leisure Sciences*, 13, 185–204.

Ajzen I., & Madden, T. J. (1986). Prediction of goal-directed behavior: Attitudes, intentions, and perceived behavioral control. *Journal of Experimental Social Psychology*, 22, 453–474.

American College of Sports Medicine Physical Activity Guidelines for Americans (2011).

Arkowitz, H., Westra, H.A., Miller, W.R., & Rollnick, S. (Editors). (2008). *Motivational interviewing in treating psychological problems*. New York: Guilford Press.

Bandura, A. (1982). Self-efficacy mechanism in human agency. *American Psychologist*, 37, 122–147.

Bandura, A. (1986). *Social foundations of thought and action: A social cognitive theory*. Prentice-Hall.

Bandura, A. (2004). Health promotion by social cognitive means. *Health Educ Behav*, 31, 143-164.

Beck, J. S. (2011). *Cognitive behavior therapy: Basics and beyond* (2nd Ed.) (pp. 19-20). New York, NY: The Guilford Press.

Brisson, C., Larocque, B., Moisan, J., Vézina, M., Dagenais, G.R. (2000). Factors at work, smoking, sedentary behavior, and body mass index: a prevalence study among 6995 white collar workers. *J Occup Environ Med*, 42(1):40.

Carver, C.S., & Scheier, M.F. (1998). *On the self-regulation of behavior*. New York, NY: Cambridge University Press.

Carver, C. S., & Scheier, M. F. (1999). Themes and issues in the self-regulation of behavior. In R. S. Wyer, Jr. (Ed.), *Advances in social cognition* (Vol. 12, pp. 1-105). Mahwah, NJ: Erlbaum.

Centers for Disease Control and Prevention. (2011). Quitting Smoking Among Adults--United States, 2001–2010. *Morbidity and Mortality Weekly Report*, 60(44):1513–9.

Deci, E. L., & Ryan, R. M. (1985). *Intrinsic motivation and self-determination in human behavior*. New York: Plenum Publishing Co.

Deci, E. L., & Ryan, R. M. (2000). The 'what' and 'why' of goal pursuits: Human needs and the self-determination of behavior. *Psychological Inquiry*, 11, 227-268.

Deci, E. L., & Ryan, R. M. (2012). Self-determination theory in health care and its relations to motivational interviewing: a few comments. International Journal of Behavioral Nutrition and Physical Activity, 9, 1-6. doi: 10.1186/1479-5868-9-24

DiClemente, C. C., & Prochaska, J. O. (1982). Self change and therapy change of smoking behavior. A comparison of processes of change in cessation and maintenance." *Addictive Behavior*, 7, 133–142.

Elliot, A., Niemiec, C. P., La Guardia, J. G., Gorin, A. A., & Rigby, C.S., & Williams, G. C., (2015). Brief report on a virtualized intensive lifestyle intervention in type 2 diabetes.

Elfhag, K, & Rössner, S (2005). Who succeeds in maintaining weight loss? A conceptual review of factors associated with weight loss maintenance and weight regain. Obesity Review, 6(1): 67–85.

Fishbein, M. (ed.). (1967). *Readings in Attitude Theory and Measurement*. New York: Wiley.

Fishbein, M., & Ajzen, I. (1975). *Belief, attitude, intention, and behavior: An introduction to theory and research*. Reading, Mass.: Addison-Wesley, 1975.

Fortier, M.S., Duda, J.L., Guerin, E., Teixeira, P.J. (2012). Promoting physical activity: development and testing of self-determination theory-based interventions. *International Journal of Behavioral Nutrition and Physical Activity*, 9:20.

Fortier, M.S., Williams, G.C., Sweet, S.N., & Patrick, H. (2009). Self-Determination Theory: Process models for health behavior change. In R. J. DiClemente, R. A. Crosby, and M. C. Kegler (Eds.), *Emerging theories in health promotion practice and research*. 2nd ed. San Francisco, CA: Jossey-Bass, pp. 157-183.

Gollwitzer, P.M. (1999). Implementation intentions: Strong effects of simple plans. *American Psychologist*, 54, 493-503.

Gollwitzer, P.M., & Sheeran, P. (2006). Implementation intentions and goal achievement: A meta-analysis of effects and processes. *Advances in Experimental Social Psychology*, 38, 69-119.

Gourlan, M., Sarrazin, P., & Trouilloud, D. (2013). Motivational interviewing as a way to promote physical activity in obese adolescents: A randomized-controlled trial using self-determination theory as an explanatory framework. *Psychology & Health*, 28:11, 1265-1286, doi: 10.1080/08870446.2013.800518

Gray, C.M., Hunt, K., Bunn, C., La Guardia, J., Andersen, E., & Wyke, S. on behalf of the EuroFIT consortium. (2015). European Fans in Training (EuroFIT): A socio-psychological approach to the development of the healthy lifestyle programme to engage an at-risk group in sustained behavior change. Poster presented at the annual conference of the International Society of Behavioral Nutrition and Physical Activity. Edinburgh, Scotland, UK.

Groesz, L.M., McCoy, S., Carl, J., Saslow, L., Stewart, J., Adler, N., Laraia, B., & Epel E. (2012). What is eating you? Stress and the drive to eat. *Appetite*, 58(2):717-21. doi:10.1016/j.appet.2011.11.028. Epub 2011 Dec 4. 60.

Haerens, L., Aelterman, N, Vansteenkiste, M, & Van Petegem, S. (2014). Do perceived autonomy-supportive and controlling teaching relate to physical education students' motivational experiences through unique pathways? Distinguishing between the bright and dark side of motivation. *Psychology of Sport and Exercise*, 16, 26-36. doi: 10.1016/j.psychsport.2014.08.013.

Hagger, MS, & Chatzisarantis, NLD. (2009). Integrating the theory of planned behaviour and self-determination theory in health behavior: A meta-analysis. *British Journal of Health Psychology*, 14(2), 275-302. DOI: 10.1348/135910708X373959

Hagger, M. S., & Chatzisarantis, N. L. (2007). Self-determination theory and the theory of planned behavior: An integrative approach toward a more complete model of motivation. In L. V. Brown (Ed.), *Psychology of motivation* (pp. 83-98). Hauppauge, NY: Nova Science.

Heckhausen, H., & Gollwitzer, P. M. (1987). Thought contents and cognitive functioning in motivational versus volitional states of mind. *Motivation and Emotion*, 11, 101-120.

Hochbaum, G. M. (1958). Public Participation in Medical Screening Programs: A Socio-Psychological Study. Washington, D.C.: U.S. Dept. of Health, Education, and Welfare.

La Guardia, J. G. (2014). *Reducing Stress and Building Resilience Program*. Washington, DC: U.S. Copyright Office.

La Guardia, J. G., Cook, K., Stanford, C. N., Potter, L.J., & Povec, K.M. (2015*). Bringing a motivational lens to health behavior change: Integrating evidence based approaches to create an effective employee wellness program for weight loss*. Unpublished manuscript.

La Guardia, J. G., & Patrick, H. (2014).The Influence of the Social Environment on Health Behavior. In N. Weinstein (Ed.), *Integrating Human Motivation and Interpersonal Relationships: Theory, Research and Applications,* (pp. 299-315). Springer Publications, Inc.

La Guardia, J. G., Sharp, DL, & Ryan, RM, & Lewis, V. (2015). *In support of underrepresented professionals in academia: Self-determination Theory's CARES model of mentoring.*

Markland, D., Ryan, R. M., Tobin, V. J., & Rollnick, S. (2005). Motivational interviewing and self-determination theory. *Journal of Social and Clinical Psychology*, 24, 811–831. doi:10.1521/jscp.2005.24.6.811

Miller, W.R., & Rollnick, S. (2013). *Motivational Interviewing: Helping People Change, 3rd Edition.* Guilford Press.

Moller, A. C., Buscemi, J., McFadden, H.G., Hedeker, D., & Spring, B. (2013). Financial motivation undermines potential enjoyment in an intensive diet and activity intervention. *Journal of Behavioral Medicine*, 1-9. doi: 10.1007/s10865-013-9542-5

Moller, A. C., McFadden, H. G., Hedeker, D., & Spring, B. (2012). Financial motivation undermines maintenance in an intensive diet and activity intervention. *Journal of Obesity*, 2012, 1-8.

Moller, A. C., Ryan, R. M., & Deci, E. L. (2006). Self-determination theory and public policy: Improving the quality of consumer decisions without using coercion. Journal of Public Policy & Marketing, 25, 104-116.

Mouchacca, J., Abbott, GR, & Ball, K. (2013). Associations between psychological stress, eating, physical activity, sedentary behaviours and body weight among women: a longitudinal study. *BMC Public Health*, 13:828, http://www.biomedcentral.com/1471-2458/13/828

National Institutes of health Office of Behavioral and Social Sciences Research. (2015). *https://obssr.od.nih.gov/scientific_areas/methodology/mhealth/*

National Heart, Lung, and Blood Institute (NHLBI) and the North American Association for the Study of Obesity (NAASO). (2000). The practical guide: Identification, evaluation, and treatment of overweight and obesity in adults. Bethesda, MD: National Institutes of Health.

Ng, D.M., & Jeffery, RW. (2003). Relationships between perceived stress and health behaviors in a sample of working adults. *Health Psycholology*, 22(6):638.

Ng, J. Y. Y., Ntoumanis, N., Thogersen-Ntoumani, C., Deci, E. L., Ryan, R. M., Duda, J. L., & Williams, G. C. (2012). Self-determination theory applied to health contexts: A meta-analysis. *Perspectives on Psychological Science*, 7, 325-340. doi: 10.1177/1745691612447309

Patrick, H., & Williams, G. C. (2012). Self-determination theory: Its application to health behavior and complementarity with motivational interviewing. *International Journal of Behavioral Nutrition and Physical Activity*, 9(18), 1–12. doi:10.1186/1479-5868-9-18

Prochaska, J. O., & DiClemente, C. C. (1983). Stages and processes of self-change of smoking: Toward an integrative model of change." *Journal of Consulting and Clinical Psychology*, 51, 390–395.

Prochaska, J. O., Norcross, J. C., & DiClemente, C. C. *Changing for Good*. New York:William Morrow, 1994.

Prochaska, J.O., Redding, C.A., & Evers, K.E. (2015). The transtheoretical model and stages of change. In: Glanz, K, Rimer, BK, Viswanath, K (Eds.). *Health behavior and health education: Theory, research, and practice, 4th edition* (pp. 97-121). Jossey-Bass.

Rogers, C.R. (1961). *On becoming a person: a therapist's view of psychotherapy*. Boston: Houghton Mifflin.

Rosenstock, I.M. (1960). What research in motivation suggests for public health. *American Journal of Public Health*, 50, 295–302.

Rosenstock, I. M. (1974). Historical origins of the Health Belief Model. *Health Education Monographs*, 2, 328–335.

Ryan, R.M., & Deci, E. L. (In press, 2017). Self-Determination Theory: Basic Psychological Needs in Motivation, Development, and Wellness. Guildford Press.

Ryan, R. M., & Deci, E. L. (2000). Self-determination theory and the facilitation of intrinsic motivation, social development, and well-being. *American Psychologist*, 55, 68-78.

Ryan, R. M., & Deci, E. L. (2000). The darker and brighter sides of human existence: Basic psychological needs as a unifying concept. *Psychological Inquiry*, 11, 319-338.

Ryan, R. M., Lynch, MF, Vansteenkiste, M, & Deci, E. L. (2010). Motivation and autonomy in counseling, psychotherapy, and behavior change: A look at theory and practice. *The Counseling Psychologist*, 39, 193-260.

Ryan, R.M., Patrick, H., Deci, E.L., Williams, G.C. (2008). Facilitating health behaviour change and its maintenance: Interventions based on self-determination theory. *The European Health Psychologist*, 10: 2-5.

Sharp, D.L., Bellush, N.K., Evinger, J.S., Blaakman, S.W., & Williams, G.C. (2009). Intensive Tobacco Dependence Intervention with Persons Challenged by Mental Illness: Manual for Nurses. University of Rochester School of Nursing Tobacco Dependence Intervention Program.

Sheeran, P. (2002). Intention-behavior relations: A conceptual and empirical review. In. W. Stroebe & M. Hewstone (Eds.), *European Review of Social Psychology*, (Vol. 12, pp. 1-30). Chichester: Wiley.

Teixeira, P. J., Carraça, E. V., Markland, D. A., Silva, M. N., & Ryan, R. M. (2012). Exercise, physical activity, and self-determination theory: A systematic review. *Journal of Behavioral Nutrition and Physical Activity*, 9, 78. doi: 10.1186/1479-5868-9-78

U.S. Department of Health and Human Services. (2014). *The Health Consequences of Smoking— 50 Years of Progress: A Report of the Surgeon General*. Atlanta: U.S. Department of Health and Human Services, Centers for Disease Control and Prevention, National Center for Chronic Disease Prevention and Health Promotion, Office on Smoking and Health.

U.S. Department of Health and Human Services. (2008). Treating Tobacco Use and Dependence. Washington, DC.
U.S. Department of Agriculture. (2010). Dietary Guidelines for Americans. Washington, DC: USDA.

Van de Berghe, L., Vansteenkiste, M., Cardon, G., Kirk, D., & Haerens, L. (2014). Research on self-determination in physical education: Key findings and proposals for future research. *Physical Education and Sport Pedagogy*, 1, 97-121. doi: 10.1080/17408989.2012.732563

van der Ploeg, H, Gray, C., Teixeira, P., Roberts, G., Hunt, K., Gill, J., Bunn, C., Chalmers, M., van Achterberg, T., Nijhuis-van der Sanden, R, Bosmans, J., La Guardia, J., Jotdet, G., Maxwell, D., Mourselas, N., van Nassau, F., Philpott, M., Anderson, A., Treweek, S., van Mechelen, W., Clissmann, C., Mutrie, N., & Wyke, S. for the EuroFIT consortium. (2014). European Fans in Training (EuroFIT): Improving Physical Activity, Sedentary and Eating Behaviours in Football Fans. Poster presented at the annual conference of the International Society of Behavioral Nutrition and Physical Activity. San Diego, CA.

van Nassau, F., van der Ploeg, HP, Abrahamsen, F., Andersen, E., Anderson, A.S., Bosmans, J.E., Bunn, C., Chalmers, M., Clissmann, C., Gill, J.M.R., Gray, C.M., Hunt, K., Jelsma, J.G.M., La Guardia, J.G., et al. (2016). Study protocol of European Fans in Training (EuroFIT): a four-country randomised controlled trial of a lifestyle program for men delivered in elite football clubs. BMC Public, 16:598, DOI:10.1186/s12889-016-3255-y

Vansteenkiste, M., & Sheldon, K. M. (2006). There's nothing more pratical than a good theory: Integrating motivational interviewing and self-determination theory. *British Journal of Clinical Psychology*, 45, 63–82. doi:10.1348/014466505X34192

Vansteenkiste, M., Williams, G. C., & Resnicow, K. (2012). Toward systematic integration between self-determination theory and motivational interviewing as examples of top-down and bottom-up intervention development: Autonomy or volition as a fundamental theoretical principle. *International Journal of Behavioral Nutrition and Physical Activity*, 9, 1–11. doi:10.1186/1479-5868-9-23

West, D. S., Gorin, A. A., Subak, L. L., Foster, G., Bragg, C., Hecht, J., Schembri, M., & Wing, R. R. (2011). Novel motivation-focused weight loss maintenance intervention is as effective as a behavioral skills-based approach. *International Journal of Obesity*, 35, 259-269. doi: 10.1038/ijo.2010.138

Williams, G. C., Niemiec, C. P., Elliot, A., La Guardia, J. G., Gorin, A. A., & Rigby, C.S. (2014). Virtual look AHEAD program: Initial support for a partly virtualized intensive lifestyle intervention in type 2 diabetes. Diabetes Care, 37, 169-170. doi: 10.2337/dc14-0831

Wing, R.R., & Phelan, S. (2005). Long-term weight loss maintenance. The American Journal of Clinical Nutrition, 82 (1), 222S–225S.

World Health Organization. (2011). Global Status Report on Noncommunicable Diseases 2010.

APPENDICES

A. SDT Framework of the Motivations for Behavior

B. The three basic psychological needs: Autonomy, Competence, Relatedness

C. Interventions for health behavior change that employ SDT as a core theoretical foundation

D. Structure & Process of the Initial Interview

E. Practitioner dialogue revisited: Tobacco cessation

F. History of clients' experience around health behavior change

G. Balance of client's motivations

H. Details of clients' current health behaviors

I. Clients' health history questionnaire

J. Illustrating how practitioners' dialogue supports basic psychological needs: Examples from the Initial Session with clients

K. Structure & Process Issues During Treatment

L. Mapping big picture goals with clients

M. Problem solving and making a plan of action

N. Common roadblocks to behavioral change

O. Enlisting social support

P. M-health programs with SDT as the basis of design

Q. Practitioners' self-assessment of their need supportiveness of their clients

R. Self-assessment of practitioners own motivations

S. CARE self-assessment for practitioners' own psychological needs

T. Contrasting other health models with the SDT approach

Appendix A. SDT Framework of Motivations for Behavior

INTRINSIC	Behavior is engaged for the enjoyment, interest, fun inherent in the activity itself	**AUTONOMOUS**
INTEGRATED	Behavior is in harmony with other big picture values, life goals, and behaviors	*More* likely to maintain behaviors over the long term if focused here
IDENTIFIED	Value the behavior (e.g. because it improves health)	
INTROJECTED	Internal pressures to do the behavior in order to avoid feeling bad (e.g., guilt, anxiety, shame) or to feel better about oneself (e.g., pride) and maintain self-worth	*Less* likely to maintain behaviors over the long term if only focused here
EXTERNAL	Direct rewards or punishments/pressures for doing the behavior	**CONTROLLED**
AMOTIVATION	Behavior is not personally important; don't believe they have the ability to carry out the behavior; and/or don't believe that the behavior will produce the desired outcome	**DISENGAGED from behavior**

Appendix B. The three basic psychological needs: Relatedness, Autonomy, Competence

RELATEDNESS

Definition	Experience	How need is supported

Refers to the need to feel close, connected to, and valued by important others.
It is the foundation of self-worth--the sense that one is significant, lovable, and worthy of care.
	Best captured by the sense that one can be authentic, or in other words one's "true self", and have that appreciated by others.	1. Unconditional Positive Regard
		  • Warmth
		  • Genuineness
		  • Empathy
		2. Support from the practitioner
		3. Support from others outside of treatment

AUTONOMY

Definition	Experience	How need is supported
Autonomy refers to the idea that people need to feel willingly engaged in their behaviors and feel a sense of ownership over their actions. The opposite of feeling autonomous is feeling controlled or pressured to behave in a particular way.	People feel like they have a say in what they do and that their perspective and their feelings actually matter to others.	Client centered orientation 1. Understanding the client's perspective 2. Devise menu of possible behavior change options *with* clients 3. Active exploration of clients' thoughts and feelings 4. Develop *personally* relevant, meaningful health behaviors

COMPETENCE

Definition	Experience	How need is supported
Competence refers to the need to feel effective and capable and develop a sense of mastery over one's behaviors.	People have opportunities to be actively immersed and engaged in their behavior and feel optimally challenged to stretch, extend, and grow their skills and abilities.	1. Structure 2. Meeting clients at their skills and abilities 3. Formulating optimally challenging action plans 4. Translating planning into practice 5. Developing realistic expectations 6. Coping with inevitable disappointments

Appendix C. Interventions for health behavior change that employ SDT as part of their core theoretical foundation

Weight Loss
Cherrington, AL, Willig, AL, Agnel, AA, Fowler, MC, Dutton, GR, & Scarinci, IC. (2015). Development of a theory-based, peer support intervention to promote weight loss among Latina immigrants. *BMC Obesity, 2:17.*
Edmunds, J., Ntoumanis, N., & Duda, J. L. (2007). Adherence and well-being in overweight and obese patients referred to an exercise on prescription scheme: A self-determination theory perspective. *Psychology of Sport and Exercise, 8*, 722-740. doi:10.1016/j.psychsport.2006.07.006
Fenner, A. A., Straker, L. M., Davis, M. C., & Hagger, M. S. (2013). Theoretical underpinnings of a need-supportive intervention to address sustained healthy lifestyle changes in overweight and obese adolescents. *Psychology of Sport and Exercise, 14*, 819-829. doi: 10.1016/j.psychsport.2013.06.005
Silva MN, Markland DA, Minderico CS, Vieira PN, Castro MM, Coutinho SS, Santos TC, Matos MM, Sardinha LB, Teixeira PJ. (2008). A randomized controlled trial to evaluate self-determination theory for exercise adherence and weight control: Rationale and intervention description. *BMC Public Health,* 8: 234-247.
Silva MN, Vieira PN, Coutinho SR, Minderico CS, Matos MG, Sardinha LS, Teixeira PJ. (2010). Using Self-Determination Theory to promote physical activity and weight control: A randomized controlled trial in women. *Journal of Behavioral Medicine*, 33: 110-122.
Silva MN, Markland D, Carraça EV, Vieira PN, Coutinho SR, Minderico CS, Matos MG, Sardinha LB, Teixeira PJ. (2011). Exercise autonomous motivation predict 3-year weight loss in women. *Medicine & Science in Sports & Exercise*, 4: 728-737.
Teixeira PJ, Going SB, Houtkooper LB, Cussler EC, Metcalfe LL, Blew RM, et al. (2004). Pretreatment predictors of attrition and successful weight management in women. *Int J Obes Relat Metab Disorders*, 28(9), 1124-33.
Teixeira, P. J., Going, S. B., Houtkooper, L. B., Cussler, E. C., Metcalfe, L. L., Blew, R. M, et al. (2006). Exercise motivation, eating, and body image variables as predictors of weight control. *Medicine and Science in Sports and Exercise, 38*, 179-188. doi:10.1249/01.mss.0000180906.10445.8d
Teixeira PJ, Silva MN, Vieira PN, Minderico CS, Castro MM, Coutinho S, Sardinha LB. (2007). A new theory-based behavioral program to promote physical activity and long-term weight control: Results from a randomized controlled trial. *Medicine & Science in Sports Exercise*, 39(Suppl): 12.
Wasserkampf, A., Silva, M. N., Santos, I., Carraca, E. V., Meis, J. J. M., Kremers, S. P. J., & Teixeira, P. J. (2014). Short- and long-term theory-based predictors of physical activity in women who participated in a weight-management program. Health Education Research, 29, 941-952. doi: 10.1093/her/cyu060.
West DS, Gorin AA, Subak LL, Foster G, Bragg C, Hecht J, Schembri M, Wing RR. (2010). Program to Reduce Incontinence by Diet and Exercise (PRIDE) Research Group. A motivation-focused weight loss maintenance program is an effective alternative to a skill-based approach. *International Journal of Obesity*, 35(2): 259-269.
Williams GC, Grow VM, Freedman ZR, Ryan RM, Deci EL. (1996). Motivational predictors of weight loss and weight-loss maintenance. *Journal of Personality and Social Psychology*, 70: 115-126.
Diet
Resnicow, K, Davis, RE, Zhang, G, Konkel, J, Strecher, VJ, Shaikh, AR, Tolsma, D., Calvi, J, Alexander, G, Anderson, JP, & Wiese, C. (2008). Tailoring a Fruit and Vegetable Intervention on Novel Motivational Constructs: Results of a Randomized Study. *Ann. Behav. Med.*, 35:159–169. DOI 10.1007/s12160-008-9028-9
Shaikh, AR, Vinokur, AD, Yaroch, AL, Williams, GC, & Resnicow, K. (2011). Direct and Mediated Effects of two theoretically based interventions to increase consumption of fruits and vegetables in the *Healthy Body Healthy Spirit* Trial. *Health Education & Behavior*, 38(5), 492-501.

Physical Activity

Chatzisarantis, N. L. D., & Hagger, M. S. (2009). Effects of an intervention based on self-determination theory on self-reported leisure-time physical activity participation. *Psychology and Health, 24*, 29-48. doi:10.1080/08870440701809533

Duda, JL, Williams, GC, Ntoumanis, N, Daley, A, Eves, FF, Mutrie, N, Rouse1, PC, Lodhia, R, Blamey, RV, & Jolly, K. (2014). Effects of a standard provision versus an autonomy supportive exercise referral programme on physical activity, quality of life and well-being indicators: a cluster randomized controlled trial. *International Journal of Behavioral Nutrition and Physical Activity, 11:10.*

Fortier MS, Sweet S, O'Sullivan TL, Williams GC. (2007). A self-determination process model of physical activity adoption in the context of a randomized controlled trial. *Psychology of Sport and Exercise,* 8(5): 741-757.

Jolly, K, Duda, JL, Daley, A, Eves, FF, Mutrie, N, Ntoumanis, N, Rouse, PC, Lodhia, R, & Williams, GC. (2009) Evaluation of a standard provision versus an autonomy promotive exercise referral programme: rationale and study design. *BMC Public Health*, 9:176. doi:10.1186/1471-2458-9-176

Lonsdale, C., Hall, A., Williams, G. C., McDonough, S. M., Ntoumanis, N., Murray, A., & Hurley, D. (2012). Communication style and exercise compliance in physiotherapy (CONNECT). A cluster randomized controlled trial to test a theory-based intervention to increase chronic low back pain patients' adherence to physiotherapists' recommendations: study rationale, design, and methods. *BMC Musculoskeletal*, 13:104. doi: 10.1186/1471-2474-13-104

Lonsdale, C., Murray, A., Tenant Humphries, M., McDonough, S., Williams, G. C., & Hurley, D. (2010). Testing a theory-based intervention designed to increase chronic low back pain patients' adherence to physiotherapists' recommendations: A pilot study. *Journal of Sport and Exercise Psychology*, 32, S192-193.

Murray A, Hall AM, Williams GC, McDonough SM, Ntoumanis N, Taylor IM, Jackson B, Matthews J, Hurley DA, Lonsdale C. (2014). Effect of a self-determination theory-based communication skills training program on physiotherapists' psychological support for their patients with chronic low back pain: a randomized controlled trial. *Arch Phys Med Rehabil,* 96(5):809-16. doi: 10.1016/j.apmr.2014.11.007. Epub 2014 Nov 26.

Patrick, H, & Canavello, A. (2011). Methodological Overview of A Self-Determination Theory-Based Computerized Intervention to Promote Leisure-Time Physical Activity. *Psychol Sport Exerc.*, 12(1): 13–19. doi:10.1016/j.psychsport.2010.04.011.

Rouse PC, Veldhuijzen Van Zanten JJ, Metsios GS, Ntoumanis N, Yu CA, Koutedakis Y, Fenton SA, Coast J, Mistry H, Kitas GD, Duda JL. (2014). Fostering autonomous motivation, physical activity and cardiorespiratory fitness in rheumatoid arthritis: protocol and rationale for a randomised control trial. *BMC Musculoskelet Disord.*, 19;15:445. doi: 10.1186/1471-2474-15-445.

Thogersen-Ntoumani, C., Loughren, E., Duda, J. L., Fox, K. R., & Kinnafick, F. E. (2010). "Step by Step". A feasibility study of a lunchtime walking intervention designed to increase walking, improve mental well-being and work performance in sedentary employees: Rationale and study design. *BMC Public Health,* 10, 578. doi: 10.1186/1471-2458-10-578

Van Hoecke, A-S, Delecluse, C, Bogaerts, A, & Boen, F. The long term effectiveness of need-supportive physical activity counseling compared with standard referral in sedentary older adults . *J Phys Act Health,* 22(2): 186-198.

Van Hoecke, A-S, Delecluse, C, Opdenacker, J, Lipkens, L, Martien, S, Boen, F. (2012). Long-term effectiveness and mediators of a need-supportive physical activity coaching among Flemish sedentary employees. Health Promotion International, 28 (3), 407-417. doi:10.1093/heapro/das025

Wilson, P. M., Rodgers, W. M., Blanchard, C. M., & Gessell, J. (2003). The relationship between psychological needs, self-determined motivation, exercise attitudes, and physical fitness. *Journal of Applied Social Psychology, 33*, 2373-2392. doi:10.1111/j.1559-1816.2003.tb01890.x

235

Tobacco cessation

Sharp, DL, Bellush, NK, Evinger, JS, Blaakman, SW, & Williams, GC. (2009). *Intensive Tobacco Dependence Intervention with Persons Challenged by Mental Illness: Manual for Nurses.* University of Rochester School of Nursing Tobacco Dependence Intervention Program

Williams, G. C., Cox, E. M., Kouides, R., & Deci, E. L. (1999). Presenting the facts about smoking to adolescents: The effects of an autonomy supportive style. *Archives of Pediatrics and Adolescent Medicine, 153*, 959-964.

Williams GC, Gagné M, Ryan RM, Deci EL. (2002). Facilitating autonomous motivation for smoking cessation. *Health Psychology*, 21: 40-50.

Williams GC, McGregor H, Sharp D, Kouides R, Lévesque, C, Ryan RM, et al. (2006). Testing a Self-Determination Theory Intervention for motivating tobacco cessation: Supporting autonomy and competence in a clinical trial. *Health Psychology*, 25(1): 91-101.

Williams, G. C., McGregor, H. A., Sharp, D., Kouides, R. W., Lévesque, C., Ryan, R. M., & Deci, E. L. (2006). A self-determination multiple risk intervention trial to improve smokers' health. *Journal of General Internal Medicine, 21*(12), 1288-1294. PMID 16995893

Williams GC, Niemiec CP, Patrick H, Ryan RM, Deci EL. (2009). The importance of supporting autonomy and perceived competence in facilitating long-term tobacco abstinence. *Annals of Behavioral Medicine*, 37: 315-324.

Williams, G. C., Patrick, H., Niemiec, C. P., Ryan, R. M., Deci, E. L., & Lavigne, H. M. (2011). The Smoker's Health Project: A self-determination theory intervention to facilitate maintenance of tobacco abstinence. Contemporary Clinical Trials, 32, 535-543.

Dental Health

Münster Halvari, A. E., & Halvari, H. (2006). Motivational predictors of change in oral health: An Experimental test of self-determination theory. *Motivation and Emotion, 30,* 294-305.

Halvari, A., Halvari, H., Bjørnebekk, & Deci, E. L. (2012). Self-determined motivational predictors of increases in dental behaviors, decreases in dental plaque, and improvement in oral health: a randomized clinical trial. Health Psychology, 31, 777-88. doi: 10.1037/a0027062

Medical management of chronic disease

Brown, DL, Conley, KM, Resnicow, K, Murphy, J, Sánchez, BN, Cowdery, JE, Sais, E, Lisabeth, LD, Skolarus, LE, Zahuranec, DB, Williams, GC, & Morgenstern, LB. (2012). Stroke Health and Risk Education (SHARE): Design, methods, and theoretical basis. *Contemporary Clinical Trials*, 721-729.

Williams GC, Freedman ZR, Deci EL. (1998). Supporting autonomy to motivate glucose control in patients with diabetes. *Diabetes Care.* 21: 1644-1651.

Williams GC, McGregor HA, Zeldman A, Freedman ZR, Deci EL. (2004). Testing a Self-Determination Theory process model for promoting glycemic control through diabetes self-management. *Health Psychology*, 23: 58-66.

Williams, G. C., Niemiec, C. P., Elliot, A., La Guardia, J. G., Gorin, A. A., & Rigby, C.S. (2014). Virtual look AHEAD program: Initial support for a partly virtualized intensive lifestyle intervention in type 2 diabetes. Diabetes Care, 37, 169-170. doi: 10.2337/dc14-0831

Williams GC, Rodin GC, Ryan RM, Grolnick WS, Deci EL. (1998). Autonomous regulation and adherence to long-term medical regimens in adult outpatients. *Health Psychology*, 17: 269-276.

Adolescent Health

Contento, IR, Koch, PA, Lee, H, Calabrese-Barton, A. (2010). Adolescents Demonstrate Improvement in Obesity Risk Behaviors after Completion of *Choice, Control & Change*, a Curriculum Addressing Personal Agency and Autonomous Motivation. *J Am Diet Assoc., 110:1830-1839.*

Gillison, F, Standage, M, Verplanken, B. (2014). A cluster randomised controlled trial of an intervention to promote healthy lifestyle habits to school leavers: study rationale, design, and methods. *BMC Public Health, 14:221.*

Adolescent Health (cont'd)

Lonsdale, C., Rosenkranz, RR, Sanders, T, Peralta, LR, Bennie, A, Jackson, B, Taylor, IM, & Lubans, DR. (2013). A cluster randomized controlled trial of strategies to increase adolescents' physical activity and motivation in physical education: Results of the Motivating Active Learning in Physical Education (MALP) trial. *Preventive Medicine, 57, 696–702.*

Pardo, BM, Bengoechea, EG, Clemente, JAJ, & Lanaspa, EG. (2014). Empowering adolescents to be physically active: Three-year results of the Sigue la Huella intervention. *Preventive Medicine*, 66, 6–11.

Riiser, K, Løndal, K, Ommundsen, Y, Smastuen, MC, Misvær, N, Helseth, S. (2014). The Outcomes of a 12-Week Internet Intervention Aimed at Improving Fitness and Health-Related Quality of Life in Overweight Adolescents: The Young & Active Controlled Trial. *PLOS ONE.* doi:10.1371/journal.pone.0114732

Robbins, LB, Pfeiffer, KA, Vermeesch, A, Resnicow, K, You, Z. (2013). "Girls on the Move" intervention protocol for increasing physical activity among low-active underserved urban girls: a group randomized trial. *BMC Public Health*, 13:474.

Robbins, LB, Pfeiffer, KA, Wesolek, SM, Lo, Y-J. (2014). Process evaluation for a school-based physical activity intervention for 6th- and 7th-grade boys: Reach, dose, and fidelity. *Evaluation and Program Planning*, *42*, 21–31.

Rosenkranz, RR, Lubans, DR, Peralta, LR, Bennie, A, Sanders, T, & Lonsdale, C. (2012). A cluster-randomized controlled trial of strategies to increase adolescents' physical activity and motivation during physical education lessons: the Motivating Active Learning in Physical Education (MALP) trial. *BMC Public Health*, 12:834

Wilson, DK, Evans, AE, Williams, J, Mixon, G, Sirard, JR, Pate, R. (2005). A preliminary test of a student-centered intervention on increasing physical activity in underserved adolescents. Ann Behav Med, 30(2), 119-124.

Wilson, DK, Griffin, S, Saunders, RP, Evans, AE, Mixon, G, Wright, M, Beasley, A, Umstattd, MR, Lattimore, D, Watts, A, Freelove, J. (2006). Formative evaluation of a motivational intervention for increasing physical activity in underserved youth. Eval Program Plann, 29(3): 260–268. doi:10.1016/j.evalprogplan.2005.12.008.

New trials

Blackford, K; Jancey, J, Lee, AH, James, AP, Howat, P, Hills, AP, & Anderson, A. (2015). A randomized controlled trial of a physical activity and nutrition program targeting middle-aged adults at risk of metabolic syndrome in a disadvantaged rural community. *BMC Public Health*, 15: 284. DOI 10.1186/s12889-015-1613-9

Busse, M, Quinn, L, Dawes, H., Jones, C., Kelson, M, Poile, V., Trubey, R. Townson, J., Edwards, RT, Rosser, A, & Hood, K. (2014). Supporting physical activity engagement in people with Huntington's disease (ENGAGE-HD): study protocol for a randomized controlled feasibility trial. *Trials*, 15:487

Fenner, AA, Straker, LM, Davis, MC, & Hagger, MS. (2013). Theoretical underpinnings of a need-supportive intervention to address sustained healthy lifestyle changes in overweight and obese adolescents. *Psychology of Sport and Exercise*, 14, 819-829.

Gray, C.M., Hunt, K., Bunn, C., La Guardia, J., Andersen, E., & Wyke, S. on behalf of the EuroFIT consortium. (2015). *European Fans in Training (EuroFIT): A socio-psychological approach to the development of the healthy lifestyle programme to engage an at-risk group in sustained behavior change.* Poster presented at the annual conference of the International Society of Behavioral Nutrition and Physical Activity. Edinburgh, Scotland, UK.

Moreau, M, Gagnon, M-P, Boudreau, F (2015). Development of a Fully Automated, Web-Based, Tailored Intervention Promoting Regular Physical Activity Among Insufficiently Active Adults With Type 2 Diabetes: Integrating the I-Change Model, Self-Determination Theory, and Motivational Interviewing Components. *JMIR Res Protoc 4(1):e25)* doi:10.2196/resprot.4099

New trials (cont'd)
Thompson, D, Cantu, D, Bhatt, R, Baranowski, T, Rodgers, W. (2014). Texting to increase physical activity among teenagers (TXTMe!): Rationale, design, and methods proposal. JMIR Res Protoc, 3(1):e14) doi:10.2196/resprot.3074
Wilson, DK, Kitzman-Ulrich, H, Resnicow, K, Van Horn, ML, St. George, SM, Siceloff, R, Alia, KA, McDaniel, T, Heatley, V, Huffman, L, Coulona, S, Prinz, R. (2015). An overview of the Families Improving Together (FIT) for weight loss randomized controlled trial in African American families. Contemporary Clinical Trials, 42, 145–157.
van der Ploeg, H, Gray, C., Teixeira, P., Roberts, G., Hunt, K., Gill, J., Bunn, C., Chalmers, M., van Achterberg, T., Nijhuis-van der Sanden, R, Bosmans, J., La Guardia, J., Jotdet, G., Maxwell, D., Mourselas, N., van Nassau, F., Philpott, M., Anderson, A., Treweek, S., van Mechelen, W., Clissmann, C., Mutrie, N., & Wyke, S. for the EuroFIT consortium. (2014). *European Fans in Training (EuroFIT): Improving Physical Activity, Sedentary and Eating Behaviours in Football Fans*. Poster presented at the International Society of Behavioral Nutrition and Physical Activity. San Diego, CA.
van Nassau, F., van der Ploeg, HP, Abrahamsen, F., Andersen, E., Anderson, A.S., Bosmans, J.E., Bunn, C., Chalmers, M., Clissmann, C., Gill, J.M.R., Gray, C.M., Hunt, K., Jelsma, J.G.M., La Guardia, J.G., et al. (2016). Study protocol of European Fans in Training (EuroFIT): a four-country randomised controlled trial of a lifestyle program for men delivered in elite football clubs. BMC Public, 16:598, DOI:10.1186/s12889-016-3255-y

Appendix D. Structure & Process of the Initial Interview

Structure & Content

A. Provide framework or general outline for session

B. Introduce yourself and your background

C. Getting to know the client

- Gather information (personal, general health history, health behavior history)

- Understand reasons for maintaining the behavior and for wanting to change the behavior

- Understand client goals

D. Talk about program offered (if set program or other constraints as to what is offered)

E. Develop a collaborative plan for next steps, as appropriate.

Process:

A. Provide clear structure so that clients know what to expect from session

B. Provide rationale for questions you are asking or statements you are making

C. Open-ended questions in conversation form (be curious!)

D. Empathically respond--reflect client's perceptions and experiences without labeling,

lecturing, judgment and convey understanding and appreciation for their perspective

E. Provide clients opportunities to be in control of the decisions being made around their care

Appendix E. Practitioner dialogue revisited: Tobacco cessation

PROVIDER DIALOGUE PRIOR TO CHANGE ATTEMPT	NEED SUPPORTIVE PROCESS
What got you to start smoking initially? What keeps you smoking now?	Understand client current behaviors and perspective
People often have a number of things influencing their decision to quit smoking---they want to spend less money on cigarettes, they have developed physical health problems because of their smoking, they are at higher risk for disease (e.g., cardiovascular disease, cancer), they are getting pressured from others to quit, or they want to feel better physically. I'm wondering if any of these kinds of reasons, or any others, might be influencing your decision as well?	Querying about specific motivations for behavior
There a number of health risks associated with smoking. Would you be interested in talking about these?	Provides opportunity to gain knowledge
Oftentimes people experience withdrawal symptoms as they try to quit smoking....I am wondering what your experience is with this... Would you like to hear about coping strategies and medications available to help people manage withdrawal symptoms?"	Provides opportunity to gain knowledge and adding coping tools
You chose to use nicotine replacement medications to help you quit smoking. It's important for me to review the potential side effects and proper use of the medication so that you can get the safest and most effective use of it.	Provides information for building efficacy and preserving client safety
Oftentimes clients find it helpful to create a quit plan to help them make this change. Have you thought about a quit date?	Develops scaffolding for optimal challenge; provides client choice
Are there certain activities that trigger your smoking? Can you think of ways you may avoid, or minimize, them?	Help clients identify behavioral cues and problem solve
Is there anyone that you would find helpful with supporting you in your efforts to quit smoking (e.g., family members, friends, co-workers, etc.)? • *How can they help you?* • *What kinds of things would you like them to do for you?*	Assesses relatedness and support in clients' social context
Sometimes clients are unsure about what quitting will be like. Would you be willing to do an experiment and quit for half of the day to see what it feels like? You can use intermittent Nicotine Replacement Therapy (NRT), like gum, lozenge, inhaler, or nasal spray to manage withdrawal symptoms. NRTs are especially helpful if you have never made a quit attempt and need some relief from withdrawal symptoms.	Experimentation helps clients gather information on experience when they are not clear on whether they want to make changes to their current behaviors
So, it is my understanding that you want to quit smoking, but would like to wait until _____, is that right? It seems like that will be a better time for you, because... *Can you help me understand what will be different for you then that will help you to feel more confident in your ability to quit then? What is it about now that is in the way of you thinking about quitting?* *I respect your decision to not make changes right now. We can always leave the option open to make some time down the road to check back in and see if anything has changed...*	Validate clients' choice around health behavior change and attempt to understand their perspective

PROVIDER DIALOGUE DURING CHANGE ATTEMPT	NEED SUPPORTIVE PROCESS
How would you rate your level of Anxiety? Irritability? Difficulty concentrating? Cravings for cigarettes?	Awareness of mood and physical symptoms of withdrawal so that can then work to manage them
What kinds of positive changes have you noticed since you quit smoking? What kinds of negative changes have you noticed since you quit smoking?	Develop clients abilities to assess thoughts & feelings about behavior change
Are there things you miss about smoking?	Probe for motivation to return to prior behavior
How has your social circle (e.g., family, friends, co-workers) responded to your attempts to quit smoking?	Assess relatedness support in clients' social context
What are your thoughts about the medication you chose? What did you like about it? What didn't you like about it?	Learn to assess efficacy of strategies clients choose
Recall how or when you slipped? What do you think influenced why you slipped then? How could you change the situation to prevent relapse from happening again?	Learn to assess own behavior, express empathy, encourage trying behavior change again
Often plans don't always go the way we originally thought they would. What working with your current quit plan? What isn't working? How are you feeling as you are going through this process?	Refines concrete strategies but also highlights how feelings about behavior change can color the process

Some excerpts adapted with permission from Sharp et al. (2009) Intensive Tobacco Dependence Intervention with Persons Challenged by Mental Illness: Manual for Nurses.

See additional materials at www.Smokefree.gov, some of which were designed by SDT researchers and practitioners.

Appendix F. Client's Motivations for Behavior Change

What are some of the reasons that you might want to be more physically active?

	Direct pressures or rewards	Internal pressures to avoid feeling bad or to feel better about self	Big picture values & life goals, health	Enjoyment, Interest
Explanation of each category of motivation	Participate in the program because they feel direct external pressures to achieve a reward or to avoid punishment. So, they might get rewards if they exercise and lose weight (e.g., spouse stops nagging them) or they might get punished if they don't (e.g., pay extra doctor bills, expenses because they are overweight).	Feel internal pressures (e.g., "I should" or "I have to") in order to maintain their self-worth or to avoid feeling bad (e.g., guilty). So, they might exercise to lose weight so that others (e.g., doctors, family, friends) won't be disappointed with them or because they believe that working out will help them look better, others will be more attracted to them or think better of them.	Value the behaviors and how it serves other important personal goals. For example, they might exercise because they value being healthier/more fit and it is a way to lose weight. They also value playing with their kids/grandkids and doing more activities with friends—exercising & losing weight makes it physically easier to do both	They do the behavior because it is fun or interesting. That is, they might really enjoy being physically active and find it fun and challenging.
Examples of what people often say	*I have to go to the doctor more often, take medications because of my health which is costing me a lot of money*	*I have to change my behaviors, otherwise something bad is going to happen (I'm going to get sick and die early).*	*I value my health/being fit and want to be as healthy/fit as I can*	*I enjoy exercising (e.g., playing football, taking walks, swimming)*
	My partner/doctor/kids/friends get after me about being overweight and unhealthy	*Even when others aren't telling me directly, I feel pressured to exercise ("I should exercise") and feel guilty if I don't*	*Being healthier means I can contribute more to my family/others who are important to me*	*I like creating new physical challenges for myself (e.g. running a 5K)*
	Others tell me I look bad (ugly, fat, unattractive)	*I feel bad about myself (I'm ugly, fat, unattractive) and I want to stop feeling bad*	*Being healthier lets me keep up with my friends and do more things with them (e.g., play football)*	*I am really interested in trying out new exercise activities*
	I know I will feel physically bad/sick/in pain if I don't exercise.	*I want my partner/others to think I'm attractive, handsome/I look good*	*I want to be able to keep up with my kids/grandkids*	*I am really interested in developing new skills*
		I want to look like I used to when I was younger	*I want to be a good role model for my kids/grandkids*	
		I want others to think highly of me (I'm a strong man/woman)	*My body feels good/I get more energy when I exercise*	
		I want people who are important to me to be proud of me/not be disappointed in me	*I feel physically more able to live my life the way I want to*	

Appendix G. History of Client's Experience Around Health Behavior Change

Think about the questions below. In the blanks, write some notes about your thoughts.
We will talk about them together in your first session with your lifestyle counselor.

Prior successes and challenges around Weight Loss

1. If you have tried to lose weight in the past, what did you do?

2. Have you ever used dietary supplements or medications to control your weight?

3. What worked well for you?

4. What didn't work well?

5. Any new challenges for you currently that are making it difficult to lose weight?

Prior successes and challenges around changing Physical Activity

1. What kinds of things have you tried to do to in the past to be physically active (e.g., playing sports, exercising, leisure activities)?

2. How did you feel about those activities?

   a. What did you like about those activities?

   b. What didn't you like about those activities?

3. What got in the way of being more physically active regularly?

Prior successes and challenges around changing Diet

1. What kinds of things have you tried to do to in the past to change your diet (e.g., portion control, special diets, eating more fruits/veggies, cutting out particular foods)?

2. How did you feel about those changes? How well did each work for you?

3. What got in the way of making dietary changes that would last?

Prior successes and challenges around attempts to quit using tobacco

1. Can you remember when you began smoking/using tobacco?

   a. What was it like?

   b. Has anything changed in your experience of smoking/using tobacco since that time?

2. Have you ever tried to quit?

   a. What was it like for you? How did it feel?

   b. What did you do to try to quit? Did you use medications?

   c. What were the hardest parts of quitting?

   d. What were the biggest benefits of quitting?

Appendix H. Details of clients' current health behaviors

Current Physical Activity Habits

1. How physically active are you doing your workday? (not at all; moderately active; very active)

2. How physically active are you away from work? (not at all; moderately active; very active)

3. How often do you exercise each week (e.g., walk, ride bike, elliptical)? _____ days/week

4. How long did you typically exercise on those days? _____ hours _____minutes

5. What kinds of activities do you do?

6. Do you exercise with anyone? _____NO _____YES (Who?_____)

7. How did you feel about those activities?

   a. What do you like about being physically active?

   b. What don't you like about physical activity?

8. What things keep you from being active?

9. What kinds of physical activity might you be interesting in trying out? Anything new?

Current Eating Habits

Below please make some notes about your current eating patterns. On the left please jot down what a typical day looks like for you when you feel you are on target with your goals. On the right, please jot down what a day looks like for you when you are having a bad day.

	"Good" day	"Bad" day
Breakfast		
Snacks		
Lunch		
Snacks		
Dinner		
Snacks/dessert		
Any drinks (e.g., soda, specialty coffees)?		
Any alcohol?		

How many days of the week are you typically having a "bad" day? _____days/week

Current Tobacco Use

1. How many cigarettes are you smoking per day?/How often do you use tobacco each day?

2. Has it always been this amount?

3. When do you find you most use tobacco during the day? Any pattern you notice?

4. Any new challenges for you currently that are making it difficult to quit using tobacco?

Current Life Stressors & Social Supports

1. What kinds of things create stress in your life right now?

2. On a scale from 1 to 10 (with 10 being the most stressed you have ever felt in your life) what would you say is your current level of stress? (mark the number below)

    1   2   3   4   5   6   7   8   9   10

    Little or   The most stress
    no stress   I have had in my life

3. Who are the important people in your life that provide you support?

4. Are there any people in your life that are making it difficult for you to change your behaviors (e.g., to lose weight)?

Personal Goals Around [Weight Loss; Physical Activity; Dietary Change; Quitting Tobacco]

1. What are your reasons for wanting to [lose weight; be more physically active; change your diet; quit tobacco] now?

2. People often have a goal in mind that they would like to achieve by the end of the program (e.g., regain energy and mobility, reduce pain in everyday life activities, be able to be more active to play with their kids or join in activities with their partner or friends). What goal(s) do you hope to achieve through this program?

245

Appendix I. Current Health Conditions (example from weight loss program)

Information About Your Health

Some medical conditions may require us to monitor particular aspects of your health (e.g., blood pressure; nutritional intake) or change some of the physical activities you will be doing in this program (e.g., provide alternative stretches for those with lower back injuries). To help us understand whether you have any of these needs we need to know a little bit about your health history. Please indicate if you have any of the following conditions by placing an "x" in the box next to the conditions you have had:

☐ Headaches
☐ Dizziness
☐ Fatigue
☐ Numbness
☐ Neck pain
☐ Sinus troubles
☐ Temporomandibular joint dysfunction (TMJ)
☐ Skin disorder (e.g. psoriasis)
☐ Arm/shoulder pain
☐ Abdominal pain
☐ Back pain/injury
☐ Sciatica
☐ Spinal Disc Injury
☐ Hip or leg pain
☐ Knee pain
☐ Swollen joints (e.g., arthritis, bursitis)
☐ Joint replacements
☐ Sore Feet

☐ Asthma
☐ Chronic bronchitis
☐ Emphysema
☐ Other lung or bronchial disorders
   Specify:_____

☐ High blood pressure (hypertension)
☐ Low blood pressure
☐ Chest pain/angina
☐ Thrombosis (blood clots)
☐ Circulatory issues
☐ Cold Hands/Feet
☐ Fibromyalgia
☐ Varicose Veins

☐ Diabetes/sugar diabetes
☐ Kidney Disease
☐ Liver disease (e.g., cirrhosis)
☐ Thyroid disease

☐ Hepatitis

☐ Chronic Infection

☐ Digestive disorder
   ☐ Crohn's disease
   ☐ Celiac disease
   ☐ Colitis
   ☐ Other: _____

☐ Neurological conditions
   ☐ Epilepsy
   ☐ Seizures (non-Epilepsy)
   ☐ Multiple Sclerosis
   ☐ Alzheimer's or other dementias
   ☐ Parkinson's disease
   ☐ Other: _____

☐ Serious head injury
☐ Brain tumor
☐ Cancer (please describe)

Type of cancer_____
Year diagnosed_____
☐ Cardiovascular disease
☐ Angina (chest pain related to your heart)
☐ High cholesterol (> 200)

☐ Cardiovascular event
   (please write in year it happened)
   ☐ Heart attack
   ☐ Stent
   ☐ Angioplasty
   ☐ CABG (bypass)
   ☐ Valve replacement
   ☐ Congestive heart failure
   ☐ Stroke
   ☐ Mini-stroke (TIA: transient ischemic attack)
   ☐ Other: _____

☐ Other conditions not listed:
_____

1. Do you currently see a health care practitioner for any of the conditions listed on the previous page?

   ☐ NO
   ☐ YES → Please describe what conditions you are currently being treated for and what kind of treatment you are receiving:

   CONDITION: TREATMENT:

   _____   _____
   _____   _____
   _____   _____

2. Are you taking any medications currently?

   ☐ NO
   ☐ YES → Please list all medications you are currently taking and their dosages:

Medication Name	Dosage (mg.)	# of pills per dose	Times per day	Reason for Taking

3. Are you taking steroid pills or shots such as prednisone or cortisone?
   (NOTE: do not check "YES" if this is for hormone replacement)

   ☐ NO
   ☐ YES → What condition(s) are you taking this for? _____

4. Do you have any activities that are painful or uncomfortable for you to do?

   ☐ NO → Go to question 5.
   ☐ YES → Please indicate which of the following activities are painful for you:

   ☐ Sitting   ☐ Climbing stairs
   ☐ Standing   ☐ Crouching
   ☐ Rising from the chair   ☐ Kneeling
   ☐ Walking   ☐ Pushing
   ☐ Bending   ☐ Pulling
   ☐ Rising up from bending   ☐ Lifting
   ☐ Reaching above shoulder level   ☐ Repeated lifting
   ☐ Reaching below shoulder level

5. Do you have any other physical limitations that restrict your movement or prevent you from engaging in regular physical activity?

   ☐ NO
   ☐ YES → Please list these limitations: _____

6. Are you currently taking any weight loss medications?
   ☐ NO
   ☐ YES → What medications are you on?

      ☐ Orlistat (Alli, Xenical)
      ☐ Metformin (Fortamet, Glucophage, Glumetza)
      ☐ Bupropion (Aplenzin, Wellbutrin, Wellbutrin SR, Wellbutrin XL)
      ☐ Metformin + bupropion
      ☐ Other: _____

7. Are you currently participating in another weight loss program such as Weight Watchers, Jenny Craig, or another program that promotes weight loss through physical activity or nutrition counseling?
   ☐ NO
   ☐ YES → Have you been active and using their services within the past month?   ☐ No   ☐ Yes

8. Have you lost weight in the past 3 months?
   ☐ NO
   ☐ YES → Was it more than 10 pounds?   ☐ No   ☐ Yes

9. Have you ever had, or has a doctor ever told you, you had:

☐ Insomnia	☐ YES	☐ NO	☐ DON'T KNOW
☐ Mania	☐ YES	☐ NO	☐ DON'T KNOW
☐ Depression	☐ YES	☐ NO	☐ DON'T KNOW
☐ Anorexia	☐ YES	☐ NO	☐ DON'T KNOW
☐ Bulimia	☐ YES	☐ NO	☐ DON'T KNOW

10. Have you ever had a major accidents or injuries?
    ☐ NO
    ☐ YES →   Please list all accidents/injuries and when they happened.

       ACCIDENT/INJURY: YEAR:
       _____   _____
       _____   _____
       _____   _____

11. Have you ever had a major surgery?
    ☐ NO
    ☐ YES →   Please list all surgeries and when they happened.

       SURGERY: YEAR:
       _____   _____
       _____   _____
       _____   _____

ARE YOU CURRENTLY A SMOKER? (check one below)

☐ **No, I have never smoked** → **GO TO THE NEXT PAGE**

☐ **No, I quit within the last 6 months**

     a. When did you quit? ___ / ___ / _____ (fill in date)

     b. In your life, how many years did you smoked altogether? _____ years

     c. During a typical 7 day period, how many cigarettes did you smoke per day?
        _____ cigarettes per day

     d. Have you smoked 100 cigarettes in your entire life?   ☐ Yes
                                                 ☐ No → **GO TO the next page**

☐ **No, I quit more than 6 months ago**

     a. When did you quit? ___ / ___ / _____ (fill in date)

     b. In your life, how many years did you smoked altogether? _____ years

     c. During a typical 7 day period, how many cigarettes did you smoke per day? _____ cigarettes per day

     d. Have you smoked 100 cigarettes in your entire life?   ☐ Yes
                                                 ☐ No → **GO TO the next page**

☐ **Yes, I currently smoke**

• Smoke a pipe?	☐ Yes	☐ No
• Smoke cigars?	☐ Yes	☐ No
• Use snuff?	☐ Yes	☐ No
• Use chewing tobacco?	☐ Yes	☐ No
• Use electronic cigarettes?	☐ Yes	☐ No

     a. In your life, how many years have you smoked altogether? _____ years

     b. During a typical 7 day period, how many cigarettes did you smoke per day? _____ cigarettes per day

     c. Have you smoked 100 cigarettes in your entire life?   ☐ Yes   ☐ No

     d. In the last year, how many times have you quit smoking for at least 24 hours? _____ times

     e. Are you seriously thinking of quitting smoking (check one)?

         ☐ No, I am not thinking of quitting → **GO TO the next page**
         ☐ Yes, within the next 30 days   → **GO TO f**
         ☐ Yes, within the next 6 months   → **GO TO f**

f. How much do you want to quit smoking? (circle a number from 1 to 10 below)

1	2	3	4	5	6	7	8	9	10
Don't want to quit				Somewhat want to quit					Very much want to quit

g. As of now, how confident are you that you can quit smoking? (circle a number from 1 to 10 below)

1	2	3	4	5	6	7	8	9	10
Not at all confident				Somewhat confident					Very confident

---

FOR WOMEN ONLY:
1. Are you currently pregnant?
   ☐ DON'T KNOW
   ☐ NO   1st day of your last period? ____/____/____
   ☐ YES

2. Are you currently nursing?   ☐ NO   ☐ YES

3. Do you take birth control pills?   ☐ NO   ☐ 1st day of your last period? ____/____/____
                                        ☐ YES

4. Are you post-menopausal?   ☐ NO
                                        ☐ YES
                                                Do you now or have you in the past taken
                                                hormone replacements?   ☐ No   ☐ Yes

---

Appendix J.   Illustrating how practitioners' dialogue supports basic psychological needs: Examples from Initial Session with Clients

A.   Provide framework or general outline for session

PROVIDER DIALOGUE	NEED SUPPORTIVE PROCESS
Thanks so much for coming in today	Warm regard
Today we have about 50 minutes to talk. In this first session I typically like to use this time to learn a little more about you—your background, your health, and your experiences around [insert health behavior, e.g., trying to lose weight], both the challenges you have encountered and what has worked well for you. I also like to spend some time learning about your goals and what you hope to get out of our work together.	Provides clear structure so that clients know what to expect from session
All of this information will help us to understand a bit more about how to create a plan that best addresses your needs and make changes more manageable.	Provide rationale for questions you are asking
Near the end of the session we can discuss some potential ways to address some of your goals and determine what we want to do in terms of next steps.	Lets clients know they are in charge of choices around their health
What do you think of that plan for today? Anything else you think I missed that we should add to our agenda?	Elicits input from client to craft the session agenda
Because our work together is about managing your health it is helpful to have your inputs throughout our work together. So I'll do my best to check in with you about your thoughts and feelings throughout the session but please also feel free to stop me at any time while we are talking to ask questions or to let me know other thoughts you might have.	Sets up collaborative, open dialogue and encourages client inputs

B.   Introduce your background and role.

PROVIDER DIALOGUE	NEED SUPPORTIVE PROCESS
Before I ask you more about yourself, I wanted to let you know a little about my background and the team we have here to assist you in your care. I am a registered dietitian by training...	Provides information on provider expertise, connect personally
We don't need to just explore changes to your diet. We can talk about incorporating physical activity, managing stress, or other health behaviors, like smoking that might also be impacting your health. It's up to you how much or little we might work on these different aspects of your health.	Gives clients information on potential menu of options to support holistic care
...we also have other teams members—an exercise physiologist, nurse, and psychologist—who can consult with us on any specific area of concern so that we can ensure we are doing the best in terms of your care	Explains how provider can draw on other expertise to support care
With your permission, we can also work closely with your primary care physician to coordinate your care.	Ensures client of consent in collaboration
Do you have any questions?	Offers opportunities for client input to shape dialogue

C.   Getting to know the client (personal, general health history, health behavior history)

PROVIDER DIALOGUE	NEED SUPPORTIVE PROCESS
Tell me a little about yourself. • *What do you do for a living? What's your workplace like?* • *Family? (Note: for some people their pets are their family so consider asking about pets. "Any pets?")*	Open-ended questions in conversation form (be curious!)
I heard you say that having kids has really made it challenging to have time for yourself. It sounds like this stress has contributed to not always eating very well or getting time to exercise.	Brief summary of information from client. Helps them to know that they are heard, understood
It sounds like you felt like you had a better handle on your weight in your 20s because it was easier to exercise and lose the weight. But that doesn't seem to be working well now. Is that right?	Check information from client. Helps them to know that they are heard, understood
My understanding is you have been struggling with your weight since childhood and that it made you feel not so good about yourself, especially when you were a teenager. And from what you said, it sounds like some of those feelings continue even today.	Reflect the meaning of clients' disclosures. Helps them to know that they are heard, understood
It seems that you might have been pretty disappointed by that experience. Often people feel pretty frustrated and defeated when they try a bunch of ways to lose weight and run into a lot of obstacles. I'm wondering if you might have had this experience as well.	Wondering with clients about feelings to connect thoughts and affect; Deepen understanding of experience
So I'm curious about what is making you want to [lose weight] now? [Alternative: What are your reasons for wanting to lose weight now?]	Assessing motivation for seeking treatment
So people often have a number of things influencing their decision to lose weight---they want to get better health benefits or spend less money on health care, they are getting pressured from others to lose weight, they want to feel better physically, or they want to do other things that are important to them (e.g., travel) and losing some weight will help them to do that more easily. I'm wondering if any of these kinds of reasons or any others might be influencing your decision as well?	Querying about specific motivations for behavior
Any reasons for not wanting to change your current behaviors? Anything you think you'll miss or miss out on if you change your behavior?	Querying about motivations to NOT change behavior
On one hand you have some reasons to change your behavior such as (insert what they said) and on the other hand there are some pulls such as (insert what they said) that might make you not want to change.	Showing understanding of the client's perspective and acknowledging various motivational pulls
I'm wondering what you think about the balance of these different motivations? How strong is each side pulling right now?	Understanding the strength and relative balance of different motivations from the clients' perspective

C.   Getting to know the client (cont'd)

PROVIDER DIALOGUE	NEED SUPPORTIVE PROCESS
Sounds like you feel pretty pressured to change your behaviors right now. One of the things that we know is that pressure can kick us into gear to get started with behavior change but we also need other reasons to keep doing the behavior over the long term. So, as we work together I am wondering if we try to see if there are some ways to help you feel less pressured and find your own personal value for these behaviors (and maybe even find ways to help you like it too). How does that sound to you?	Appreciates current client feelings; introduces how treatment can support internalization towards more autonomous motivation; checks in with client about reactions
Sounds like changing your behaviors right now is really important to you personally. That personal value and interest in changing your behavior that you have right now will be important to sticking with these behaviors over the long term. Sometimes over the course of treatment clients find that they might start to feel more pressured to change their behaviors. As we work together if you start to feel more pressure to engage in these health behaviors let's talk about how that is affecting you. That way we can try to see if there are some ways to help you feel less pressured and rediscover your own personal value, interest, and enjoyment of the behaviors. How does that sound to you?	Appreciates current client feelings; introduces how treatment can support continued growth of autonomous motivation; checks in with client about reactions
Transition Statement: In the next bit of time I would like to learn more about you're current health behaviors. If you can help me get the most accurate picture of your current [eating, physical activity, smoking] patterns, this will help us to identify some potential opportunities for change.	Helps to create structure so they know what is coming
You said that your current level of stress is pretty high. How do you think that might impact the changes you are hoping to make?	Use reflections to gain a greater understanding of how they anticipate stress to impact their efforts
I'm wondering...in general, who are the important people in your life that provide you support? Who do you think you can count on for support around changing your behaviors so you can lose some weight?	Assesses relatedness and support in clients' social context
I noticed that when I asked you about who are your best supports you mentioned two of your close friends, but that your husband/wife was not someone you listed. I'm wondering how he/she fits in the picture?	Assesses when need support may be absent or needs are being thwarted
People often have a goal in mind that they would like to achieve (e.g., regain energy and mobility, reduce pain in everyday life activities, be able to be more active to play with their kids or join in activities with their partner or friends). What goal or goals do you hope to achieve through our work together?	Supports clients identifying personally meaningful goals
We have covered a lot of territory today. I want to take a moment to check back in with you to summarize what I've heard and see if I have a good sense of important information.	Ensures that you have accurately understood the client's point of view and conveys to the client that you have listened

253

D. Discussing options for treatment

PROVIDER DIALOGUE	NEED SUPPORTIVE PROCESS
There are different options we can explore to help you to lose weight. Are you interested in hearing information about some potential options?	Provides option to receive information/input rather than just offer it
One way to go about losing weight is to focus on eating healthier. There are many ways to eat healthier... Another way to go about losing weight is to focus on getting more physically active. When we focus on physical activity we typically look for ways to increase your daily activity and incorporate exercise routine into your week...We also can tackle weight loss by doing a combination of healthy eating and physical activity strategies.	Provides menu of treatment options--with complete information so client can be thoroughly informed about each option
The potential benefit of changing up your diet and level of physical activity is that it can lower your cholesterol...which are all important in lowering your risk for developing heart disease, diabetes, and some cancers. People also report that changing diet and physical activity also helps to improve energy levels, improve mood, and make it easier to do everyday activities.	Providing a meaningful rationale for changing behaviors
These are the typical ways that we address weight loss. Are there other ideas or strategies that you are interested in talking about?	Offers opportunities for client input to shape treatment menu of options

E. Develop a collaborative plan for next steps, as appropriate.

PROVIDER DIALOGUE	NEED SUPPORTIVE PROCESS
So we've discussed a number of options, do any of these approaches sound appealing? Any sound more manageable for you right now?	Elicit clients' initial thoughts/feelings
Because we have talked about a lot today I am wondering whether it would be helpful to give you some information about each of these options and then we can make an appointment to talk again about what seems most appealing and doable for you.	Allows clients to review/ add to information at a pace that feels manageable before making decisions
Some people consider all of their options but decide that making a change isn't something that they want to do right now. So, we can always leave that option open too and make some time down the road to check back in and see if anything has changed. What's important to know is that the option of how we proceed is up to you and I will do my best to offer support around whatever you choose.	Advocates for clients autonomous decisions, including offering "not changing" a viable option
Do you have a sense of whether you would like more information and talk again in a week or two or would you rather hold off on considering making changes right now?	Provides client opportunity to direct decision making process
I respect your decision to not make changes right now. I am wondering if you can help me better understand what led you to that decision?	Attempts to understand decisions
I am wondering whether it would be helpful to you if we make some time down the road to check back in? [if yes, then schedule an appointment in a month or two from now. This can be a simple phone check in or a formal face to face appointment.] What's important to know is that the option of whether we follow-up is up to you and I will do my best to offer support around whatever you choose.	Offer continued contact, invitation for support if interested at any time

254

Appendix K. Structure & Process Issues During Treatment

Outline of Structure:

A. Identify scope of what you will tackle

B. Goals

    1. Seeing health behavior in context in big picture life goals

    2. Macro-level health goals

    3. Micro-level goals--small, specific problems to tackle

C. Gaining knowledge

    1. Identify basic educational content needed for foundational knowledge

    2. Select potential behavioral change tools to choose from to gain knowledge

D. Engage in plan of action, including

- Problem solving

- Identifying needed social supports

- Skill building through experimentation
  - Understanding experience of experimentation, including emotional impact
  - Fostering positive self-relevant feedback
  - Revision of goals and strategies
  - Expansion of goals (beginning to do more challenging, interesting)

E. Communicating needs for support to important others

F. Examining the role of stress and promoting optimal coping

G. Preparing for maintenance

- Revisiting motivation for health behavior and their connection to "big picture" goals

- Plans for sustaining and expanding current behaviors, including new goals/optimal challenges and building vitality

- Social support to continue behavior

- Revisiting role of life stress & how those things derail the process of behavior change

- Prevention: return to treatment for booster sessions if on slide backwards (red flags)

Appendix L. Mapping Big Picture Goals with Clients

1. In the chart below, first just write down some of your "big picture" goals and values for different aspects of your life. These are things you are trying or would like to do, regardless of whether or not you are actually successful at them. (e.g., "Spend quality time with my family.")

2. Once you've completed that side of the chart, consider the following questions:

   • How does your health fit into the big picture?
     ○ How can being healthier help you to better meet these goals?
     ○ How can being healthier help you do what is most important to you?
   • Ideally, how would daily life look different if your health goals got more attention?
   • How are other goals or aspects of life potentially derailing attention to your health?

	GOALS AND VALUES	HOW CAN BEING HEALTHIER HELP YOU TO BETTER MEET THESE OTHER GOALS?
Work/school		
Home/family		
Friendships/ other relationships		
Leisure/recreation		
Other life areas		

Appendix M. Problem solving and making a plan of action

Successfully reaching your goals often requires you to make a series of small changes. Making small, manageable changes that _you_ choose can help you to feel a sense of accomplishment and get your important needs met.

Steps to making an action plan of small changes:

STEP 1: Select the 1 thing you would like to work on changing. Write this goal/priority at the top of the blank worksheet page

STEP 2: Write down the things that are making it difficult to meet that goal. Make sure to write down all the challenges that are getting in your way. NOTE: If you are having trouble breaking this down, take a look at Appendix N. We have given you a list of some of the commons things that people say create challenges for them. Not everything that makes it difficult to reach your goals is found on this page so make sure to write down whatever is making it difficult for you to meet your goal.

STEP 3: Next to each challenge that you wrote down, write down how you would like things to be different---so, if you woke up tomorrow and things were different, what would that look like? What would happen? (Be realistic!). This is what you wish for. (HINT: Think about how you want your needs to be met.) Don't worry too much right now about whether these things will actually come true. You first need to define what you want before you can ask for it.

STEP 4: For each challenge brainstorm some small changes that you could make to tackle the challenge. You likely already have some ideas about how you might want to go about changing some things, but if you get stuck use some of the ideas that we provided in the examples.

A few points to remember....

1. **Be specific.** The more you can think through the specifics of a plan ahead of time, the more likely you will be able to follow through. Consider the following questions: What are you going to do? When? Are there other things do you need to do to make this plan happen?

2. **Be realistic.** Many people want a carefree, easy life---less work, more money, and more fun. But for most of us, we can't just leave all responsibilities behind. So given your life circumstances, think about the possibilities of what you _can_ do.

3. **Pace yourself.** It's great to have a bigger end goal. But to reach that goal you will need to identify sets of small, manageable steps to reach that ultimate goal. Setting expectations that that are too big or too difficult to reach can lead to disappointment, which often leads people to just give up. Remember, you didn't get to where you are in a day—the challenges you are facing have likely built up over time. It will probably take some time, several sets of small changes, and some revisions to your plans to reach your end goal. For example: If you say "I want to lose 30 pounds" but you aren't physically active at all, the first step might be to find ways to work a walk around the block 15 minutes each day.

4. **Remember that not everything will be in your control.** We can't control how other people act or we can't control some of the events that happen in our lives. But, we can control how much energy and investment we put into aspects of our lives, such as our health. Choices aren't always obvious and sometimes we need others help to figure out what to do next. For starters, try to focus your energy on the things that you can readily control---the small changes that you can make to better satisfy your basic needs.

GOAL/PRIORITY: Reduce the number of cigarettes I smoke

Challenges making it difficult to reach my goal	How would I like this to be different?	Small changes I can make	What can others do to help?
My friends all smoke so when we go out I want to	I would like to be able enjoy going out with friends without feeling the need to smoke	Suggest going out to places that are non-smoking. Chew gum when I feel the urge to smoke when I am out with my friends.	

GOAL/PRIORITY: Get more physically fit.

Challenges making it difficult to reach my goal	How would I like this to be different?	Small changes I can make	What can others do to help?
I get winded really easily and my body hurts when I get more active	I would be able to breathe easier and not be in so much pain.	Try out other ways to be physically active (e.g., swimming) that might be easier on my body. Start at a slower pace, take breaks when I need to.	

GOAL/PRIORITY: Cook healthier meals.

Challenges making it difficult to reach my goal	How would I like this to be different?	Small changes I can make	What can others do to help?
I don't have enough time to cook healthy meals every night.	Eat home cooked, healthy meals every night without too much fuss.	Prep snacks and meals on Sunday and Wednesday so that I can just grab a snack and heat meals up on the other days.	

Appendix N. Common Roadblocks to Behavioral Change

- Time management of home/work/social or personal interests
    - Difficult/challenging work, family, or other responsibility that is draining
    - Overwhelmed by total number of responsibilities (e.g., family, work, etc.)
    - No personal time
    - No time to do any leisure/recreational fun activities

- Social support for behavioral change
    - Conflict with your spouse/partner or kids around incorporating valued health behaviors
    - Social time encourages current behavioral patterns and changing behavioral patterns elicit conflict with social group
    - Workplace culture not readily adaptable to needed change (e.g., schedule/structure; traditions around celebrations)

- Culture and traditions
    - Want to preserve important cultural traditions and not sure how to integrate this with healthier lifestyle
    - Role changes to create healthier lifestyle requires renegotiation of relational contracts

- Behavior features
    - Not finding things I enjoy doing right now (e.g., type of exercise)
    - Financial problems/don't have $ to do what I want to do

- Emotional coping related to the health behavior
    - Other coping tools not well-developed to replace behavior (e.g., smoke to de-stress)
    - Changing behaviors creates anxiety, distress and other coping tools not well-developed to manage stress around behavior change

- Emotional coping with life stressors in other domains makes it difficult to take in new information, make changes
    - $$$$
    - Conflict in personal relationships (partner, other family members, friends, co-workers)
    - Time with spouse/partner and/or kids (not enough quality time; don't have shared activities; don't like shared activities)
    - Don't have personal connections at work/school; have few friends, feel disconnected; desire romantic partner but don't have one
    - Not doing what I am most interested in or want to do for work

- Personal health
    - Physical disability or injury limitations
    - Complex health issues
        - Managing chronic disease (e.g., diabetes, high blood pressure, high cholesterol; Crohn's disease) or acute physical Illness (e.g., cardiovascular disease, cancer)
        - Managing psychological challenges (e.g., depression, anxiety)

Appendix O. Enlisting social support

We all need supportive people to help us meet our goals. But, sometimes getting the support that we need can be challenging. In some cases, people hesitate to ask for support. Sometimes people aren't sure who to turn to for support. And sometimes, even when people are willing to ask for support and have people to turn to, the support doesn't turn out to be what they had hoped for. Below we address how to choose the right people to turn to for support and how to ask for their support.

Choosing the right people to turn to for support

Relationships that are good for you will support you, not tear you down, especially at times when you are struggling to reach your goals or when you're not feeling so great about yourself. Supportive others (e.g., friends, spouse, family, etc.) are the people that can help you remind you of your strengths and join forces with you to fight the challenges that come your way.

- *Who are the people that have been the sources of strength and support along the way?*

- *Who would be most helpful for the current challenges you are facing?*

A few important points to remember…

- Different people might help you to tackle different challenges. So, think about who might be most helpful for a particular challenge.

- Sometimes the people who have been most supportive to you in the past may not be able to provide the support you need right now. Don't write them off forever. It just means you will need to find another resource for now.

- If you don't get the support you are hoping for, use this as information for the next time you need support. Perhaps this person isn't truly the best one to turn to.

- Sometimes people think that they "should" seek support from particular people (e.g., family, friends). But these folks may not be the best supports and/or they may be too invested in a particular outcome. Perhaps consider a neutral person (e.g., counselor) who might be able to provide an unbiased listening ear.

Asking for support: How to increase your chances of getting the support you need

We often assume that others know what to do to be supportive. Although they might have some ideas about how to be supportive, others really need you to provide them with information. They need to know what you are feeling, when you need support, and what specifically they can do to be most supportive. They cannot adequately respond to your needs if you don't share them!

STEP 1: **First, do some work on your own--focus on understanding your own feelings & needs before you talk to others.** You have already articulated what your challenges are, how you would like things to be different, and what others can do to be helpful in your Making a Plan for Change worksheet. Use this as a guide.

STEP 2: **Timing is everything!** Have you ever been bombarded with questions or requests right as you walk in the door? Unless you are prepared, this approach can feel pretty overwhelming and the likelihood of you responding well is low. So, make sure to let others know that you would like to talk and what you would like to talk about, and set up an uninterrupted time to do it. Giving others a heads up gives them a chance to think about how they feel about what you are asking from them. And by setting aside some uninterrupted time you both have a better chance of responding more thoughtfully to each other.

STEP 3: **Talk with others about <u>your</u> own feelings and needs**. No one will be receptive if you focus on what they are doing wrong. This will just raise their defenses and lessen the chance that you will be heard. Focus on what has been challenging for *you*, how *you* are feeling, and how *you* hope things might be different. Use what you wrote down earlier to help you to clearly express these things.

STEP 4: **Communicate with others about what they can do to be more supportive.** We all have expectations about how we want others to help. Sometimes you want others to just listen, sometimes you want their help to problem solve some creative solutions. Others may not be sure what to do or how to best be supportive. So, giving them some guidance as to how they can be helpful can make it easier for them to respond in the way that you need them to. To help you complete this step, fill in the final portion of your Making a Plan for Change worksheet with these specifics. Take a look at how we completed the examples in the worksheet on the next page.

STEP 5: **Make sure to check in to see if what you are asking from others is manageable for them**. Remember that others may not be able to be responsive in the way that you had hoped. Brainstorm with them about other ways they could manage to help. Also be open to hearing about what they need too!

STEP 6: **Make a plan of action together and try it out.** Once you have decided on a course of action, try out the plan. Make sure to decide on a time to check back in to see how the plan is working for each of you, that way you can work on how to fix the things that aren't working well and strengthen the things that have worked.

GOAL/PRIORITY: _Reduce the number of cigarettes I smoke_

Challenges making it difficult to reach my goal	How would I like this to be different?	Small changes I can make	What can others do to help?
My friends all smoke so when we go out I want to	I would like to be able enjoy going out with friends without feeling the need to smoke	Going out to places that are non-smoking. Chew gum when I feel the urge to smoke when I am out with my friends.	Tell my friends about my efforts to try to quit and ask them to go to some places that are non-smoking or at least smoke away from me so I'm not as tempted.

GOAL/PRIORITY: _Get more physically fit._

Challenges making it difficult to reach my goal	How would I like this to be different?	Small changes I can make	What can others do to help?
I get winded really easily and my body hurts when I get more active	I would be able to breathe easier and not be in so much pain.	Try out other ways to be physically active (e.g., swimming) that might be easier on my body. Start at a slower pace, take breaks when I need to.	See if my friend wants to go to the pool and walk with me. Ask for help from my doctor to get advice on how to exercise safely.

GOAL/PRIORITY: _Cook healthier meals._

Challenges making it difficult to reach my goal	How would I like this to be different?	Small changes I can make	What can others do to help?
I don't have enough time to cook healthy meals every night.	Eat home cooked, healthy meals every night without too much fuss.	Prep snacks and meals on Sunday and Wednesday so that I can just grab a snack and heat meals up on the other days.	Get my spouse and kids to help decide on menus and prep meals with me. Ask my spouse to get dinner on the table a few nights a week.

Appendix P. Examples of m-health programs designed in part using principles of SDT

Program	Description
European Fans in Training (EuroFIT) http://eurofitfp7.eu/	EuroFIT tests the utility of a culturally- and gender- sensitized lifestyle program aimed at improving physical activity and reducing sedentary time in middle aged men across 4 countries. Men are engaged through 'live' programs held in their football clubs and continued engagement is promoted through mobile technologies that provide real-time, self-relevant feedback on health behaviors as well as connections to other participants through social media and online football matches. Thus, the strong affiliation and loyalty to clubs is leveraged as well advances in technology to create and sustain interest and engagement--core motivational challenges for lifestyle behavior interventions. (Gray et al., 2015; van der Ploeg et al., 2014; van Nassau et al, 2016).
Digital Innovations and Self-determined Exercise motivation (GoDIS)	The main aim of the project is to design, test and evaluate a digital exercise motivation m-health intervention. In collaboration with the three healthcare companies in Sweden a large sample (N > 10,000) from primary care will receive the intervention, and both subjective (self-reports) and objective measures (accelerometers) will be used as outcomes. Prior iterations of this work have been tested in smaller samples (see Weman-Josefsson et al., 2014, 2015).
Smokefree.gov Initiatives (SfGI)	SfGI is the U.S. Department of Health and Human Services' premier smoking cessation intervention. It consists of 4 websites, 11 SMS (text messaging) programs (see example below), and multiple social media pages. Specialized programs are available for women, teens, veterans, and Spanish-speaking populations. Programs address not only tobacco cessation but also weight management, physical activity, dietary intake, and stress reduction. These m-health interventions have had wide population reach and great success, with more than 4 million unique visitors to SfGI resources in 2014 alone.
	HealthyYouTXT (www.smokefree.gov/healthyyou) is one of the mobile text messaging services offered through Smokefree.gov that is designed to help men and women across the U.S. live a healthier lifestyle. This 6-week program is entirely modeled on SDT principles. The program allows participants to address diet and/or physical activity goals and provides 24/7 encouragement and tips to help participants achieve their health goals and stay on track.

Examples of texts targeting physical activity from HealthyYouTXT, a 6-week SMS-based intervention using principles of SDT

User chooses a goal	
TEXT PROMPT	**REPLY**
What's your activity goal? Move more, sit less or a mix of both?	• MOVE • SIT LESS • MIX of BOTH

Support the user in exploring their motivation
TEXT PROMPT
Why do you want to be more active & move more? Make a list of your reasons and post it on the fridge or at your desk so you have a reminder.

Provide an opportunity to explore expectations
TEXT PROMPT
Hoping you'll go from couch potato to fitness buff in a few weeks? Start with smaller goals & expectations so you don't get discouraged.

Check in and provide supportive feedback		
TEXT PROMPT	**REPLY**	**TEXT RESPONSE TO REPLY**
How's it going with adding 10 minutes of cardio activity 1-2 days this week?	• EASY	• If increasing cardio by 10 minutes has been super easy for you, challenge yourself! Go for 15 minutes, 30 minutes or more!
	• HARD	• Cardio can be intense. Increasing cardio time can be hard. If 10 minutes is too much for now, start with 5 minutes & work your way up
You've spent the week learning more about your activity & sitting patterns. How do you feel about what you've learned?	• GOOD	• Knowledge is power! Knowing your patterns will help you choose your goals. What will you try next week?
	• OK	• Learning about your patterns can feel good and bad, but it also gives you the power to make new choices. What will you try next week?
	• BAD	• Try not to be too hard on yourself. Learning about your patterns gives you the power to make new choices. What will you try next week?

Appendix Q. Practitioners' self-assessment of their need supportiveness of their clients

This assessment is designed to help you to reflect on your thoughts and feelings about your client and how your reactions might be affecting your work with this client. It is also designed to help you to lay out potential plans of action when appropriate. Some people might simply start by reading through each question and jotting down notes about their experience. Then, after they have had some time to reflect on their thoughts and feelings, they return to the exercise to formulate their preferred plans of action. Others might just work on a single section at any one sitting, writing down their thoughts and feelings as well as a preliminary plan of action. Work through this exercise at your own pace and approach it in the way that best fits you.

1. ## NOTES ABOUT MY EXPERIENCE WITH THIS CLIENT
   In this section simply write down your thoughts and feelings in response to each question. Try to be as honest as you can. Awareness of your thoughts and feelings will help you to identify both how you appreciate your client and how you might feel challenged by him/her.

2. ## POTENTIAL IMPACT ON MY WORK WITH MY CLIENT
   Oftentimes when we have strong positive or negative reactions to our clients it can cause us to act in ways that may not be optimal for helping them. For example, when people have strong positive reactions to a client, sometimes it can create blindspots and discourage some of the dialogue you might typically have (you may not probe about things that might get uncomfortable for the client). With strong negative reactions you may be more likely to be more controlling and defensive, rather than open and supportive.

   In this section, write down any ways that your thoughts and feelings about your client might be disrupting your connection to him/her. Make sure to pay attention to both the obvious ways that your reactions might disrupt your connection with your client (e.g., cutting him/her off while talking) as well as the subtle ways that this might happen too (e.g., tuning out; "leaking" judgments through non-verbal cues).

3. ## PLAN OF ACTION
   This section helps you to think about the ways to better engage with your client. Check out Chapter 13 for some potential ways to do this.

265

	NOTES ABOUT MY EXPERIENCE	IMPACT ON MY WORK WITH CLIENT	PLAN OF ACTION
RELATEDNESS			
Do you like your client?			
How connected do you feel to your client? Do you feel disengaged from your client? If yes, how do you make sense of that?			
Are there things that he/she is doing that you disapprove of or frustrate you?			
Are you genuine with your client?			
AUTONOMY			
What do you think of your client's personal goals?			
Who is your client making changes for?			
How do you feel/what do you do when your client hasn't worked on what he/she was going to do?			
COMPETENCE:			
Do you/your workplace have adequate structure and resources to provide what this client needs?			
What are *your* expectations about your client's goals? What are *your client's* expectations about his/her own goals? Is there a mismatch?			
What are *your* expectations about your client's progress? What are *your client's* expectations about his/her own progress? Is there a mismatch?			
What is your sense of how well evaluation of progress on goals will go?			

Appendix R. Self-Assessment of Practitioners' Own Motivations

1. *What are some of the reasons that fuel why you do the work that you do?* We have listed some of the common things that practitioners say drives their behavior. Select those things that resonate with you and add to the chart if something is missing.

	AMOTIVATED	CONTROLLED		AUTONOMOUS	
	Disengaged	Direct pressures or rewards	Internal pressures to avoid feeling bad or to feel better about self	Big picture values & life goals, health	Enjoyment, Interest
Explanation of each category of motivation	Work is not important/interesting; Don't feel very capable or effective.	Feel direct external pressures to achieve a reward or to avoid punishment.	Feel internal pressures (e.g., "I should/have to") in order maintain your self-worth or to avoid feeling bad (e.g., guilty).	Value the work and how it serves other important personal goals.	Work is fun or interesting. That is, they enjoy it and/or find it challenging.
Examples of what practitioners say	*I don't know why I am doing this work. I don't feel connected to it.*	*I am pressured to clock enough billable hours to meet my client quota, or else there will be consequences*	*If my clients show up and perform well I will look more competent.*	*I value being healthy and want to help other people be healthier as well.*	*I am passionate about helping others be healthier.*
	I don't feel very capable in what I am doing. I am over-challenged	*I have to get clients to attend more sessions and/or complete programs or else there will be consequences*	*If my clients show up and perform well I will be well-regarded by my colleagues.*	*By doing this job I make sure to attend to my own health too, which helps me to do the other things that are important to me in my life*	*I find the work that I do interesting and challenging.*
	I don't think what I do actually helps anyone. I don't feel very effective in what I do.	*If I don't perform well it might cost me (my salary, membership on insurance panels, program funding, keeping my job).*	*I need to be successful at my job to feel good about myself.*	*I feel connected and a part of team.*	*I enjoy working with clients and helping them achieve things that are important to them.*
		If I perform well it will get me benefits (e.g., salary, funding).	*I like to be an authority on how to make people healthier*	*The work that I do is meaningful to me, gives me a sense of purpose.*	

2. Now, take a look at what you have endorsed above. Ask yourself the following question: "Overall do I mostly feel disengaged, pressured, or willingly engaged and interested in my work? In other words do you feel more **amotivated, controlled, or autonomous in general?**

Appendix S. "CARE" Self-Assessment for Practitioners' Own Needs

This worksheet is designed to help you to reflect on the key ways that your own psychological needs are being met or not adequately met in your current workplace. It will also help you to make a plan of action--identifying social supports to enlist for help and doing something about the things you can control—in order to better get your needs met.

Some people simply start by reading through each question and jotting down notes about their experience. Then, after they have had some time to reflect on their thoughts and feelings, they return to the exercise to formulate their preferred plans of action. Others might just work on a single section at any one sitting, writing down their thoughts as well as a preliminary plan of action.

Work through this exercise at your own pace and approach it in the way that best fits you.

1. NOTES ABOUT MY EXPERIENCE

In this section simply write down your thoughts and feelings in response to each question. Try to be as specific as you can—the more specific you can be, the easier it will be to formulate a plan of action.

2. ACTION PLAN: What can I control?

- What things so I need to happen to better this situation? Be specific and realistic. (What can you realistically do? When? Are there other things you need to do to make this plan work?)

- If bigger changes are required, what resources might I access to get some assistance?

3. WHO CAN I TURN TO?: Enlisting social support

We all need supportive others to help us navigate life. Sometimes getting the support we need can be challenging. In some cases people hesitate to ask for support. Sometimes people aren't sure who to turn to for support. When you identify a challenge in this exercise, consider the following….

- Who might I talk to about this issue? Talking through the issue often provides greater clarity. Others might also offer useful perspectives.

- Who are the important people that can help me get my needs met? How can I enlist their support in this situation?

NOTE: Tackling the issues that arise from this exercise will be a process. Take it slow! Tackle the plans that seem the most manageable or attend to the one area that seems to be wreaking the most havoc on the other areas. Small steps will help you to be more effective in carrying out your plans and making longer lasting changes.

	NOTES ABOUT MY EXPERIENCE	ACTION PLAN	WHO CAN I TURN TO?
RELATEDNESS			
How connected do you feel with others in your department or work group? How "at home" do you feel? How does that impact you and your experience at work?			
Are you recognized and known to others? Do you ever feel invisible, alone, or alienated?			
Do you have colleagues to whom you can turn when you feel stressed or frustrated?			
Do you have colleagues that make you feel stressed or frustrated? What do they do that makes it difficult to interact with them?			
To what extent are you satisfied with your interactions in your workplace?			
AUTONOMY			
What areas do you feel most interest and value in your professional pursuits?			
Are you able to pursue your interests and valued goals? If not, what is getting in the way of pursuing these interests/goals?			
Is there anything or anyone hindering your ability to pursue valued goals at present?			
Are there tasks or duties that you feel pressured or compelled to do that you wish you didn't' have to perform?			
Have there been any ways in which you have felt constrained, controlled, or pressured to perform in your work?			

269

	NOTES ABOUT MY EXPERIENCE	ACTION PLAN	WHO CAN I TURN TO?
COMPETENCE:			
What are areas where you feel most confident or competent in your work?			
Any there areas where you feel over-challenged in your skills/abilities or where you sometimes doubt your competence?			
How is your workload-- too much, too little, or just right? If too much, what seems to be taking up most of your time?			
How available are opportunities for professional development?			
Is there additional personnel, help, and/or technical resources you need to best function in your current role? If yes, what do you need?			
What kind of feedback have you received about your work? • What's your sense of how you are doing? • Do you feel you are getting enough feedback to support your development? • What about the quality of the feedback? What do you need more/less of?			

	NOTES ABOUT MY EXPERIENCE	ACTION PLAN	WHO CAN I TURN TO?
EXTRINSIC COMPENSATION & EQUITY			
How satisfied are you with your current pay and benefits? How does it affect your work?			
Are you given enough resources and training to do your work? How does this affect your work?			
Do you see resources and compensation as being fair and equitable? If not, where do you see the imbalance?			
Is your workload fair and equitable as compared to your colleagues? If not, where do you see the imbalance?			
How fair and consistent does the advancement process seem to you?			
WORK-LIFE BALANCE			
To what extent are you putting your energy towards the things that are most important to you in life? If the balance is off.... • What important things are getting pushed to the side? • How would you like things to be different?			
Any positive ways that you can/do create some balance?			

NOTES ABOUT MY EXPERIENCE	ACTION PLAN	WHO CAN I TURN TO?
ISSUES OF DIVERSITY		
Are there any issues that have arisen for you as a result of your gender, race, ethnicity, sexual orientation, socioeconomic status, disability, political or scholarly views, or other factors that makes you diverse? If yes: How has it impacted… • Feeling welcome and accepted? • Your relationships with others? • Your sense of competence? • Your work productivity?		

Appendix T. Contrasting other health intervention models with the SDT approach

	SDT
Health Belief Model	
Emphasis is on cognitive processes (beliefs)	Broader focus including emotional connections to motivation
Focus on competence solely	Focus on competence, autonomy, and relatedness
Readiness to take action can only be sparked by cues to take action → threat and a perceived benefit to change	Motivation includes identified (e.g., value) and intrinsic motivation
Theory of Reasoned Action/ Theory of Planned Behavior	
A person who believes that others think she should perform a behavior AND is motivated to meet expectations of the others will hold a positive subjective norm	Example is not viewed as positive, but rather controlling and thus less likely to persist in the long term. Growing greater autonomous motivation is the focus
Control + intention = greater likelihood to engage in behavior	Accounts for variations in the type of goals pursued and the likelihood of persistence
Intention is best predictor of engaging in a behavior	Autonomous motivation is best predictor of initiation and persistence
Transtheoretical Model (Stages of Change)	
Bottom up approach; descriptive	Top down approach; prescriptive
How interventions are delivered has potential for being controlling (e.g., feedback, confrontations)	Intervention techniques focused on supporting autonomy
Emphasis of maintenance is behaviorism in its approach (e.g., counterconditioning, reinforcement management, stimulus control)	Emphasis in maintenance is building greater autonomous motivation – identification, integration, intrinsic motivation
Meaning of "process"	Process focuses on creating need supportive environment

	SDT
Social Cognitive Theory	
Mostly focused on competence building	Focus on competence, autonomy, and relatedness
If you change the thoughts or expectations, that will change behavior	Emphasis on person <u>and</u> context→ enhance supportiveness of social context
Some techniques are not need supportive (e.g, thought stopping)	Do not judge thoughts and feelings that emerge…in fact, these thoughts and feelings are instructive about the perceived supportiveness social context
Structure, delivery is often dictated by practitioner	Structure, delivery is collaborative
Self-Regulation Theory	
Focus mainly on competence building	Focus on competence, autonomy, and relatedness
Success at goal is key to change	The type of goal matters as to whether behavior will persist
Structure, delivery is often dictated by practitioner	Structure, delivery is collaborative
Cognitive Behavioral Approaches	
Uses external contingencies, rewards, and punishments will indeed move behavior	Maintains that external prompts and prods are not necessary to produce behavioral changes
Beliefs or appraisals about self and social context are thought to be maladaptive	Likely some reality to perceptions (e.g., social environment is not being supportive). Focus is on enhancing supportiveness of the social context
Techniques, such as thought stopping, are useful in modulating behavior.	Some techniques, such as thought stopping, are harmful to clients (e.g., judging their thoughts are "bad"/"wrong") and are not used.

	SDT
Motivational Interviewing (MI)	
Expressedly atheoretical	Strong theoretical base with empirical work to back up the model
Explicit focus is on initiation of change	Focus on initiation <u>and</u> maintenance
Focus largely is on the client only	Focus on social-contextual factors that support vs. undermine motivation
Move clients toward change talk, without regard for the reasons behind change; all movement toward change is equal, as long at the endpoint is change	Quality of motivation matters. Thus, reasons for wanting to change, goal types are important for sustained motivation
"MI is about influencing choice" specifically in the direction of change (Miller & Rollnick, 2012, p. 231). Fundamental disconnect between MI "spirit" and directing change	*Not changing* has to be considered a valid choice that clients can autonomously endorse; also explore "sustain talk"
Narrow boundary conditions where neutrality is appropriate	Do not add another source of pressure for clients or convey conditional regard (e.g., change is what is acceptable)
Once change has been committed to then other counseling approaches or therapies (e.g., CBT) may be applied or perhaps no further intervention may be needed	Coherent model of motivation; cannot simply add on motivational techniques to other forms of treatment that do not share the same core foundations or intervene in ways inconsistent with the core philosophy

ABOUT THE AUTHOR

Jennifer La Guardia, Ph.D.
Licensed Psychologist California #27223, New York #016109-1

Motivated for Health (www.motivated4health.com)

Dr. Jennifer La Guardia is a licensed clinical psychologist, research scientist, and educator with an expertise in Self-Determination Theory (SDT) and its applications to wellness and healthcare. Over the past 15+ years she has designed and implemented 'live', web-based, and m-Health interventions to promote health behavior change, manage chronic illness, and improve personal well-being. She has also worked directly with individuals and couples to help them better manage emotional and physical health transitions that occur as a result of a new health event (e.g. heart attack) or chronic illness (e.g., cancer, cardiovascular disease, diabetes, obesity).

Dr. La Guardia completed her graduate work at the University of Rochester under the supervision of Dr. Richard Ryan, one of the creators of SDT. She also completed clinical postdoctoral training in the Department of Psychiatry at University of Wisconsin-Madison Hospitals & Clinics and NIH-sponsored postdoctoral research training on emotion at the Department of Psychology at the University of Wisconsin-Madison. She was formerly a tenured professor at the University of Waterloo in Ontario, Canada and has held Associate Professor, Research Scientist, and adjunct positions at top institutions, including the University of Rochester Medical Center and UC Santa Barbara. She is the founder and primary consultant for Motivated for Health (www.motivated4health.com).

92404379R00168

Made in the USA
Middletown, DE
08 October 2018